Adobe After Effects
A Complete Course and
Compendium of Features

Ben Goldsmith

Adobe After Effects

A Complete

Course

and

Compendium

of Features

rockynook

Adobe After Effects: A Complete Course and Compendium of Features
Ben Goldsmith

Editor: Jocelyn Howell
Project manager: Lisa Brazieal
Marketing coordinator: Katie Walker
Interior and cover design and type: Steve Laskevitch

ISBN: 978-1-68198-865-8
1st Edition (1st printing, November 2022)
© 2023 Ben Goldsmith
Rocky Nook Inc.
1010 B Street, Suite 350
San Rafael, CA 94901
USA

www.rockynook.com

Distributed in the UK and Europe by Publishers Group UK
Distributed in the U.S. and all other territories by Ingram Publisher Services

Library of Congress Control Number: 2021944846

Printed in China

About the Author

Ben Goldsmith tells stories and shares ideas through editing videos and designing motion graphics. After receiving his BA at Hampshire College in digital media production, Ben developed and created immersive media experiences for historic and scientific museums nationwide, including the Franklin D. Roosevelt Presidential Library and Museum and the Boston Museum of Science. He then schlepped over to Seattle, where he lives today with his wife, Dylan. Ben now produces videos for Sparkworks Media—where he creates content for Amazon, Alaska Airlines, and other local businesses—and is an Adobe Certified Instructor, teaching motion design at Luminous Works, the School of Visual Concepts, and Seattle University. When he's not churning out the good stuff, you might find him bouldering, brewing ales, or playing ABBA songs on the piano.

Acknowledgments

It all started at Luminous Works, where Steve Laskevitch and Carla Fraga invited me to teach. I think we were about fifteen minutes into introductions before Steve asked me if I had any interest in writing a book on Premiere. The Premiere book happened under Steve's tutelage and mentorship. Perhaps there was a week of downtime afterward, but the most obvious follow-up was a book on After Effects—which again, couldn't have happened without Steve's help.

Another huge thanks goes to Rocky Nook, in particular this book's editor, Jocelyn Howell. Without her finely honed attention to detail, htis book wuld look l8ke ths,

Many fine artists generously donated the artwork used for these lessons. Chapter 1's UFO was created by Jason Hoppe, Chapter 2's Grow Your Career plant by Keeli McCarthy, and Chapter 5's campfire scene by Steven Leonti.

The artwork seen on the Compendium pages came from a wide swath of fantastic designers from around the world. Check out the annotations on those pages to see some truly great designs.

My students were also instrumental in helping me refine these lessons—even if they weren't aware they were guinea pigs for this book. If you find yourself asking a question that is then answered in this book, it's likely because a student asked the same question.

Lastly, I'd like to thank my wonderful wife, Dylan. A writer herself, she was a reliable sounding board for the exclusion of this book's worst ideas. It takes considerable patience to write a book, but arguably more so to be married to the person writing it.

Ben Goldsmith
Seattle, May 2022

Contents

The Course

The Compendium

Introduction
Start Here

In this book, you will be working your way through a full course curriculum that will expose you to all of the essential features and functions of Adobe After Effects. Along the way, you'll learn the concepts and vocabulary of digital video. There are five Course chapters that teach you steps as you go. In those lessons, each action that I'd like you to try looks like this:

➡ This is what an action looks like.

The paragraphs surrounding the action explain some of the why and how. For greater depth, the second section of this book is a Compendium of those features and functions, providing the "deep dive" needed for true mastery of this powerful application. Throughout the Course section, I will suggest readings in the Compendium section. Just remember that everything in the Course is explained in further detail later in the book, so if you're curious for more, or want to discover other options that might better suit your workflow, check the corresponding section in the Compendium.

Software and Files

Have you installed After Effects yet? If you work for a company with an enterprise license, it's likely your IT people have installed it for you. We will be using the Creative Cloud app as our hub for launching Adobe applications and accessing the services that come with a Creative Cloud (CC) license. This app also checks to make sure your software license is up to date, so it should remain running whenever you use your creative applications. I use the CC app's Preferences to have it launch on startup.

I most often launch After Effects by clicking the Open button next to the After Effects icon. If there's an update available, it'll be available in the Updates section.

Please note that After Effects is regularly updated, and discrepancies between interface elements may exist between your screen and the images in this book.

To follow along with the projects and lessons in this book, you'll need the Course Files. Launch your favorite web browser and go to rockynook.com/AfterEffectsCandC, answer

The Interface & Editing

Animation

Text

Shapes, Masks & Mattes

Effects

3D

Special Tools & Features

Expressions

a simple question, and download the files. Save the files somewhere memorable. If you can't store them on your internal hard drive, make sure you're using a fast and reliable external drive.

A Note Regarding Keyboard Shortcuts

To be efficient in After Effects, or any application, we should take advantage of time-saving features like shortcuts. I will always share menu-driven ways to achieve our ends (when such exist), but I'll encourage faster ways too. An extensive reference for shortcuts can be found in After Effects' Edit menu. Wherever shortcuts appear, the Mac shortcut precedes the shortcut for Windows.

Note that keyboard shortcuts usually involve holding down a modifier key (outlined in red here) while pressing other keys. Since the modifiers appear on both sides of the keyboard, almost all shortcuts can be performed with one hand.

Mac users should note the cryptic symbol used in menus to denote each modifier key.

THE
COURSE

1 Layout and Basic Animation

Let's get started. To kick things off, we'll need to first dive into how After Effects works and how to import and organize files, then we'll get to the fun stuff—layout and basic keyframe animation.

Project Organization

In After Effects, organization is crucial—even before you open the software. Let's look at some best practices to keep track of where things are.

Folder Structure

Make sure you've downloaded the assets for this lesson (see the Introduction). You'll see a set of folders that looks like this:

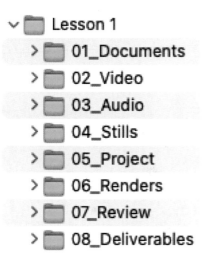

I start every project by duplicating this exact empty folder structure. This way, all my projects are organized the same way, and I know where to find my stuff.

Make sure you keep this folder somewhere memorable, and on a device that has a decent amount of space. If you're using an external drive, make sure it's something fast. Thunderbolt, USB 3, and USB C connections are often indicators of fast drives.

Move Your Folder Now, Not Later

You don't want to move your folders around after you begin working. That will cause some grievances. Why? Well, After Effects doesn't actually import files—it makes a reference to where a file lives on your computer. If that file moves, After Effects won't know where it is and will call it "offline," replacing the file with ugly color bars.

Offline Media

If you do get offline media, simply right-click the missing asset from the Project panel and select Replace Footage. You'll then be prompted to point After Effects to where your file currently lives. If you've moved several things together, After Effects is pretty smart about automatically relinking multiple offline assets at once.

And whatever you do, don't rename your assets in the Finder after they've been imported. Not only will this make objects offline, but you'll also have to remember the new name of the object, and automatic relinking won't work.

The Interface & Editing

Animation

Text

Shapes, Masks & Mattes

Effects

3D

Special Tools & Features

Expressions

Setting Up the After Effects Project

⮑ Open After Effects, either from your Applications folder or directly from the Creative Cloud app.

The lessons in this book are constructed with a factory-fresh version of After Effects, meaning that I've reset all my preferences and After Effects will operate as if I'm opening it for the first time. While not completely necessary, you may wish to reset your After Effects preferences if you've already been tinkering with it and you want to make sure our screens look as similar as possible. To do so, hold down ⌘-opt-shift/Ctrl-Alt-Shift before opening After Effects and while it loads, until prompted to reset your preferences.

This book was written using After Effects version 22.3. In the coming years, you may notice some slight features that have debuted since this book was written. Check the What's New folder in the course downloads to see the latest features, and note any discrepancies between our screens. You can also do a web search for "What's new in Adobe After Effects" to get a succinct list of new features from Adobe.

Create a New Project

Once AE is launched, you'll be greeted with the Home screen.

⮑ Select New Project.

Let's go ahead and save this project. Per the project structure template, AE files ought to go into the 05_Project folder.

⮑ Go to File > Save As or hit ⌘-shift-S/Ctrl-Shift-S.
⮑ Navigate to Lesson 1 > 05_Project, name this project Lesson 1, then hit Save.

We've just created an AEP file, or an After Effects Project file. This file stores all of our stuff. Since After Effects doesn't actually import assets, AEPs remain fairly small file sizes, making them easy to back up and send off.

If you've been tinkering with After Effects already, you may wish to reset your workspace to the Default layout, so our screens look the same. If this is your first time opening After Effects, you can skip these steps.

⮑ Select Window > Workspace > Default.
⮑ Select Window > Workspace > Reset "Default" to Saved Layout.

Import Assets

Before we can start working with assets, such as images or videos, we have to import the assets into After Effects. All of your assets are then stored in the Project panel, which should be on the left-hand side of the After Effects interface.

There are several ways to import assets. For now, do this:

- ➦ Select File > Import > File or ⌘-I/Ctrl-I.
- ➦ Navigate to Lesson 1 > 04_Stills and select UFO.ai. Don't select Open just yet.
- ➦ In the Import dialog box, under Import As, choose Composition – Retain Layer Sizes.
- ➦ Click Open.

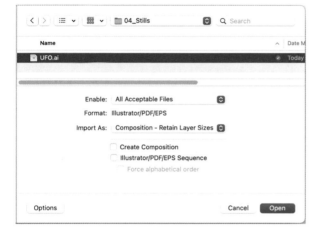

We've just imported a layered Adobe Illustrator file. After Effects can import Illustrator and Photoshop documents with layers, allowing you to select and animate layers individually. However, you have to ensure that After Effects imports the layered object as a composition to have access to those layers. In other cases, selecting Import As > Footage will flatten the object, treating it as a single layer.

The Project panel now has two items: a composition, in which our layered Illustrator files are laid out exactly as they were in the original file, and a Folder containing our individual layers.

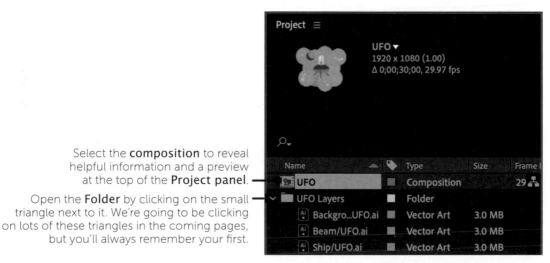

Select the **composition** to reveal helpful information and a preview at the top of the **Project panel**.

Open the **Folder** by clicking on the small triangle next to it. We're going to be clicking on lots of these triangles in the coming pages, but you'll always remember your first.

The Interface & Editing

Animation

Text

Shapes, Masks & Mattes

Effects

3D

Special Tools & Features

Expressions

The Composition Panel

⮕ Double-click the UFO composition from the Project panel to open it.

This loads the UFO composition in the timeline. We can see what the timeline is doing in the Composition panel.

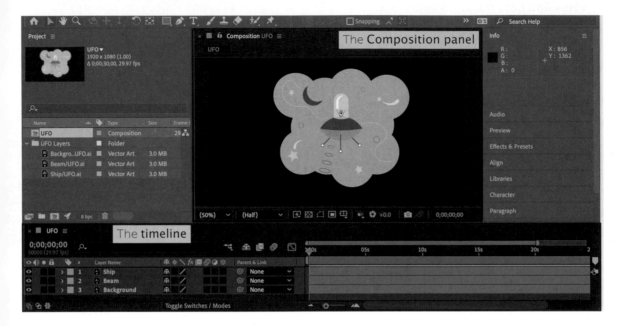

Configure the Comp Panel to Your Liking

Let's note some important things about the Composition panel. None of the features in this section actually change your image or animation—these are merely navigational tools to help you work on your project.

Zooming In and Out

If you want to take a closer look at what's going on in your image, there are a ludicrous number of ways to enlarge the image within the Composition panel.

The first is the Magnification Ratio Popup, which is in the lower-left corner of the Composition panel. It should show a percentage.

This defaults to Fit, which automatically sizes your composition to fit the size of the panel. While convenient, you may wish to change this to 100% at certain times to view your composition in full resolution—that is, maximum quality.

You can also zoom by hovering your cursor over the Composition panel and scrolling with your mouse. This is my favorite method. The same thing can be achieved by pressing ⌘-=/Ctrl-= to zoom in and ⌘--/Ctrl-- to zoom out.

My least favorite way of zooming in and out is using the Zoom tool. I hate this so much that I'm going to make you refer to Compendium Chapter 1 to learn it. Better yet, don't.

Moving the Composition Panel

Zooming in zooms toward the center of the Composition panel. But what if you want to see something else?

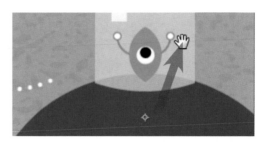

Press and hold the spacebar to temporarily switch to the Hand tool. With the Hand tool, you can click and drag within the Composition panel to move the viewport around.

If you're using a trackpad (which I wholly don't recommend), I believe it is physically impossible to hold

down the spacebar while clicking and dragging, especially if there's a bagel in your other hand. Sometimes, you may wish to manually switch to the Hand tool. You can do this by selecting it from the Toolbar at the top of the screen, or by pressing the hotkey H.

With the Hand tool selected, you'll find you can do little but move the viewport. Make sure you switch back to the Selection tool by selecting it from the Toolbar, or with the hotkey V.

The **Selection tool** should almost always be selected. If you can't click on stuff, it's probably because you need to select this.

Resolution

This is important, so listen up. The only certainties in life are death, taxes, and After Effects running slowly. The fix for this is the Resolution/Down Sample Factor Popup. Chances are, you don't need After Effects to produce every pixel perfectly. By lowering your composition's resolution, After Effects can skip pixels and render your image faster, at the expense of image quality.

The Resolution/Down Sample Factor Popup is found next to the Magnification Ratio Popup.

The default setting is Auto, in which the resolution changes depending on your zoom amount. I don't like this. While working, I often set my resolution to the lowest it can go (usually Quarter), and I only increase it if I need to work out details. I'll leave you to decide which settings you find most agreeable for your computer. If yours is packed to the brim with RAM, set this to Full and blast off!

Toggle Transparency Grid

Selecting this button ▓ at the bottom of the Composition panel changes how After Effects handles transparency. If it's deselected, transparent pixels will display whatever color is set to the composition's Background Color (ours has defaulted to black). For now, I'll save a little ink by selecting this, so my transparent pixels are now displayed with a checkered grid.

Does using less black ink reduce carbon emissions? I'm going to pretend it does.

The Interface & Editing

Animation

Text

Shapes, Masks & Mattes

Effects

3D

Special Tools & Features

Expressions

Layout in the Comp Window

Now, let's get to doing some actual editing within the composition. We'll start with the three basic transformation tools: position, rotation, and scale.

Changing an Object's Position

First, we must select a layer.

- ➡ Make sure the Selection tool is selected by pressing V or selecting it from the Toolbar ◣.
- ➡ Select the UFO, either by clicking on it in the composition, or clicking on the Ship layer in the timeline.

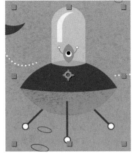 The eight points around the layer indicate that it's currently selected.

- ➡ Click and drag the UFO to move it around. Whee!

We've just changed the position of the layer.

Changing an Object's Scale

Scale refers to the size of an object. Scaling is easy.

- ➡ Click and drag one of the corners of the bounding box to scale an object.

Scaling without the **shift** key.   Scaling with the **shift** key.

Hmm, this doesn't look great.

➡ Undo with Edit > Undo, or ⌘–Z/Ctrl–Z.
➡ Scale again, but this time hold down shift while doing so.

This scales proportionally, meaning the object retains its ratio of width to height as it scales. Sorry, Photoshop users, holding down the shift key is backward from what you're used to!

➡ Undo until the alien is back in its original position and scale.

Changing an Object's Rotation

We can't actually rotate with the Selection tool. We'll have to switch to the Rotation tool.

➡ Select the Rotation tool by either pressing W or selecting it from the Toolbar .

Since the hotkey for this tool is W, it's often referred to as the Wotation tool. We're going to stick to that convention, since it's funny.

➡ Click and drag on the UFO to wotate it.
➡ Play with this tool a little, then undo until it's back at its original wotation.

Changing an Object's Anchor Point

Did you notice that the alien was spinning about the center of the image? Notice the crosshair dead center on the alien.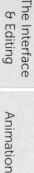

This is the object's Anchor Point. All assets have one. This is the point about which the object wotates—and actually, scales and positions. Think of it as a pencil stuck in a piece of paper. When you spin the paper, it will spin around the point where the pencil is stuck.

When it comes to still images, the Anchor Point isn't important, since you can just place an object anywhere you want. However, we will be animating this UFO shortly, and we'll want it to wotate in a specific way. I don't wan't the UFO to wotate about the center of the layer; I want it to wotate about the center of the ship. So, I'll want to move my Anchor Point down slightly.

➡ Select the Anchor Point tool with the hotkey Y, or from the Toolbar .

The Interface & Editing

Animation

Text

Shapes, Masks & Mattes

Effects

3D

Special Tools & Features

Expressions

- ⮕ Click and drag the Anchor Point until it is where the two blues of the ship meet. Do so while holding shift so it moves in a straight line.
- ⮕ Switch back to the Wotate tool.
- ⮕ Wotate the object and see how it moves about the Anchor Point.
- ⮕ Undo your wotation, but keep the Anchor Point where we moved it to.

The Anchor Point is very important. It can be difficult to change after you've added animation. **Set your Anchor Point before you begin animation.**
      Once more for good measure.

Set your Anchor Point before you begin animation.

Transform Controls in the Timeline

Accessing position, scale, and rotation in the Composition panel is a great way to quickly move assets around and get your layout where you want it visually. When it comes time to animate, we need a more precise and numeric interface. Accessing the same controls as above, but in the timeline, allows for just that.

Configuring the Timeline

The timeline is where we do most of our work in After Effects. We currently have three layers—one for the ship, one for the beam, and one for the background. This is because the Illustrator file we imported was created with three top-level layers.

Let's organize the timeline a little. I'm not worried about the Beam layer just now.

Timecode. Click and drag to change.
Click with ⌘/Ctrl to switch to frame count.

Playhead

Labels

Layers

The triangle

Toggle track visibility, mute, solo, and lock

⮕ Temporarily turn off Beam by clicking on its Toggle Track Visibility, or Eyeball button 👁.

It's easy to accidentally click a background layer, which can be annoying. Let's prevent us from selecting and making any changes to the Background layer.

⮕ Click on the box next to Background under the Lock icon 🔒.

Since the UFO is so important, let's make it stand out a little bit more in the After Effects interface. I'll change the layer's label color, which just helps me see it a little better.

⮕ Click the purple square on the Ship's layer ◼, and change the label color to orange.

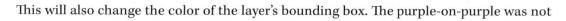

This will also change the color of the layer's bounding box. The purple-on-purple was not

The Interface
& Editing

Animation

Text

Shapes, Masks
& Mattes

Effects

3D

Special Tools
& Features

Expressions

working for me.

Transform Controls

The little triangle on each layer contains all editable parameters.

➡ Unfurl Ship's triangle ▶.

All assets have Transform controls listed here. It's basically the same stuff we were editing in the Composition panel— Anchor Point, Position, Scale, and Rotation. These controls also reveal Opacity, which is one thing we cannot edit in the Composition panel, just here.

These controls are another way of changing a layer's transform. Try this:

➡ Under Rotation, click and drag the number that says 0.0° to the right to increase the rotation value.

You can also manually type in a value.

➡ Click once on the blue Rotation value that you just edited.
➡ Type in 90.
➡ Hit return/Enter.

Rotation is measured in degrees, so you'll typically type in anything from 0–360. Can't remember your high school geometry class? No problem. These number fields also accept math functions. To rotate a third of the way around…

➡ Click once on the blue Rotation value.
➡ Type in 360/3.
➡ Hit return/Enter.

360 divided by 3 is 120, and your object will rotate a third of the way around a full circle. Math! Let's reset our alien, who's probably nauseous by now.

➡ Right-click on Rotation.
➡ Select Reset.

Rotation should now be back to 0°.

PARTS

Accessing these Transform controls is essential to animation, so we'll be doing it a lot. Clicking on the triangles to get here is too time-consuming, so let's use hotkeys instead.

I like the mnemonic device PARTS to remember the five hotkeys for our five parameters:

- P - Position
- A - Anchor Point
- R - Rotation
- T - opaciTy (or, Transparency)
- S - Scale

With a layer selected, selecting one of our PARTS keys will quickly display that Transform control. If you already have an attribute open and you'd like to view an additional one, holding down shift and typing one of your PARTS keys will add it to the display.

Zoom In and Out of the Timeline

Depending on the size of your monitor, your timeline might be scaled a little differently from mine. There are several ways to zoom in and out of your timeline, which might help with a detailed view of the next few sections. Just like when we zoomed into the Composition panel, this is just an interface option and won't affect your layout or animation.

The following steps are only necessary if your timeline doesn't quite look like mine. If that's the case, refer to the following section.

To zoom into the timeline, do one of the following:

- Press =.
- Slide the timeline scaler toward the big mountain.
- Click and drag the end of the timeline navigator inward.

It's the one on the top; not the one on the bottom.

To zoom out of the timeline, do one of the following:

- Press – (dash).
- Slide the timeline scaler toward the small mountain.
- Click and drag the end of the timeline navigator outward.

To scroll through the timeline, do one of the following:

- Use the scroll wheel on your mouse while holding shift.
- Scroll horizontally, if that's a thing your mouse can do.
- Click and drag the scroll bar (right).
- Click and drag the timeline navigator.

The Interface & Editing

Animation

Text

Shapes, Masks & Mattes

Effects

3D

Special Tools & Features

Expressions

Keyframe Animation

Let's get to animating. In the previous section, we discovered that pretty much all attributes in After Effects are controlled by a number. In this section, we'll add keyframes to those numbers. Keyframes are what control animation, and allow us to change those numbers over time.

Prepping for Animation

We're going to have the UFO fly in from off-screen, pause, then fly off. Let's make sure we've done everything we need to do to be prepared.

➡ Make sure the playhead is at the beginning of the timeline.

The timecode at the top-left of the timeline should read 0;00;00;00, and the blue playhead should be at the far left of the timeline. If they've shifted while you've been playing around, do any of the following:

- Click and drag the playhead until it's at the start of the timeline.
- Click and drag the blue timecode numbers until they read 0;00;00;00.
- Press the home key on your keyboard.

➡ Make sure the Anchor Point is in the center of the ship.

Remember, set your Anchor Point before animating!

➡ Make sure the Selection tool is selected.
➡ Click and drag the UFO until it's outside of your composition, toward the top-right of the comp.

We've just set the starting position of the UFO at the beginning of this animation.

Animating Position

The placement of the UFO on-screen is the object's position, which we'll want to animate. We don't need to bother ourselves with the other transform controls just yet, so let's hide them.

➲ With the UFO selected, tap P to reveal just Position transforms in the timeline.

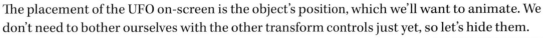

Position is composed of two numbers—the first indicating X, or horizontal value, and the second for Y, or vertical value. After Effects starts this count in the top-left corner of the composition window. So, my numbers are telling me that my object's Anchor Point is 2146.9 pixels away horizontally from the top-left corner of the composition window, and 16.6 pixels lower. It's okay if your numbers don't match mine precisely.

➲ Click the stopwatch next to Position.

We've just turned on keyframes and enabled animation for this layer's position. Our adventure into animation has begun!

There are four important things to note:

- We've created a keyframe for the layer's position.
- That keyframe lives at the time of 0;00;00;00.
- That keyframe is holding a value of [2146.9,16.6] (or whatever your values are).
- Keyframes are now enabled for this parameter. Any change we make to this parameter will create a new keyframe, or edit the existing one.

In order for animation to happen, we need at least two keyframes and two different times holding two different values. After Effects will automatically animate between those keyframed values over time.

➲ Click and drag the blue playhead to 2s on the timeline.

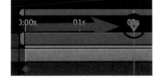

The timecode should read 0;00;02;00. We've just advanced two seconds into the timeline. Timecode is measured in hours ; minutes ; seconds ; frames.

➲ Click and drag the UFO back into the center(ish) of the composition.

The Interface & Editing

Animation

Text

Shapes, Masks & Mattes

Effects

3D

Special Tools & Features

Expressions

Let me reiterate what I stated before: Because the stopwatch has been clicked, keyframes are now enabled for this parameter. Any change we make to this parameter will create a new keyframe, or edit the existing one.

So, we now have a new keyframe at two seconds into our timeline, holding a new value.

It's Playback Time

Let's watch our glorious animation.

➲ Get back to the beginning of the timeline by doing one of the following:

- Click and drag the playhead to the start of the timeline.
- Click and drag the blue timecode numbers until they read 0;00;00;00.
- Press the home key on your keyboard.

➲ Press the spacebar to play the timeline.

And we have animation! Remember, two keyframes at two different times holding two different values means After Effects automatically animates from one to the other. So, After Effects is taking two seconds to go from our first keyframe of position value [2146.9,16.6] to the second keyframe of position value [992.9,540.6], or whatever your values are.

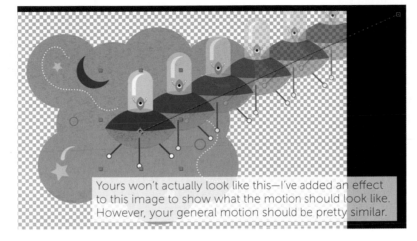

Yours won't actually look like this—I've added an effect to this image to show what the motion should look like. However, your general motion should be pretty similar.

Configuring Playback

Depending on the power of your computer, your first time pressing the spacebar may have been a little choppy. In fact, the Info panel that should be open in the top-right of the After Effects interface may have displayed something like the figure at right.

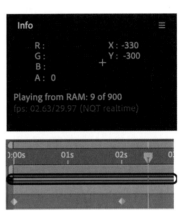

The first time you play your animation might not be in real time, which means playing at the proper frame rate of your final video. However, you should also see a little green bar shooting across your timeline.

Once the bar has traveled down your timeline, it's an indication that After Effects has processed those frames and is ready to likely play them back in real time. This is called the RAM preview, because these frames are stored in your computer's Random Access Memory. The more RAM your computer has, the faster the RAM preview will generate, and the more frames it can hold.

Don't have a ton of RAM? Remember to change the Resolution of your comp to something your computer can comfortably handle.

The Preview Panel

While I rarely touch this, you may enjoy navigating the timeline with the Preview panel. Find it by opening the tab on the right-hand side of the After Effects interface.

Move the **playhead** back one frame   Start/Stop   Move the **playhead** forward one frame

Jump to **timeline** start ——   —— Jump to **timeline** end

The Interface & Editing

Animation

Text

Shapes, Masks & Mattes

Effects

3D

Special Tools & Features

Expressions

All these playback functions can be done with keystrokes.

- Jump to timeline start: home key.
- Move the playhead back one frame: ⌘–left arrow/Ctrl–left arrow or PageUp.
- Start/Stop: spacebar.
- Move the playhead back one frame: ⌘–right arrow/Ctrl–right arrow or PageDown.
- Jump to timeline end: end key.

A detailed overview of the rest of these features, which allow you to tailor exactly what happens when the spacebar is pressed, can be found in chapter 1 of the Compendium.

Work Area

We're now examining a two-second animation in a thirty-second long composition. While the Preview panel loops playback indefinitely, twenty-eight seconds is an awfully long time to wait. Let's tell After Effects that we're only interested in a small section of this animation. The Work Area does just that.

➥ Click and drag the playhead until it's at the exact same time as your second keyframe (two seconds in). Do this while holding shift so the playhead snaps to the keyframe.

Holding down shift is a universal feature throughout After Effects that has your playhead snap to various things in your timeline, such as the ends of clips, keyframes, and markers.

➥ Tap N to bring the Work Area end to the playhead.

Now, playing our composition back, we'll loop just this section of animation.

➥ Bask in your fantastic loop.
➥ Double-click within the Work Area boundaries to reset the Work Area to the length of the composition.

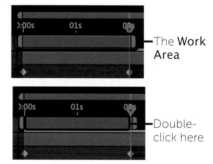

The **Work Area**

Double-click here

Adding a Pause in Animation

Let's add to this. After the UFO lands, let's have it pause for two seconds, then continue to fly away. How do we do this?

Well, remember that in order for animation to happen, we need two different keyframes with two different values at two different times. However, if we have two different keyframes with the *same* value, no change will occur and our animation will be static between those identical keyframes.

➥ Navigate to four seconds into your composition.
➥ Click the Add Keyframe button, to the far left of the Composition panel.

This button adds a **keyframe** wherever the **playhead** is, or removes a **keyframe** if there's already one there.

These two **keyframes** are identical in value, so no movement will happen between them.

➡ Navigate to six seconds into your composition.

➡ Move the UFO off-screen, to the bottom-left of the composition.

➡ Tap N to set the Work Area end to six seconds.

Top-right...   Center hold...   Bottom-left

Remember, since keyframes are enabled for position, any change we make to this layer's position will automatically add a new keyframe. That's why when we got to six seconds and simply moved the UFO off-screen, a new keyframe was automatically created. This is great—but be careful! If you tweak the placement of this layer's position, you'll write or edit keyframes.

Editing Keyframes

Want to change keyframes after they've been created? Simple. First, let's look at a new way to navigate keyframes.

➡ Press the Go To Previous Keyframe button until you're at the beginning of the composition.

The Interface & Editing

Animation

Text

Shapes, Masks & Mattes

Effects

3D

Special Tools & Features

Expressions

Notice how the Add Keyframe button is now blue, indicating that the playhead is on a keyframe.

➡ Move the off-screen UFO until it's in the bottom-right corner of the composition.

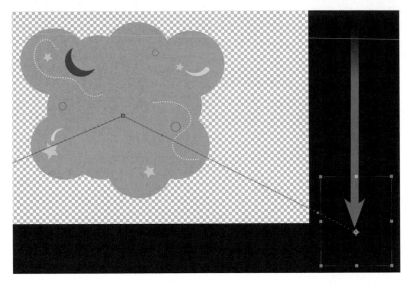

Because our playhead was on a keyframe, editing that position edited the current keyframe. Using the Go To Previous and Go To Next Keyframe buttons is a great way to make sure that the playhead is exactly on a cursor. You can also drag the playhead while holding shift, or use the hotkeys J and K.

Position keyframes can also be edited, even if you're not on the current time. By now, you've likely noticed these little dots all over our composition indicating the path that our image is traveling. And those squares along the path indicate where the keyframes land.

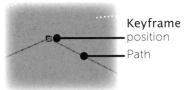

Keyframe
position
Path

We can simply drag these keyframe squares around the Composition panel to change where our position keyframes land. Let's try it.

➡ Drag the keyframe in the bottom-left corner up to the top-left corner.

Our ship now flies from the bottom-right to the top-left. Easy! Now, take a little break.

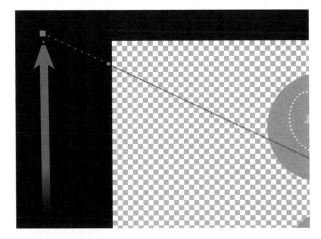

Adding Finesse

You hopefully now have a basic understanding of keyframes. Let's go ahead and make this animation look a little more interesting, and explore a few more things we can do with keyframes.

Curved Position Paths

The alien flies in a straight line. That's boring. Let's turn this line into a curve.

➡ Select the first keyframe from either the Composition panel or the timeline. It doesn't matter what time the playhead is set to.

It might be a little difficult to see, but in the Composition panel you should see a handle sticking out of that keyframe, pointing in the direction of the path.

➡ Click and drag the ball at the end of the handle to change the curve of the path. Adjust the curve so it forms a nice big arc.

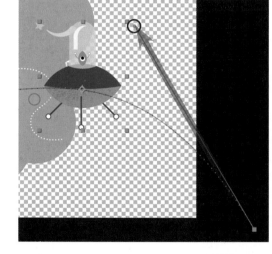

➡ Do the same for keyframe 4. Whee!

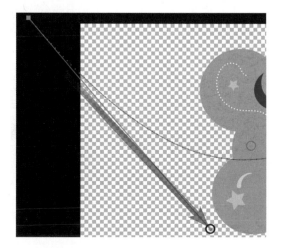

The Interface & Editing

Animation

Text

Shapes, Masks & Mattes

Effects

3D

Special Tools & Features

Expressions

Add Rotation

Since we've already made sure this UFO rotates nicely, it'd be a shame to waste that. Let's have it rotate a little after it lands.

Since we're messing with rotation, we need to see the parameter in the timeline. Think PARTS—R for Rotation. However, we don't want to hide Position—we want to see both Position and Rotation at the same time in the timeline.

➡ With the Ship layer selected, press shift-R.

Now, let's add a quick rotate during that pause. This is familiar territory.

➡ Make sure Rotation is currently set to 0°.

➡ Navigate to two seconds, either by dragging the cursor with shift, pressing the J or K hotkeys, or clicking on the Go To Previous or Go To Next Keyframe buttons.

➡ Click the Rotation stopwatch to enable keyframes for rotation and write one at two seconds.

➡ Navigate to three seconds.

➡ Press the Add Keyframe button to write a second rotation keyframe at three seconds, holding a value of 0°.

➡ Navigate to 0;00;02;15, or the midpoint between the two rotation keyframes.

➡ Either use the Wotate tool or simply click and drag the blue rotation value in the timeline to write a third keyframe between the two. I'll make mine wotate about 20°.

The alien should now fly in, do a quick rotation (resetting back to 0° at the end), pause for a second, then fly off again.

Note how I placed my two 0° keyframes before placing my 20° keyframe. This just saved me a tiny amount of time, as it's slightly faster to use the Add Keyframe button than it is to recreate a keyframe value from scratch.

Trimming Clips

Let's get back to our forgotten Beam layer.

➡ Click the Eyeball 👁 on the Beam layer to switch it back on.

The beam is visible during the entirety of the composition, which we don't want. Let's have it just appear after the ship rotates.

➡ Move the playhead until it's on the last rotation keyframe.

➡ Click and drag the start of the Beam layer in the timeline until it reaches the playhead. Hold shift to enable snapping.

As you can see, the duration of the bars in the timeline shows when the clip is visible. Now, let's have the beam disappear before the ship flies off, this time using hotkeys.

➡ Move the playhead to four seconds.
➡ With the Beam layer selected, press opt–]/Alt–].

You should now have a silly yet functional animation of an alien flying in, rotating, creating a beam, then flying off. It's not spectacular, but it's plenty for our first chapter. In the next, we'll make our animation really shine.

Here are our main takeaways on keyframe animation:

- Clicking the stopwatch enables keyframes for that parameter.
- Once keyframes are enabled, any change you make to that parameter adds or edits keyframes.
- Animation requires at least two keyframes with two different values at two different times.
- Duplicates of the same keyframe provide no change, and therefore will hold still.

2 Advanced Animation, Parenting & Text

Now that we know how to move things around on the screen, let's make those things look good. If you watch a motion graphics animation—or any animation for that matter—notice the way objects move from point A to B. Is it smooth? Snappy? Jerky? Thinking about these options will breathe life into our animation. In this chapter, we'll look at how to achieve such things, and look at many more ways to gain control of our keyframes.

This chapter will also cover creating text, text animation presets, and exporting.

Set Up the Project

Make sure you have the Lesson 2 files downloaded.

Import the Asset

- Fire up a new After Effects project, either by clicking New Project from the splash screen, or with File > New Project.
- Save this project into Lesson 2 > 05_Project, naming it Lesson 2.

We'll now import the image in the Stills folder, but with a different approach than last time.

- Drag the file called GrowYourCareer.ai from the Stills folder in the Finder or Explorer into the Project panel.

You'll see a dialog box that asks us to select import options, but it's asking the same thing as the Import window.

- Be sure to change Import Kind to Composition.
- Make sure Footage Dimensions is set to Layer Size.
- Click OK.

Open the Composition

- Double-click on the GrowYourCareer composition that has been automatically created.

Just like last time, we've imported an Adobe Illustrator project, and After Effects arranged it nicely into a composition, just the way it looked in Illustrator.

However, in Lesson 1, the Illustrator file was 1920 x 1080 pixels, which is a standard size for video. This is rarely the case with Illustrator files. GrowYourCareer.ai was not designed for video, and is a very small size. I know this by checking the Project panel with the composition selected.

This composition is only 448 x 303 pixels. This would make for a teeny-tiny video that would look pretty bad if enlarged to fill a screen. Let's make this composition bigger.

The Interface & Editing

Animation

Text

Shapes, Masks & Mattes

Effects

3D

Special Tools & Features

Expressions

Composition Settings

➡ Make sure either the timeline or Composition panel is active by clicking on either one—there should be a blue box surrounding the active panel.

➡ Go to Composition > Composition Settings, or press ⌘–K/Ctrl–K.

The Composition Settings dialog is where we can change many aspects of our composition, notably the dimensions, frame rate, and duration. Let's make this a normal size for video.

➡ Uncheck Lock Aspect Ratio.
➡ Set Width to 1920.
➡ Set Height to 1080.

If done correctly, the Preset should now read HDTV 1080 29.97. Selecting this as a preset from the drop-down is another way we could have set this common setting.

Frame Rate

A quick note on frame rate, which is how many frames per second a video plays. The most common frame rates for video are 29.97 (often referred to as 30) and 23.976 (often referred to as 24). If you're adding animation to a video, it's best practice to match the frame rate of the composition to the frame rate of the video (and clicking the video in the Project panel will show what the frame rate is). If you're making an animation without video, you have the freedom to choose a frame rate. Let's stick with 29.97, as the higher frame rate will give us a smoother animation.

⬅ Click OK.

Our composition is now a good size, but we haven't changed the size of the stuff within it. Let's make it bigger.

The Interface & Editing

Animation

Text

Shapes, Masks & Mattes

Effects

3D

Special Tools & Features

Expressions

Null Objects

Our next step is to scale everything in our composition. However, selecting all layers and scaling them together would be a disaster—every object has its own Anchor Point, and each would scale differently. Instead, we want to link all layers to a controller layer. With the proper linking, we should be able to manipulate just the controller, and the rest of the layers should follow.

In this case, I like to create what's called a Null Object. A Null Object is a dummy layer—it's invisible on export, and doesn't do much on its own. However, with the proper linking, we can use a Null Object as a controller for all our layers.

Create a Null Object

➡ Go to Layer > New > Null Object.

We'll now see the Null Object in the top layer of the timeline, and visualized as a red square in the Composition panel.

➡ With the layer [Null 1] selected in the timeline, press return/Enter to rename it.
➡ Name the layer Scene Scaler.
➡ Press return/Enter to confirm.

Parenting

The next step is to link the other layers to the Scene Scaler Null Object. The idea is for all the layers to follow the scale (and if we wanted them to, the position and rotation) of the Null Object.

In After Effects, this type of linking is called parenting. It's a simple yet powerful way to make layers follow other layers. We'll make the Null Object the parent of all the other layers, so wherever the Null Object goes, the other layers will follow.

Parent with Pickwhipping

➡ Select the topmost art layer, called GROW YOUR.

➡ Hold down the shift key.

➡ Select the bottom-most art layer, BACK-GROUND BURST.

Every layer except for the Null Object should be selected.

Each layer has a Pickwhip icon:
◉ Find that now.

➡ Click and drag from the Pickwhip icon of any selected layer to the Scene Scaler Null Object.

➡ Release your mouse.

All art layers should now be children of the Null Object, as indicated by the Parent & Link drop-down.

What does this mean for us? Well, here's the rule of thumb with parenting: Wherever the parent goes, the children will follow. In just a bit, we'll scale the Scene Scaler, which will scale all linked children. However, child layers can also have their own animation as well. Picture a bouncing ball on a moving platform. The bouncing ball is the child, with its own position animation. The platform is the parent that can float around space, bringing the child with it.

The Interface & Editing
Animation
Text
Shapes, Masks & Mattes
Effects
3D
Special Tools & Features
Expressions

Scale the Null

Now, we just have to scale the Scene Scaler Null Object so our stuff fills the frame. Do either of the following:

➡ In the Composition panel, click and drag the corner of the red Scene Scaler Null, while holding shift, until the background touches the top and bottom of the composition frame.

➡ Or, in the timeline, select Scene Scaler.
➡ Tap S to reveal the Scale parameter.
➡ Set Scale to 384.

Regardless of the method, the result should be the same: scaling the Null Object also scales the layer's children, resulting in a single action that scales all linked layers evenly. The image should now fill the frame—at least, vertically.

You'll notice the image has the wrong aspect ratio—that is, the relationship of width to height is off. Let's stretch the background so it fills the frame.

➡ Select the background layer.

It might be easiest to select it from the timeline rather than the Composition panel, as there's stuff on top of it.

➡ In the Composition panel, click and drag the corner of the layer's bounding box to stretch the image horizontally.

Note that we're scaling *without* holding shift, in order to scale disproportionately. We only want to scale about the X-axis.

The Interface & Editing

Animation

Text

Shapes, Masks & Mattes

Effects

3D

Special Tools & Features

Expressions

Continuous Rasterization

Does your image look crunchy? This is an Illustrator file, which is a vector format. This means that we should be able to scale this up infinitely without losing quality, as the image is made of a series of points, not pixels. However, we have to tell After Effects to interpret the artwork as such.

Enable Continuous Rasterization

Find the box underneath the Continuous Rasterization icon in the timeline, which looks like this: ☀.

➡ Select the Continuous Rasterization box for all art layers.

The fastest way to do this is to click in the top box and drag the cursor all the way down to the bottom before releasing. Or you can select all art layers and click the box for any of them. See the difference?

Here's the takeaway: When scaling an Illustrator file over 100%, make sure you switch on Continuous Rasterization so you can take advantage of that sweet vector ability to keep lines crisp.

Note that enabling this feature might increase render times. If this project is running slowly for you, feel free to switch this off. Just make sure to turn it back on before you export.

Animating Scale

Let's make our big Career plant sprout up from the ground. We'll do this by animating scale.

Don't Forget to Set Your Anchor Point
…before animation.

- ➡ Select the Career layer.
- ➡ Switch to the Anchor Point tool by either selecting it from the Toolbar or pressing Y.
- ➡ Drag the Anchor Point down so it's at the bottom of the dirt pile.
- ➡ Tap V to switch back to the Selection tool.

Scale in the Timeline

- ➡ With the Career layer still selected, tap S to reveal the scale parameters in the timeline.

I want to animate this growing from the ground, but only about the Y-axis—a disproportional scale. In order to do this, I must deselect Constrain Proportions next to Scale.

- ➡ Deselect the Constrain Proportions button by clicking on the link icon ⚭.

| 10 | Ⓐ Career | ⊕ ✳ / |
| | Ö Scale | 100.0,100.0% |

Deselecting this box allows you to animate the X and Y scales separately.

The Interface & Editing

Animation

Text

Shapes, Masks & Mattes

Effects

3D

Special Tools & Features

Expressions

Keyframe It

I'm going to add keyframes backward this time. Since my current scale value is what I want for my ending, I'll make this look like the end of my animation.

➥ Navigate to 2 seconds in the timeline.
➥ Click the stopwatch next to Scale to enable scale keyframes and set one at 2 seconds.
➥ Go back to the very beginning of the timeline.
➥ Set the scale's Y value to 0, so the first keyframe holds a Scale value of [100,0]%.

You should now have two keyframes. At 0 seconds, the Y scale of the Career layer should be 0, and at 2 seconds, the Y scale of the Career layer should be 100. The X should remain 100% throughout.

Scale is [100,0]% [100,100]%

Eased Animation

Watch your animation. The plant grows, and you've done such an amazing job. But let's make this even better.

Interpolation refers to *how* keyframe 1 gets to keyframe 2. The default interpolation in After Effects is called linear. This means, all data between two keyframes is equally spaced. Animation happens at a constant rate.

However, nothing organic moves this way. Objects have inertia; they often start slow, pick up speed, and end slow. This is a way we can imply weight to our objects, even if they technically don't have any. This type of keyframe is called Bezier. Let's introduce this into our animation.

Easy Ease

⬆ Right-click your first keyframe.
⬆ Select Keyframe Assistant > Easy Ease.

This can also be called with the hotkey F9. However, on many Mac computers, you must hold down the fn key to make sure F9 calls the function associated with F9, instead of skipping to your next song. This can be configured in your System Preferences, or you can remap this hotkey in Edit > Keyboard Shortcuts.

So, what happened? We've switched this keyframe from a linear keyframe ◆ to an eased keyframe ◀. This object now starts off moving slowly, then picks up speed. Play the animation back to see the difference.

Let's do the same to the second keyframe.

⬆ Right-click your second keyframe.
⬆ Select Keyframe Assistant > Easy Ease.

The plant starts off slow, picks up speed, then eases into its final scale. The effect might be subtle, but it's there. At the very least, I'll throw Easy Ease on nearly all my keyframes. It's easy!

The Interface & Editing

Animation

Text

Shapes, Masks & Mattes

Effects

3D

Special Tools & Features

Expressions

Keyframe Velocity

Easy Ease actually does two things: it converts keyframes to the Bezier interpolation method, then applies a certain amount of influence to the ease. Let's visualize this.

The Graph Editor

We can visualize the values of our keyframes over time in a very nifty interface called the Graph Editor. Find the Graph Editor by clicking on the Graph icon 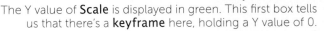 at the top of the timeline.

➡ Open the Graph Editor.
➡ Make sure that the Scale parameter of the Career layer is selected.
➡ You may wish to zoom in on the timeline with = to better see the graph.

Here, we can actually see the values of our keyframes.

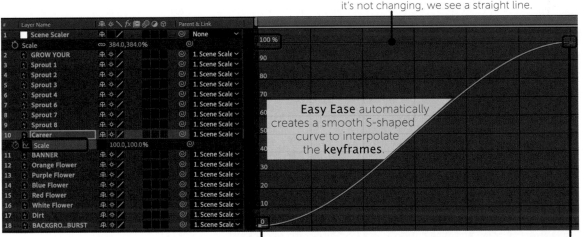

Our X value is represented in red, and since it's not changing, we see a straight line.

Easy Ease automatically creates a smooth S-shaped curve to interpolate the keyframes.

The Y value of **Scale** is displayed in green. This first box tells us that there's a **keyframe** here, holding a Y value of 0.

And Y lands at 100.

Pay attention to the shape of the green line. Because we've applied Easy Ease, we can see a gentle curvature to this line. The curve gently leaves 0% and enters 100%, with a bit of a steeper angle in the middle.

Compare that to a linear graph, which would look like this:

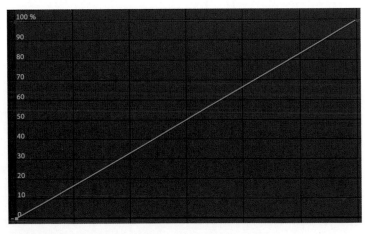

The Interface & Editing

Animation

Text

Shapes, Masks & Mattes

Effects

3D

Special Tools & Features

Expressions

Adjusting Keyframe Velocity

While Easy Ease is great, it might be a little too gentle for some animations. Adjusting keyframe velocity is a great way to quickly change the steepness of this curve. Let's punch up this animation.

➦ Select both keyframes in the Graph Editor.

There are a few ways to do this. You can select both boxes while holding shift, or draw a marquee selection around both keyframes, or click on the Scale parameter in the timeline. Either way, you'll know they're both selected when you see the bounding box around the keyframes:

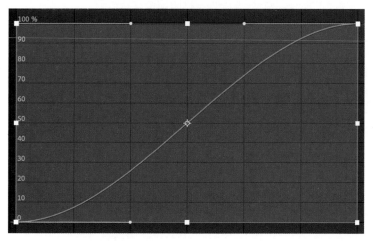

➦ Right-click any keyframe.

Make sure you right-click a keyframe in one of the corners, and not in the center of the graph.

➦ Select Keyframe Velocity.

If you don't see Keyframe Velocity, make sure that you're selecting the keyframe, and not the graph itself.

It's also worth noting that you don't have to be in the Graph Editor to bring up Keyframe Velocity. The same context menu will pop up if you right-click a keyframe in the timeline.

Keyframe Velocity

Keyframe type: Scale

Incoming Velocity   Outgoing Velocity
☑ Lock Dimensions   ☑ Lock Dimensions

   Dimension: X 0 percent/sec   Dimension: X 0 percent/sec
     Influence: 33.33333 %   Influence: 33.33333 %

   Dimension: Y 0 percent/sec   Dimension: Y 0 percent/sec
     Influence: 33.33333 %   Influence: 33.33333 %

☐ Continuous (Lock Outgoing to Incoming)

                                           Setting velocity for 2 keyframes

                                      (Cancel)   (OK)

In this interface, we can adjust for both Incoming Velocity (that is, graph stuff that happens before a keyframe) and Outgoing Velocity (graph stuff that happens after a keyframe). We can also choose to adjust X and Y velocity separately. Let's ignore this precision for now, and crank up all the values.

➡ Set all Influence parameters to 90.

Since Lock Dimensions is checked, you should only have to type it in once in Incoming, and once in Outgoing. Or, check Continuous to only have to type it in once.

➡ Click OK.

And here's our new graph:

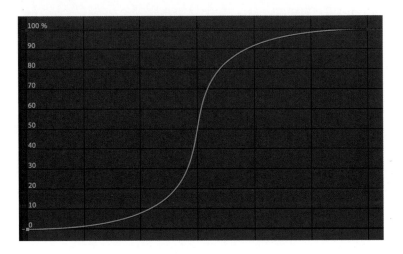

Playing this back, we can see the punchiness of this new animation—it starts off very slow, then gets very fast for a short amount of time, then gets slow again.

Here's the takeaway: while Easy Ease is nice, it's only one default value for Keyframe Velocity. Right-clicking a keyframe and adjusting its Keyframe Velocity (from either the timeline or the Graph Editor) is one way to make the curve of a Bezier keyframe more extreme.

Editing Graphs

The next level in power is to actually edit the Graph Editor itself. This allows for absolute control over how our animation lands.

Graph Bezier Curves

⮞ Select the bottom-left green keyframe in the Graph Editor (if the bounding box is visible, you may have to first deselect, then reselect a single keyframe).

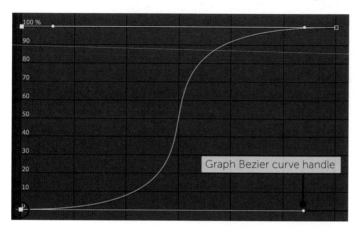

Doing so reveals the Bezier curve handles for your graph, which are the yellow balls at the end of the yellow line pointing outward from the keyframe. Manipulating this handle allows us to directly change the curve of our interpolation graph.

Let's change this graph so our Y scale overshoots—that is, goes beyond the initial value—as it leaves the first keyframe.

⮞ Click and drag the Bezier curve handle for the first keyframe until the curve projects above the 100% line.

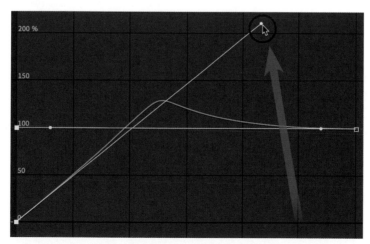

Playing the animation back, we can see the plant now hitting above 100% as it leaves the first keyframe (mine peaks at around 130%), then head back down to rest at 100%.

Let's now make the plant undershoot as it approaches the last keyframe by manipulating the second Bezier curve handle.

The Interface & Editing

Animation

Text

Shapes, Masks & Mattes

Effects

3D

Special Tools & Features

Expressions

Click and drag the second Bezier curve handle to move it out of the way. It's sitting on the 100% line, closer to the left side of the graph.

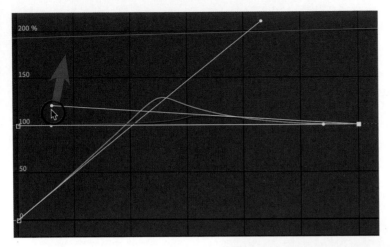

We've actually just manipulated the red X graph, not the Y graph. Since the X graph sits on top of the Y graph, it's necessary to move it out of the way to access the Y graph.

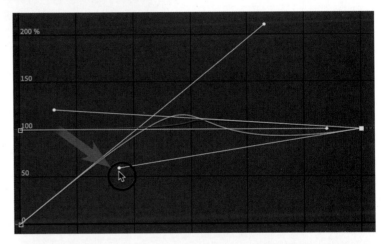

➡ Now, we can click and drag the second Y handle so the graph curves below 100% as it approaches the second keyframe.

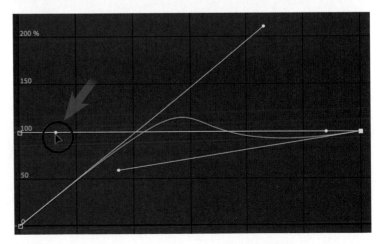

➡ Move the X handle back into its original spot so there's no curve on the X-axis.

➡ Play the animation back.

Now, we're starting to get some personality out of this plant! Things like bouncing, squashing, stretching, and overshooting are some animation fundamentals that breathe life into graphics.

What Is Bezier?

Graphs are made of Bezier curves, and we're going to be seeing a lot more of them. Bezier curves are a simple yet powerful way to gain control of the shape of a curve. There are two elements to a Bezier curve:

- The angle of the handle relative to the origin. In this case, the angle defines the amount of change in the graph values.
- The distance from the handle relative to the origin. In this case, the distance defines the timing of the graph values.

➡ Take some time to play with the graph and refine it so the plant is moving in a playful way.

If you're looking for some direction, you can make your graph look like mine:

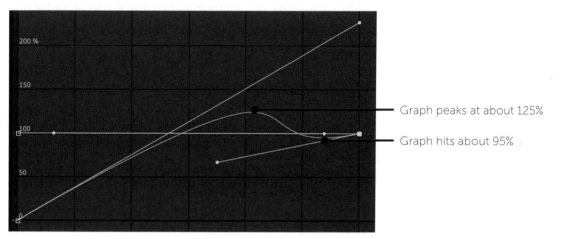

In summary, the **Graph Editor** is an extremely powerful way to detail exactly how **keyframes** interpolate. By creating this overshoot with just two **keyframes**, we keep our **timeline** simple and our animation smooth.

➡ Exit the **Graph Editor** by selecting the **Graph Editor** button again.

The Interface
& Editing

Animation

Text

Shapes, Masks
& Mattes

Effects

3D

Special Tools
& Features

Expressions

Finalize the Animation

Let's make this look nice. This section won't introduce any brand-new concepts—it's more of an application of what we've already learned, and a way to put it all together to make stuff look cool. Feel free to experiment and improvise here.

More Parenting

Let's make it so the leaves follow the stalk. Parenting, once again, is the key.

- ➡ Ensure the playhead is on the last keyframe, or later.
- ➡ Select layer Sprout 1.
- ➡ Hold down shift and select layer Sprout 8.
- ➡ Pickwhip any of the Sprout layers to the Career layer.

Now, the sprouts are parented to the stalk. They should animate perfectly with the stalk's overshoot animation, as if they're one layer.

Is yours looking weird? Make sure that you set the parent while the stalk is at 100% Scale—that is, at the end of the animation. Parented animation is inherited at the frame where the parent is set. So, if you parent when the Scale is at 0%, that scale boost will also apply to the sprouts, and they'll move unpredictably.

Also, note the new parenting hierarchy. The Career layer is still parented to the Scene Scaler Null. If we were to move the Scene Scaler, it would still move the Career layer, and since the sprouts are parented to *that* layer, they would move as well. Basically, the Scene Scaler Null is the grandparent, the Career layer is the parent, and the sprouts are the children.

Reusing Animation

Let's animate the sprouts unfolding (Scale and Rotation) as the plant grows. There are eight sprout layers—animating each of these could take a lot of time. Let's set things up so we can copy and paste animation onto each of these. Lucky for us, each sprout ought to end at a Scale value of 100% and a Rotation value of 0°. So, we can reuse the same keyframes for each.

Create the First Animation

➡ Set the playhead to 3 seconds into the timeline.

➡ **Set the Anchor Point before you animate.** Use the Anchor Point tool to place the Anchor Point of each sprout to the point where they meet the stalk.

➡ When you're done, switch back to the Selection tool.

➡ Select Sprout 1.

➡ Tap R to bring up its Rotation parameter.

➡ Press shift–S to also bring up its Scale parameter.

➡ Click the stopwatch for both Rotation and Scale.

➡ Navigate to 2 seconds in the timeline.

➡ Set the Rotation to around -150°.

➡ Set the Scale to 0%.

➡ Click and drag in the timeline to draw a box around all four keyframes, selecting them all.

➡ Right-click any keyframe and select Keyframe Assistant > Easy Ease, or tap F9.

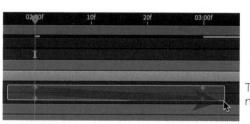

This is called a marquee selection.

➡ Open the Graph Editor.

➡ Select the Rotation parameter in the timeline (you may have to deselect, then reselect).

➡ Using the Bezier curves, add a little overshoot to the rotation, just like we did in the previous section. The amount is up to you.

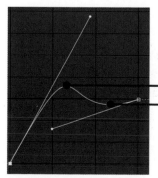

Mine peaks around 30° and then goes down to -12°.

The Interface & Editing

Animation

Text

Shapes, Masks & Mattes

Effects

3D

Special Tools & Features

Expressions

➡ Select the Scale parameter in the timeline.
➡ Add a little overshoot to the scale.

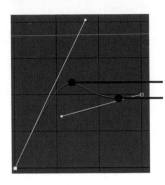

Mine peaks around 115% and then goes down to 95%. Since we have **Constrain Proportions** selected by default, this graph affects both X and Y, and should be simpler to use.

➡ Make sure the movement is to your liking before moving on.
➡ Click the Graph Editor button to close the Graph Editor.

Copy and Paste Keyframes

Now that we're happy with the animation of this one sprout, we can reuse the same animation for all.

➡ Click and drag in the timeline to marquee-select all four keyframes on Sprout 1.
➡ Copy them all with Edit > Copy, or ⌘–C/Ctrl–C.
➡ Navigate to 2 seconds into the timeline.
➡ Select layers Sprout 2 through Sprout 8.
➡ Paste the copied keyframes with Edit > Paste, or ⌘–V/Ctrl–V.
➡ Tap U to reveal all keyframes.

● ◀) ● 🔒	●	#	Layer Name	🐠 ✦ ↘ fx 📦 ◎ ● ⊕	Parent & Link	
●		3	Sprout 1	🐠 ✦ /	◎ 10. Career ∨	
◀ ◆ ▶			Scale	∞ 0.0,0.0%	◎	
◀ ◆ ▶			Rotation	0x-150.0°	◎	
●		4	Sprout 2	🐠 ✦ /	◎ 10. Career ∨	
◀ ◆ ▶			Scale	∞ 0.0,0.0%	◎	
◀ ◆ ▶			Rotation	0x-150.0°	◎	
●		5	Sprout 3	🐠 ✦ /	◎ 10. Career ∨	
◀ ◆ ▶			Scale	∞ 0.0,0.0%	◎	
◀ ◆ ▶			Rotation	0x-150.0°	◎	
●		6	Sprout 4	🐠 ✦ /	◎ 10. Career ∨	
◀ ◆ ▶			Scale	∞ 0.0,0.0%	◎	
◀ ◆ ▶			Rotation	0x-150.0°	◎	
●		7	Sprout 6	🐠 ✦ /	◎ 10. Career ∨	
◀ ◆ ▶			Scale	∞ 0.0,0.0%	◎	
◀ ◆ ▶			Rotation	0x-150.0°	◎	
●		8	Sprout 7	🐠 ✦ /	◎ 10. Career ∨	
◀ ◆ ▶			Scale	∞ 0.0,0.0%	◎	
◀ ◆ ▶			Rotation	0x-150.0°	◎	
●		9	Sprout 8	🐠 ✦ /	◎ 10. Career ∨	
◀ ◆ ▶			Scale	∞ 0.0,0.0%	◎	
◀ ◆ ▶			Rotation	0x-150.0°	◎	

Now, you should see a beautiful burst of all sprouts moving with the same motion.

The Interface
& Editing

Animation

Text

Shapes, Masks
& Mattes

Effects

3D

Special Tools
& Features

Expressions

Offset

Let's not have all sprouts burst at the same time—it makes it obvious that the animation was reused, and overlapping animation will add to the organic motion of this piece.

Retiming animation generally happens in one of two ways. You can click and drag just the keyframes you want to move around, or move the entire layer. In this case, it doesn't really matter, but shifting the layer itself is slightly easier. Let's do that.

➡ Have all Sprout layers selected. If 2–8 are currently selected, you can add Sprout 1 to the selection by holding ⌘/Ctrl and clicking on Sprout 1.

➡ Navigate to 2 seconds into the timeline.

➡ Trim all selected layers so they start at this time. Do so by either clicking and dragging the ends of the layers, or with opt-[/Alt-[.

➡ Tap U to hide the keyframed parameters.

We've now trimmed our layers so the animation starts where the layer starts. This way, even if my keyframes are hidden, I know where my animation begins. This makes editing timing a little simpler, and lets me keep my timeline a little cleaner.

➡ Navigate to 1 second into the timeline.

➡ Select layer Sprout 1. You may have to deselect and reselect it.

➡ Tap [to shift the layer's In point to the current time.

You can also click and drag a layer in the timeline to change its timing, but hotkeys are neat.

➡ Retime sprouts 2–8 so the layers' In points are staggered.

➡ Play your animation back and reflect on how clunky your alien animation was, and how far you've come in a single chapter. Bully for you!

Adding Text

The layer GROW YOUR is an Illustrator layer. We can animate it just like any other layer. However, it's difficult to animate each letter at a time. If we instead recreate this layer as a text layer, not only do we have options to change the font and style, but we can also add a powerful text animator that lets us animate on a per-letter basis.

Creating a Text Layer

- Click the eyeball on the GROW YOUR layer to switch it off. We won't be needing that anymore.
- Select the Type tool, either from the toolbar  or with ⌘–T/Ctrl–T.
- Click once on the left side of the blue banner in the Composition panel.
- Type GROW YOUR.
- Click anywhere in the timeline to finish typing.

Editing Text

Ok, I've just made things much worse. Let's fix that.

- In the timeline, select the red GROW YOUR 2 text layer that we've just created.
- On the right side of the After Effects interface, find the Character panel. If it's not already open, open it by clicking on it.
- Under the font drop-down (mine says Helvetica), change this font to something more interesting. For Mac/PC agnosticism, I'll just go with Courier New for now.
- Under the style drop-down, I'll change mine from Regular to Bold.
- For font size, I'll increase mine to about 255.
- Click this white box to quickly set your font color to pure white.

➡ Use the Selection tool to move the text to a good spot.

A full list of features of the Character panel can be found in chapter 3 of the Compendium.

Text on a Path

Let's make this text land on a curved line, just as it did in the original version.

➡ Double-check that the text layer GROW YOUR 2 is still selected.

➡ Select the Pen tool, either from the toolbar 🖊 or with G.

➡ In the Composition panel, click and drag under the G to create your first path point.

➡ Release your mouse.

We've just added a path point to this layer. Since we clicked and dragged, we automatically converted that path point to a Bezier curve—just like the ones in the Graph Editor. Yours will likely be a different color from mine, as it's randomized.

➡ Click and drag in the center of the banner to create a second path point.

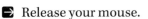

➡ Release your mouse.
➡ Click and drag under the R to create a third path point.

➡ Release.

You should now have three path points that create a curved line that may or may not resemble the curve of the banner. We'll fix that in a second.

Are any of your points hard corners? We want each point to be a Bezier. If you didn't drag your mouse when you created the path, the point will be a hard corner. That's easily fixed. With the Pen tool still selected, click on a path point while holding opt/Alt to convert it.

Edit the Path
No one gets this right on their first try. Let's make the path align more closely with the banner.

➡ Switch to the Selection tool.
➡ Select a path point to reveal its Bezier handles.
➡ Just like in the Graph Editor, click and drag the Bezier handles until the curve of this path is similar to the curve of the banner.

We've added a path to this text layer, which does…absolutely nothing. Let's now tell After Effects to align the text to the path.

Align the Text to the Path

➡ In the timeline, unfurl the text layer's Triangle > Text > Path Options.
➡ Under Path, switch the drop-down from None to Mask 1. The text should now be aligned to the path.

The Interface & Editing

Animation

Text

Shapes, Masks & Mattes

Effects

3D

Special Tools & Features

Expressions

Animating Text

Now that we have a text layer, we can animate the letters or words individually. A full description of creating a custom text animation is detailed in chapter 3 of the Compendium. For now, let's use a preset to make our lives simpler.

The Effects & Presets Panel

After Effects has a number of pre-built animations and effects. These can be accessed in the Effects & Presets panel.

- ⮑ Open this panel by clicking on its tab in the right side of the interface.
- ⮑ Unfurl *Animation Presets > Text > Animate In.
- ⮑ Bring the playhead to the beginning of the timeline.
- ⮑ Make sure the text layer GROW YOUR 2 is selected.
- ⮑ From the Effects & Presets panel, double-click Drop In By Character to apply the preset to that layer.

You should now have each letter drop into the frame, one at a time. There might be some things we ought to tweak.

First, let's adjust the timing. How does this preset work? The way all things work in After Effects: keyframes.

- ⮑ With GROW YOUR 2 selected, tap U to reveal key-frames on the layer.
- ⮑ Slide the second keyframe inward so it lands at 2 seconds.

Now that we've fixed the speed, we need to fix the fact that the letters start on-screen (at least, they do in my case).

- ⮑ Navigate to the beginning of the timeline.
- ⮑ With GROW YOUR 2 selected, tap U twice (like a double-click) to reveal all edited parameters of the layer.
- ⮑ Under the Animator 1 category, find Posi-tion (not the Position under Transform).

➡ Decrease the Y value until the letters start off-screen.

Here's the deal with presets: at best, they're a one-click solution to achieve complicated or time-consuming results. The problem is, you don't have access to the mind of the person who created it, and sometimes one click doesn't fit all. However, remember that tapping U reveals all keyframes on a layer, and tapping U twice reveals every edited parameter of the layer. This might be a quick way to reverse-engineer a preset.

Retiming, Again
Let's make room for our new animation so the text lands, then we see the rest of the animation.

➡ With GROW YOUR 2 selected, tap U to hide all that junk.
➡ Tap U again to reveal just the keyframes on that layer.
➡ Move the playhead to 2 seconds into the timeline.
➡ Select all the Sprout layers, plus the Career layer.
➡ Click and drag all selected layers so Career begins at 2 seconds, and the other layers move with it.

Trim the Comp
The composition is too long. Let's cut it down.

➡ Navigate to 7 seconds.
➡ Tap N to set the Work Area end to the playhead.
➡ Right-click within the gray Work Area bar and select Trim Comp to Work Area.

The Interface & Editing

Animation

Text

Shapes, Masks & Mattes

Effects

3D

Special Tools & Features

Expressions

Exporting

Now that we're "done," let's export this video so you can send it to your grandma. She'll be thrilled to hear from you.

Note that the following section covers exporting, which is the process of making a stand-alone video to be shared on the web. If working in Premiere is a big part of your workflow, you should use the rendering process instead to export a higher-quality video. We'll go over that in the next chapter.

Add to Adobe Media Encoder Queue

⇥ Select Composition > Add To Media Encoder Queue.

This will send your After Effects composition to Adobe Media Encoder, a freestanding piece of software used to queue exports for both Premiere and After Effects. Of course, this is assuming it's installed. If it's not, install it from the Creative Cloud App.

Hopefully, your settings default to these—if not, ensure that Format is set to H.264 and Preset is Match Source – High bitrate. H.264 is a highly versatile format that is used all over the internet. It keeps files relatively small at the expense of some image quality. How much image quality? That's decided by the Preset. Match Source – High bitrate is a good high-quality file, but you can use the drop-down here if you need it smaller.

⇥ Finally, click the blue link under Output To to decide where to save your file.

You should save it in the 08_Deliverables folder for this project, but I'm not the boss of you.

⇥ When you're ready, hit enter/Return or the green Encode arrow.

It might take a minute or so, but your composition will be exported and ready for the world.

So far, we've been working with premade assets. But After Effects allows you to create your own assets from scratch. Shape layers are similar to imported Illustrator layers, but they're much more powerful. You can easily customize the shape, color, and much more.

This chapter will also teach you how to apply and modify an effect. We'll then look at a different way to export.

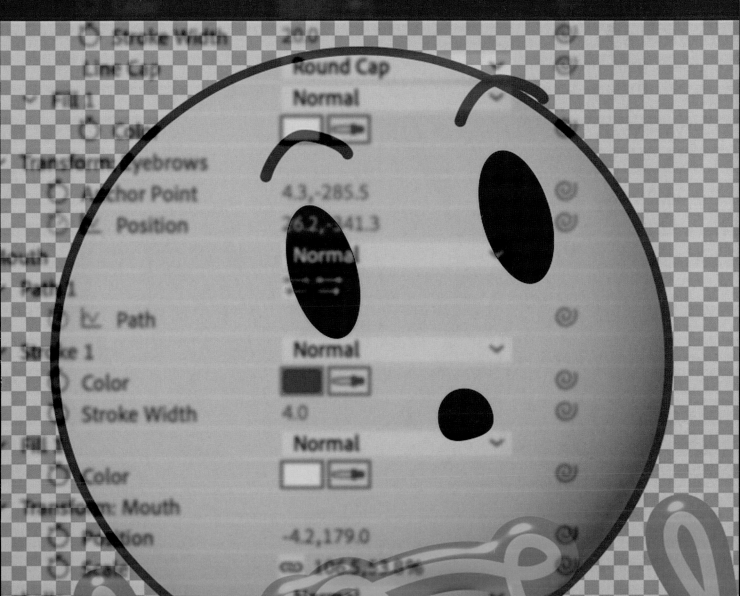

The Course

Set Up the Project

The Lesson 3 project file is completely empty! We'll be making our own kombucha today.

➥ Fire up a new After Effects project, either by clicking New Project from the splash screen, or with File > New Project.

➥ Save this project into Lesson 3 > 05_Project, naming it Lesson 3.

Creating a New Composition from Scratch

So far, we've been opening compositions based on imported Illustrator files. Since we're starting from scratch, we'll need to make a brand-new composition.

➥ Either select Composition > New Composition (⌘–N/Ctrl–N) or select the composition icon 🖼 at the bottom of the Project panel.

You'll see the New Composition panel, which is nearly identical to the Composition Settings panel we saw in the last chapter.

➥ Name the composition Emoji.

➥ Make sure the Preset is HDTV 1080 29.97.

➥ Set the Duration to 6 seconds (0;00;06;00).

➥ Click OK.

Let's set up the composition for design.

➥ At the bottom of the Composition panel, click the Toggle Transparency Grid icon ▣ (if it isn't already selected) to make the background a checkerboard.

➥ Click on the Choose Grid and Guide Options icon ▦ and select Proportional Grid.

Your empty composition should look like this:

Enabling the Proportional Grid is optional, but I find it to be helpful while designing. I'll be toggling it on and off for various screenshots throughout this chapter. Note that it won't appear on export.

The Interface & Editing

Animation

Text

Shapes, Masks & Mattes

Effects

3D

Special Tools & Features

Expressions

Creating an Emoji

In this chapter, we're going to design and animate an emoji. Some say using emojis on the job is unprofessional, and to that I say 🙅.

Create an Ellipse Shape

We'll start with the emoji's big dumb yellow head.

- ➡ Find the Shape tool in the Toolbar, which should look like a rectangle 🔲.
- ➡ Click and hold on the Shape tool until you see the drop-down.
- ➡ Select the Ellipse tool.

With a Shape tool selected, clicking and dragging in the composition creates a new shape layer, which contains your shape. Let's make a perfect circle in the middle of this composition.

- ➡ Move your cursor to the center of your composition (the Proportional Grid will help here).
- ➡ Click and drag from the center of the composition out to the edge of the composition.
- ➡ Hold ⌘/Ctrl so the ellipse's center point is the first place we clicked.
- ➡ Hold shift so the ellipse scales proportionally and becomes a perfect circle.
- ➡ Release your mouse.

Your ellipse (technically a circle now) should look like this:

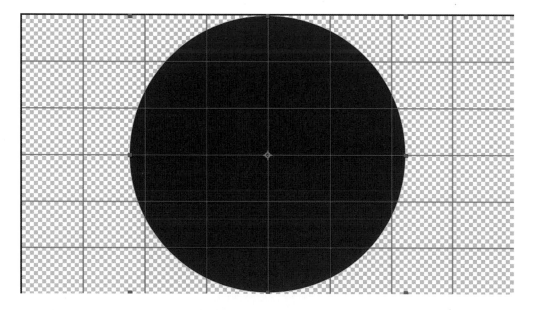

Let's rewind a little. By default, clicking and dragging with a Shape tool selected defines the top and bottom corners of the shape. However, clicking and dragging while holding ⌘/Ctrl changes this so you're defining the center and edge of your shape. This can be an easy way to center a shape around a specific point. Holding down shift while creating a shape makes the X and Y proportional, if you want to create a perfect circle or square.

Change a Shape's Fill

Congratulations, we've completed our lesson on recreating the Japanese flag 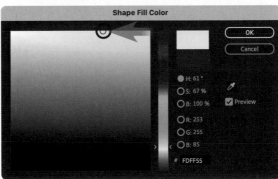. Just kidding. Let's change the fill, or the color of the shape's insides.

With this new Shape Layer 1 selected, you should see options for Fill and Stroke in the toolbar.

▶ Click the red box next to Fill ▪ to change this shape's fill color.

You'll see the Color Picker, Adobe's main way of choosing any color imaginable.

Let's make this sucker that classic Emoji yellow.

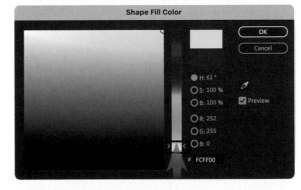

▶ Use the Hue slider in the center of the interface to choose yellow as the hue.

Let's lower the saturation, or intensity, of the yellow.

▶ Move the dot in the color field a little to the left to lower the saturation of the yellow.

Now, let's make it a little darker.

The Interface & Editing

Animation

Text

Shapes, Masks & Mattes

Effects

3D

Special Tools & Features

Expressions

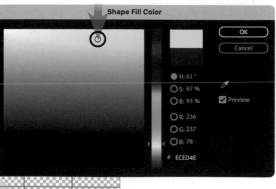

➡ Move the dot in the color field downward to lower the yellow's brightness.

➡ Click OK.

We now have a big yellow circle.

Hmm…flat solid color design is so 2022. Let's bring this graphic back into the early '00s with a gradient.

Gradient Fill

We're going to change the type of fill on this shape from Solid to Gradient.

➡ Click on the word Fill 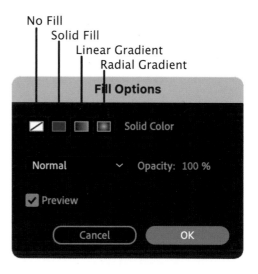 in the Toolbar.

We'll see the Fill Options dialog.

➡ Select Radial Gradient .
➡ Click OK.

Our circle is now filled with a Radial Gradient. A Radial Gradient is a fill that transitions from at least one color to another, doing so in outward concentric circles.

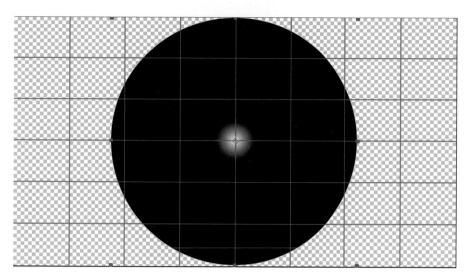

Gradient Placement

We have the option to place the gradient anywhere we want within the shape. Right now, mine isn't filling the entirety of the shape. Let's fix that.

➡ Switch to the Selection tool.
➡ Make sure that either Ellipse 1, or any content underneath it, is selected in the timeline.

You should see the Gradient Editor in the Composition panel. If not, double-check the above steps. Note that the Gradient Editor will not appear if you have a Shape tool selected.

Gradient Editor start
Gradient Editor end

➡ Click and drag the Gradient Editor end handle until the gradient fills the entire shape.

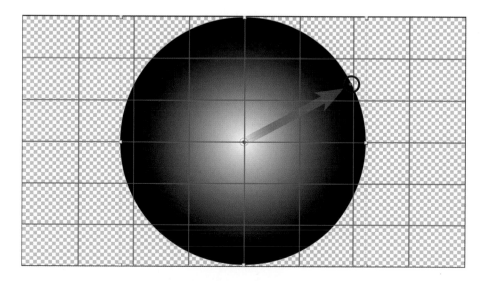

The Interface & Editing

Animation

Text

Shapes, Masks & Mattes

Effects

3D

Special Tools & Features

Expressions

Gradient Colors

Let's make this gradient not black and white.

➡ Select the Gradient Fill icon ▣ from the Toolbar.

We'll now see the **Gradient Editor** dialog, which is very similar to the **Color Picker**.

The difference is that instead of editing the entire color at once, we'll edit multiple color stops. The gradient will automatically transition from one color stop to the next.

➡ Make sure the first color stop is selected. It's the white box underneath the gradient stripe.

➡ Choose a shade of yellow that makes you happy.

➡ Select the second color stop, the black box underneath the gradient stripe.

➡ Choose a slightly darker shade of yellow. I'm a fan of sublety here.

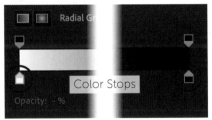

Once you've chosen two shades, your gradient stripe might look something like this:

Let's do one more thing before we finalize this. Note that gradients don't have to go evenly from one color to the next. They can favor one color versus the other. We achieve this with the Color Midpoint ◈ .

➡ Slide the Color Midpoint to the right, until the Location reads about 90%.

➡ Click OK to confirm and close this dialog.

Now that's looking more like an Emoji!

I want to make one final tweak.

➡ Move the Gradient Editors around so the gradient falls more in the lower-right area of the shape.

The Interface & Editing

Animation

Text

Shapes, Masks & Mattes

Effects

3D

Special Tools & Features

Expressions

Change a Shape's Stroke

This shape also has a stroke, which is an outline around the shape. It might be a little difficult to see, since it's white and thin. Let's make it more prominent.

➡ In the Toolbar, click the white square next to the word Stroke ▣ to edit the stroke's color.
➡ Make it a light brown.
➡ Click OK.
➡ Find the Stroke Width setting, which should say 2 px next to the box we just clicked `2 px`.
➡ Increase the Stroke Width to 15.

Our Emoji face should look like this:

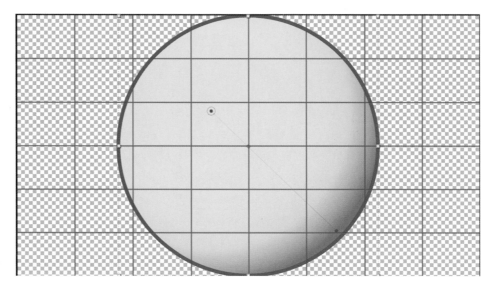

Rename Your Stuff

Let's name this layer and the shape within it so we can stay organized.

➡ In the timeline, select the layer Shape Layer 1.
➡ Press return/Enter.
➡ Type in Emoji.
➡ Press return/Enter.
➡ Find Shaper Layer 1 > Contents > Ellipse 1.
➡ Click on the text that reads Ellipse 1.
➡ Press return/Enter.
➡ Type in Head.
➡ Press return/Enter.

Add More Shapes

A single shape layer can contain multiple shapes. Just for fun, we're going to make this entire Emoji a single layer.

Let's give it an eyeball.

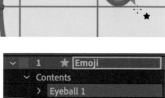

⮕ Select the Ellipse tool  from the Toolbar.
⮕ Make sure the shape layer, now called emoji, is selected.
⮕ Draw an eyeball.

Since the shape layer was selected, we've added this shape to the same layer. Let's rename it.

⮕ In this layer's Contents, rename the newly created Ellipse 1 to Eyeball 1.

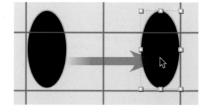

Now, let's make it look the way we want it.

⮕ With Eyeball 1 still selected, change the Fill type to Solid.
⮕ Change the Fill color to black.
⮕ Change the Stroke to white.
⮕ Decrease the Stroke Width to around 4.

Duplicate the Eyeball

To make the two shapes "eye-dentical," we can simply duplicate what we've already created.

⮕ In the timeline, select Eyeball 1.
⮕ Duplicate it with either Edit > Duplicate or ⌘-D/Ctrl-D.

After Effects automatically renamed our new shape Eyeball 2, which is pretty cool. Now, let's reposition it.

⮕ Switch to the Selection tool.
⮕ Select Eyeball 2 and move it over. Holding down shift while doing so will move it in a straight line.

Duplicate Again for the Mouth

The mouth is just going to be another duplicate of one of our eyeballs.

⮕ In the timeline, select either Eyeball shape.
⮕ Duplicate it with either Edit > Duplicate or ⌘-D/Ctrl-D.
⮕ Rename the shape to Mouth.
⮕ Reposition it.

Resize the Mouth

Let's make the mouth more of an even circle. With the Mouth

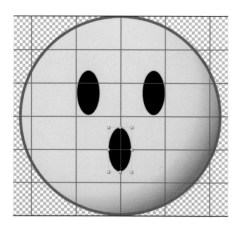

The Interface & Editing

Animation

Text

Shapes, Masks & Mattes

Effects

3D

Special Tools & Features

Expressions

shape selected in the timeline, you should see a bounding box around it. This bounding box lets you rotate and scale a shape. Let's scale it down.

➡ Select the corner of the bounding box and drag it inward to scale the mouth down vertically.

Add a Custom Shape

We don't have to use After Effects' prebuilt shapes—we can create our own. Let's do that to add some eyebrows.

➡ Select the Pen tool in the toolbar , either by clicking on it or with the hotkey G.

The Pen tool lets us draw our own Bezier shapes—just like in the previous section when we created the path for our text. Again, with a shape layer selected, the Pen tool will add a new shape to the selected layer.

➡ Click and drag above the eyebrow to draw a new path point and convert it to Bezier.

➡ Add two more path points to draw an arc—both Bezier as well, with a click and drag.

Often, one will complete the shape by selecting the first point they drew. This will close the shape, so the stroke travels around the whole thing. We're not going to do that this time—we want to just keep this a simple stroke outline, with no fill.

➡ Complete the shape by switching to the Selection tool.

Are any of your points hard corners? We want each point to be a Bezier. If you didn't drag your mouse when you created the path, the point will be a hard corner. That's easily fixed. With the Pen tool selected, click on a path point while holding opt/Alt to convert it.

➡ Rename Shape 1 to be Eyebrow 1.

Stroke Settings

Let's make this look halfway decent.

➡ Under Fill Options, set the Fill to No Fill ▱.
➡ Open the Stroke Color Picker ▣.
➡ Click on the Eyedropper ✒.
➡ Click on the brown outline of the Emoji's face. This will set this stroke to the same color as the face stroke.

➥ Click OK.

➥ Increase the Stroke Width to around 20.

Strokes have their own suite of customization options.

➥ In the timeline, unfurl Emoji > Contents > Eyebrow 1 > Stroke 1.

This is another way to access the controls in the **Toolbar**, plus many more.

➥ Find Line Cap. Switch this from Butt Cap to Round Cap.

This rounds the ends of our stroke, which I often find to be a nice look. Make sure you're happy with the look of your eyebrow before moving on. You can edit a Bezier shape's path points with the Selection tool if needed. I find it easiest to select Path 1 from the timeline to see my path points.

➥ Once you're happy with the look, duplicate Eyebrow 1 and move it over.

That's it for the design of the emoji! Feel free to polish it up to your liking.

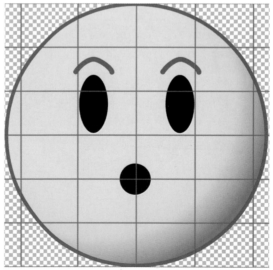

The Interface & Editing

Animation

Text

Shapes, Masks & Mattes

Effects

3D

Special Tools & Features

Expressions

Organizing Shape Layers

Keeping your shape layers organized can help with animation. Let's say I always want my eyebrows to move together—how would I achieve that? Since everything is in one layer, I can't easily parent them. However, I can move my eyebrows into a single group, and then animate the group.

Grouping Shapes

Let's do just that—place both eyebrow shapes into a group.

- Select Eyebrow 1.
- Hold shift and select Eyebrow 2, so they're both selected.
- Right-click either Eyebrow and select Group Shapes, or hit ⌘–G/Ctrl–G.

Both eyebrow shapes are now in a group called Group 1. What's special about this? Well, groups have their very own transform controls. This means I can animate the transform for the group itself, which will move all shapes within the group.

- Unfurl Group 1, then unfurl Transform: Group 1.
- Let's also rename Group 1 to Eyebrows.

Group the Eyes

Let's also put the eyeballs in a group.

- Select both Eyeball shapes.
- Place them in a group.
- Rename the group to Eyeballs.

Group All the Facial Features

Now let's put all facial features into one group.

➡ Select the Eyebrows group, Mouth, and the Eyeballs group.

➡ Group them.

➡ Rename this group to Face.

The final heirarchy of our shapes should look like this before moving on:

Contents has two top-level items, **Face** and **Head**.

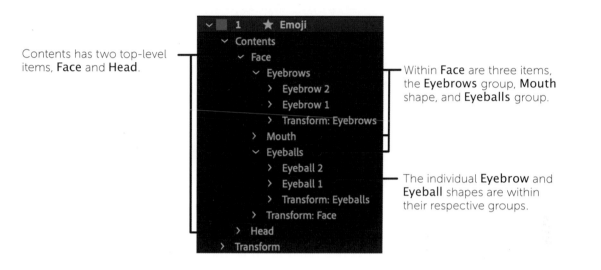

Within **Face** are three items, the **Eyebrows** group, **Mouth** shape, and **Eyeballs** group.

The individual **Eyebrow** and **Eyeball** shapes are within their respective groups.

Is the word group starting to look weird? It's time to move on.

The Interface & Editing

Animation

Text

Shapes, Masks & Mattes

Effects

3D

Special Tools & Features

Expressions

Animating an Emoji

Let's animate this. This section doesn't contain a lot of new information, but it's good practice.

Using Markers

Sometimes, I like to block my animation out so I have a plan. One way I do this is with markers. Markers are simply little flags on the timeline that can be reminders or bookmarks. They're helpful for plotting out where you want animation to land, especially because the playhead can snap to a marker if you move it while holding shift.

- To set the first marker, make sure the playhead is at the beginning of the timeline.
- Click the Marker icon ▽, which is at the far right of the timeline.

You should see a marker at your current time.

- Set more markers at 2, 4, and 6 seconds.

If the composition is 6 seconds long, and the first frame starts at 0;00;00;00, then the last frame of the composition is actually 0;00;05;29, not 0;00;06;00. That's fine.

We can also rename markers to tell us what they stand for. In this case, each marker will be a different direction that the face looks at.

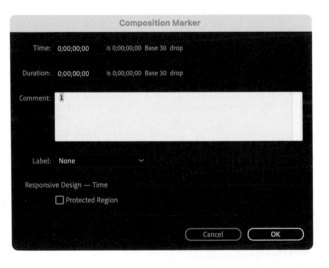

- Double click on the first marker you created, Marker 1.

This opens the Composition Marker dialog. In the Comment field, type Forward (because at this time, our emoji will be facing forward).

- Click OK.

The marker displays your comment. This is helpful—markers can store notes, reminders, and directions.

- Set the marker at 2 seconds to say Left, the marker at 3 seconds to say Right, and the final marker to say Forward.

Animate the Face Group

The reason we spent the time grouping the facial features is so we can easily animate the entire face moving with just a few keyframes.

➡️ Move the playhead to the beginning of the timeline, at the first Forward marker.
➡️ Unfurl the Transform controls for the Face group. It should be the last thing listed in the Face group.
➡️ Set a keyframe for Position and Rotation.

Align the playhead with the Left marker (remember, holding shift helps).

➡️ Select Transform: Face in the timeline to make sure the Face group itself is selected.
➡️ Using the Selection and Wotate tools, move the Face group so the face is looking left and rotated slightly.

Fun fact: You actually don't need to use the Wotate tool to rotate a shape layer. You can simply click and drag just outside a bounding box corner.

Double-check that Position and Rotation keyframes have been added to the Transform: Face control. If not, you've moved the wrong element, or haven't properly keyframed within the Face transforms.

➡️ Move the playhead to the Right marker.
➡️ Position and rotate the Face group so it's looking to the right.

When your first and last keyframes are identical, you get a perfectly looping animation. Let's copy-paste our first keyframes to the end.

➡️ Use a marquee selection to select the first Position and Rotation keyframes in the timeline.
➡️ Copy these two keyframes with Edit > Copy or ⌘–C/Ctrl-C.
➡️ Move the playhead to the end of the timeline.
➡️ Paste the first two keyframes at the end of the timeline with Edit > Paste or ⌘–V/Ctrl-V.
➡️ Play it back and make sure it's a perfect loop.

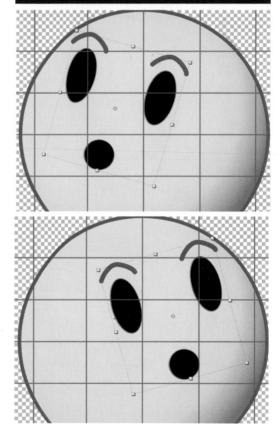

The Interface & Editing

Animation

Text

Shapes, Masks & Mattes

Effects

3D

Special Tools & Features

Expressions

Animate the Eyebrows

We've also grouped our eyebrows, making animating the two very easy.

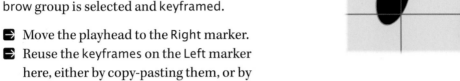

- ⮞ Jump to the beginning of the timeline.
- ⮞ Unfurl the Transform controls for the Eye-
  brows group.
- ⮞ Set a Position keyframe.
- ⮞ Move the playhead to the Left marker.
- ⮞ Move the Eyebrow group up slightly, for a
  raised eyebrow expression.

Again, you should double-check that the Eyebrow group is selected and keyframed.

- ⮞ Move the playhead to the Right marker.
- ⮞ Reuse the keyframes on the Left marker
  here, either by copy-pasting them, or by
  creating new keyframes with the Create New Keyframe button ◀ ◇ ▶ .
- ⮞ Navigate to the end of the timeline.
- ⮞ Copy-paste the first keyframes, from the Forward view.
- ⮞ Paste the first keyframes at the end.

The end result is this: Eyebrows are down at the beginning, get raised on the Left view, stay at
the same position for the Right view, then lower back down at the ending. The animation should
still perfectly loop.

Animate the Mouth

The mouth is a single shape, not in a group, so animating it should be easy. This time, we'll be
animating a single shape's path.

Convert a Shape to a Bezier Path

I want to change the shape of the mouth. Right now it's just an ellipse—I can't distort it to form
different mouth positions. Recall that the mouth is a preset ellipse shape. Compare that to the
eyebrows, which are a custom Bezier path that I can change to be any shape I want. If I want
to change the shape of my ellipse to something else, I first have to convert it to a Bezier path.

- ⮞ Unfurl Mouth > Ellipse Path 1.
- ⮞ Right-click on Ellipse Path 1.
- ⮞ Select Convert to Bezier Path.

Note that my Size and Position controls for the shape are gone. Instead, I just have a single
attribute for Path.

Keyframe a Path

When we keyframe a Bezier path, we can animate into any shape we want. This is a very powerful animation tool.

▶ Unfurl Mouth > Path 1.
▶ Navigate to the beginning of the timeline.
▶ Set a keyframe for Path.
▶ Navigate to the Left marker.

We now want to change the shape of the mouth. However, you likely have the Path attribute selected in the timeline. With this selected, we can't select individual keyframes. We must instead select Path 1—the category, not the keyframe.

▶ Deselect Path by clicking anywhere in the timeline, or with ⌘-shift-A/Ctrl-Shift-A.
▶ Click on Path 1.

Hollow boxes indicate that you can select individual path points.

...as opposed to solid boxes, which means all path points are selected and you can't manipulate points individually.

When animating mouths, I like to actually move my mouth to mimic what my character is doing. The Left marker should indicate the "aah" part of coming out of the W—the "Waah" of the "Wow." I'm going for an exaggerated, dumbstruck "wow," so my character's first mouth position will be a giant, goofy "aah"—jaw dropped, mouth agape. After practicing this, you might understand why many animators prefer to work in private.

▶ Move the path points to make a big, opened mouth shape, perhaps with a slight frown.

Remember, a mouth's opening is controlled by the jaw lowering, so the top point probably doesn't have to move a lot.

Now, the "ooh" of the Wow. W-aah-ooh.

▶ Navigate to the Right marker.
▶ Close the mouth some and bring back some of that circular shape to make an "ooh" shape.

Some tips: You may want to copy-paste your first keyframe here, then distort from that. Also, double-clicking a path point brings up a bounding box, which will let you scale your path points together, if you want this mouth shape to be smaller.

Finally, let's make it loop.

▶ Copy-paste your first keyframe to the end of the timeline.

Wow!

The Interface & Editing

Animation

Text

Shapes, Masks & Mattes

Effects

3D

Special Tools & Features

Expressions

Finesse the Animation

Everything is in place, but the animation is too slow. Let's make it look good.

➥ With the Emoji layer selected, tap U to hide all attributes.
➥ Tap U again to reveal just the keyframed attributes.

You should have a clean look at your entire timeline and the 16 keyframes we've created:

These keyframes could use a little Ease.

➥ Select all keyframes.
➥ Right-click any and select Keyframe Assistant > Easy Ease or tap F9.

Already, this is looking much better. If you want, you may consider playing with Keyframe Velocity for a different ease type.

Offset Animation

As you've probably figured out, I like to first set keyframes in a sort of grid, usually aligned to one- or two-second long (or even half- or quarter-second) animations. This places my keyframes in predictable spots, making them easy to align. I also find it easy to think about animations in terms of seconds, half-seconds, or quarter-seconds, since a second is pretty easy to visualize.

However, once the aligned grid has been set, it's a good idea to then break out of it. Having everything happen at the same time is boring, and inorganic. I call this process offsetting animation, and it's also referred to as overlapping animation. Let's start shifting keyframes.

First, I want to make the entirety of the eyebrow animation happen faster. Note that the Eyebrow keyframes should be the topmost one listed in the timeline. Here's a trick to squish several keyframes together, to make them play faster.

➥ Select all the Eyebrow keyframes (these should be the topmost keyframes in the timeline, or the ones listed under Transform: Eyebrows).
➥ Hold down opt/Alt.
➥ Click and drag the last keyframe inward.

Normally, clicking and dragging several keyframes moves them. However, doing so while holding opt/Alt squishes or stretches them—kind of like a scale function. This is a great way to speed up or slow down animation made up of several keyframes.

Now, let's do the same to the first keyframe.

➥ Click and drag the first keyframe inward while holding opt/Alt.

➥ Play with the eyebrow timing until it's to your liking.

Let's do the same for the mouth.

➥ Using the above technique, squish the Mouth keyframes so the mouth animation is slightly faster than the eyebrow animation.

Finally, Some Blinks

Add a couple of blinks by vertically scaling down the Eyeballs group. I'll let you figure this one out on your own. Remember: blinks are very fast. And once you've animated a single blink to your liking, you should be able to simply copy-paste the blink keyframes anywhere in the timeline.

The Interface & Editing

Animation

Text

Shapes, Masks & Mattes

Effects

3D

Special Tools & Features

Expressions

Shape Effects

Shape layers have their own suite of effects, which can only be applied to shape layers. They're really fun. Let's play with them.

Create a New Shape Layer

So far, we've been adding shapes to our preexisting shape layer because the shape layer was selected when we used either the Pen or Shape tools. This time, we want to create a brand-new shape layer. So, we have to make sure our preexisting shape layer is not selected.

➦ Deselect the Emoji layer by clicking in the timeline, or with ⌘-shift-A/Ctrl-Shift-A.

➦ Select the Pen tool.

I'm now going to ask you to do the most difficult task in this entire book.

➦ Using the Pen tool, write the word WOW in cursive.

Cruel, I know. But it's great Bezier curve practice. If you give up, feel free to just follow my path.

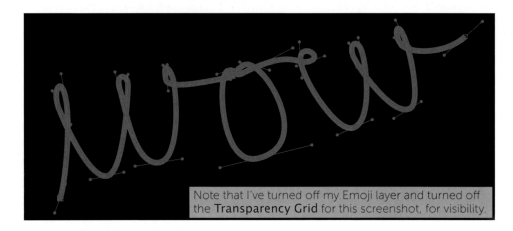

Note that I've turned off my Emoji layer and turned off the **Transparency Grid** for this screenshot, for visibility.

Is this a separate layer? Double-check before you go too far.

➦ Rename the new Shape Layer 1 to Wow.

Arrange the Elements

Since the Wow path and the Emoji are separate layers, it's very easy to arrange them.

➦ Scale and position each layer so they fit on-screen together in a nice way. You'll probably want to scale the Emoji down.

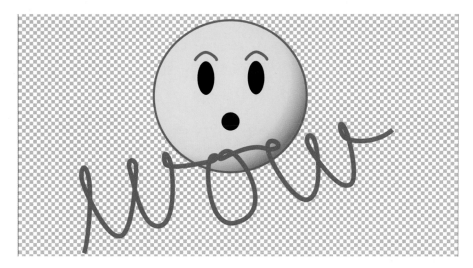

Make the Text Look Good

The Wow Bezier shape we've just created probably has the same characteristics as the last thing we drew, which were the eyebrows. Hopefully, this means our new shape doesn't have a fill. If it does, turn the Fill off.

Let's play with this a little.

- Set the color of the Stroke to one of your choosing.
- You may want to increase the Stroke Width.

I also want to change the Line Cap. Let's do this faster by using the search bar.

- Make sure the Wow layer is selected.
- In the timeline search bar, type Line Cap.
- Set the Line Cap to Round Cap.
- Click the x in the search bar to remove the search query.

Adding a Second Stroke

I heard you like strokes, so I got you a stroke for your stroke. Yep, shapes can have multiple strokes—or multiple fills, but that can get a little tricky. For now, let's add a second stroke.

- Unfurl the Wow layer's Triangle > Contents > Shape 1.

Note that Add button `Add:` when we unfurl a shape layer. This lets us add stuff—strokes, shapes, or effects—to our preexisting shape layer.

- Select Shape 1. We want to add the stroke to this shape.
- Click the triangle next to Add.
- Select Stroke.

The Interface & Editing

Animation

Text

Shapes, Masks & Mattes

Effects

3D

Special Tools & Features

Expressions

There should now be two strokes listed under Shape 1.

Editing the parameters to this stroke in the Toolbar no longer works, as this will affect all strokes in the shape. We must edit Stroke 2 individually in the timeline.

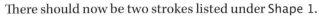

- ⮕ Unfurl Stroke 2.
- ⮕ Play with the Color, Width, Line Cap, and perhaps even the Opacity until the stroke looks the way you want it.

You can also rearrange the order of the Strokes in the timeline if you want one to be atop the other.

Here's what mine looks like, but feel free to go nuts here:

Stroke Taper

We can taper our stroke so it's not the same width throughout.

- ⮕ Decide which stroke you want to taper. I'll eventually do both.
- ⮕ In the timeline, unfurl Taper under the stroke you wish to taper.
- ⮕ Increase the Start and End Length until you find a look you like.

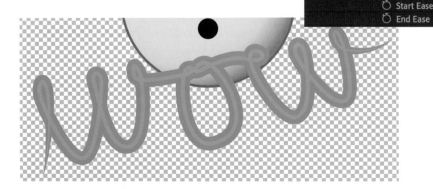

The Course

Trim Paths

Trim Paths is one of several shape effects, and it's the one I use most frequently. It's a great effect to make a stroke appear drawn on.

➥ Click the Add button `Add: ◉` and select Trim Paths.
➥ Unfurl Trim Paths.

It should sit within the Contents section of the shape layer, just below the Shape 1 category. This means the effect will affect everything above it.

Let's animate this. I'll work backward on this, since we're already seeing the end result.

➥ Move the playhead to the middle of the timeline, around 3 seconds.
➥ Enable keyframes on Trim Paths' End.
➥ Move the playhead to the start of the timeline.
➥ Set Trim Paths' End to 0%.

By animating the End of a Trim Path, we can see our stroke get drawn on.

➥ Now, keyframe the Trim Paths' Start from 0% to 100% after the End animation finishes, so we see the text get drawn off.
➥ Add Ease and play with timing until the animation writes off and writes on in a way that makes you say "wow!"

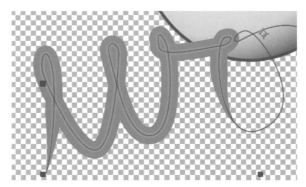

The Interface & Editing

Animation

Text

Shapes, Masks & Mattes

Effects

3D

Special Tools & Features

Expressions

Stylize It With an Effect

Just for fun, let's add a Stylize effect to give the text some texture.

📩 Make sure the Wow layer is selected.

📩 Go to Effect > Stylize > CC Plastic.

This applies the CC Plastic effect to the text layer, which makes it look like it's made out of plastic.

This will also open the Effect Controls panel on the left side of the interface, in which you can play with the effect's parameters.

📩 Tool around in the CC Plastic Effect Controls until you find a look you like.

Motion Blur

When it comes to fast animation, it's a good idea to add a little bit of blur. This smooths your animation and makes it less jerky, and a little easier on the eyes. I add motion blur to just about everything.

Enable Motion Blur

➡ To enable motion blur, click the Motion Blur box in the timeline. Do this for both layers.

Motion blur is most noticeable on fast movement, but even subtle motion blur helps.

Motion blur blends adjacent frames, which is very noticeable in my fast blink.

Optimizing Playback

Depending on the speed of your computer, After Effects might be rendering slowly at this point. Don't forget the tricks we learned in chapter 1 for making playback smooth—especially the Resolution/Downsample Factor Popup. You may want to lower this.

Motion blur will also slow down playback. Luckily, there's a great way to toggle the visibility of motion blur in the Composition panel. Do this with the Enable Motion Blur button at the top of the timeline.

Toggle this button off if you don't want to see your motion blur while working, which will speed up After Effects. If you're exporting through Adobe Media Encoder, you must make sure this switch is enabled before exporting to see motion blur. If you're exporting through the Render Queue, it doesn't matter—your motion blur will be on by default.

The Interface & Editing

Animation

Text

Shapes, Masks & Mattes

Effects

3D

Special Tools & Features

Expressions

Exporting

I know, we've already done exporting. But there are now more considerations we have to make. In some cases, we might want to export this video and upload it the way it is. For that, we'd use Add To Adobe Media Encoder, just like we did in the last chapter. However, there are some caveats to this animation that we need to be aware of.

Adobe Media Encoder Caveats

As of After Effects version 22.3, there are two big things to be aware of when exporting this through Adobe Media Encoder.

Number one: If the Enable Motion Blur button is off, this will export without motion blur. Remember to switch on the Motion Blur button before exporting.

Number two: Adobe Media Encoder exports transparent backgrounds as black. Even if you are using a composition background color, Adobe Media Encoder will ignore that.

Here's the workaround to the black background problem:

- 🡲 Go to Layer > New > Solid Layer.
- 🡲 Click the Color box.
- 🡲 Choose a nice color.
- 🡲 Click OK.

This creates a new Solid layer, which is like a very simple rectangle shape layer, with fewer features.

- 🡲 Make sure the Solid layer is the bottommost layer in the timeline.

This animation no longer has transparency, and will export with whatever color background the solid is. You can now export with Composition > Add To Adobe Media Encoder Queue, if you wish.

Exporting with Render Queue

What if you want to export this with transparency? For that, I like to use another export option—the Render Queue.

The Interface
& Editing

Animation

Text

Shapes, Masks
& Mattes

Effects

3D

Special Tools
& Features

Expressions

➡ If you've added a Solid layer in the previous section, click the Eyeball ◉ to turn the layer off, or delete it.

➡ Select Composition > Add To Render Queue.

This loads the composition into the After Effects Render Queue, which is the classic way of exporting from After Effects. The Render Queue can do a lot, but it can't export an H.264 animation. For that, we need Adobe Media Encoder.

Let's set this up so the Render Queue spits out a file with transparency. The default options here need some tweaking to make that happen.

➡ Click on Output Module > High Quality to change the format of this export.

This opens the Output Module Settings.

➡ Click on Format Options.

This opens QuickTime Options.

➡ Under Video Codec, choose Apple ProRes 4444.

⬏ Click OK.

⬏ Back in the Output Module Settings, under Channels, choose RGB + Alpha.
⬏ Click OK.

So, what was that all about? Well, we had to select a codec, or video format, that allows for an alpha, or transparency value. Not many do, but Apple ProRes 4444 does. Not only do we have to choose a codec that supports alpha, but we then have to tell After Effects to export with an alpha channel. Convoluted, I know! Chapter 1 of the Compendium details how to make Render Queue templates to make this whole process quicker the next time.

Output To

We have to then tell After Effects where to save this file.

⬏ Click on Output To > Not yet specified (yours may say Emoji.mov).
⬏ Choose where to save this file. It should go in this lesson's 06_Renders folder.
⬏ Ready to go? Hit the Render button in the top left of the Render Queue, or press return/Enter.

Once the video renders, it will be saved as a QuickTime mov. You can pop this video back into another After Effects project, or into Adobe Premiere, and it will retain its transparent background.

4 Masking, Matting & Precomps

In this chapter, we'll build a website for my dog. We'll have three main lessons: First, you'll learn how to mask, which uses Bezier curves to crop an image. A matte is similar, but it uses a second layer as a guide to another layer's visibility. We'll also learn how to precomp, which is an indispensable organization tool. And we'll look at some tricks for retiming animation.

Set Up the Project

You know the drill.

- Fire up a new After Effects project, either by clicking New Project from the splash screen, or with File > New Project.
- Save this project into Lesson 4 > 05_Project, naming it Lesson 4.
- Import Beemo.jpeg.
- Import Computer_Layers.psd. Make sure you import as a Composition – Retain Layer Sizes.

Warning: Import the JPEG and PSD files separately. Importing more than one still at a time defaults to importing them as footage instead of a composition.

Let's now drag Beemo.jpeg into its own composition.

- Drag Beemo.jpeg onto the Create New Composition icon  at the bottom of the Project panel.

You should now have an open composition with just an image of my silly dog in it.

Masking

Let's mask out Beemo, as to create a cutout of just her, without the background. This is very familiar territory using the Pen tool, so this should be a breeze.

Create a Mask

➥ Select the Pen tool in the Toolbar, either by clicking on it or with the hotkey G.

"The Pen tool? Isn't that used to create shapes?" Yes, theoretical student. However, it can also be used to create a mask. It depends on what's selected. If no layer is selected, the Pen tool draws a shape. With a layer selected, the Pen tool creates a mask. That said…

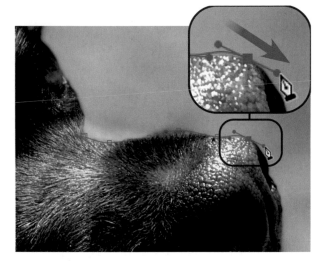

➥ Make sure the layer Beemo.jpg is selected.

➥ Use the Pen tool to draw a Bezier mask around Beemo's head.

Remember: Clicking and dragging while drawing a point with the Pen tool quickly converts the point from a hard corner to a Bezier curve. You probably want all points of this mask to be a Bezier curve. If you draw the wrong type, that's okay. You can change it later.

Try to make Beemo's face accurately with as few points as possible, taking advantage of the Bezier curve function for large areas, such as the top of her head.

➥ When you've gone around her entire head, click again on the first mask point you created, which should be outlined with a box.

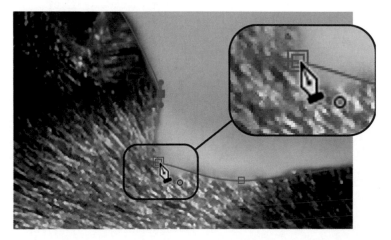

The Interface & Editing

Animation

Text

Shapes, Masks & Mattes

Effects

3D

Special Tools & Features

Expressions

This should successfully create a mask, which will chop out the background.

Editing a Mask

If you need to refine your mask after it's been created, here's how.

When the mask points are either round or hollow squares, that means you can click on the mask points and reposition them. This can be activated by clicking on the layer in the timeline.

When the mask is selected in the timeline, the mask points are solid squares. This means all points are selected. You can move all the points at once, but you can't move individual points.

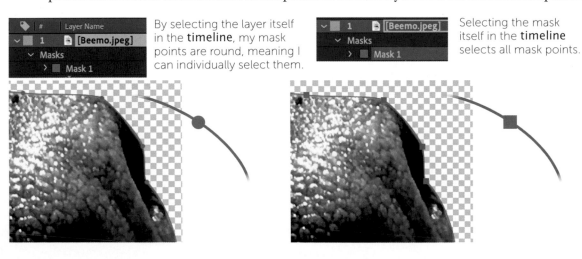

By selecting the layer itself in the **timeline**, my mask points are round, meaning I can individually select them.

Selecting the mask itself in the **timeline** selects all mask points.

Double-clicking a mask point in the Composition panel brings up a bounding box around all mask points, letting you position, scale, and rotate selected mask points.

With the Pen tool still selected, clicking on a vertex while holding opt/Alt switches it from a hard edge to a Bezier curve, and vice versa. Or, achieve the same effect by clicking and holding on the Pen tool icon in the Toolbar and selecting the Convert Vertex tool, then selecting a vertex.

Add a new point along a path by simply clicking on the path.

Delete a vertex by clicking on it while holding ⌘/Ctrl. Or, achieve the same effect by clicking and holding on the Pen tool icon in the Toolbar and selecting the Delete Vertex tool, then selecting a vertex.

Mask Options

Your mask is probably listed in the timeline—if not, select the layer and tap M. However, there are more options available.

⬕ Select the Beemo.jpeg layer and tap M twice, like a double-click.

This reveals mask options.

The Interface & Editing

Animation

Text

Shapes, Masks & Mattes

Effects

3D

Special Tools & Features

Expressions

Mask Feather is a handy tool. It softens the edge of the mask. Once we place this over a background, it will be nice to see some blending of the edge pixels.

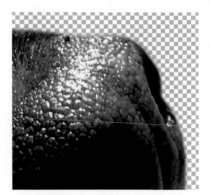

➦ Increase Mask Feather to 6 pixels.

This is good for some spots, but a little too uniform. Some areas of the image are less in focus than others—those out-of-focus areas should be feathered more. To specify feathering amounts in certain areas, we need a new tool. Something like…

The Mask Feather Tool

➦ Switch to the Mask Feather tool by clicking and holding on the Pen tool in the Toolbar, or pressing G a second time after the Pen tool is selected.

With the Mask Feather tool selected, make sure the mask you want to add feathering to is also selected in the timeline.

➦ Click near Beemo's ear on the mask path, then drag inward to create a new mask feathering path.

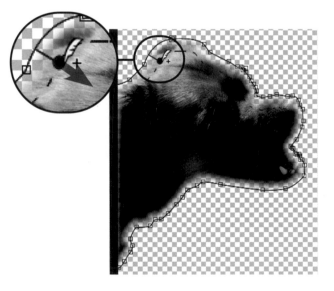

The mask is now feathered between the mask path and the mask feather path. The greater the distance between the two, the more feathering you'll get.

➦ Add a total of three points on the mask feather path—one on either side of the ear, and one in the middle.

➦ Drag the middle point inward to increase the feathering on just the ear.

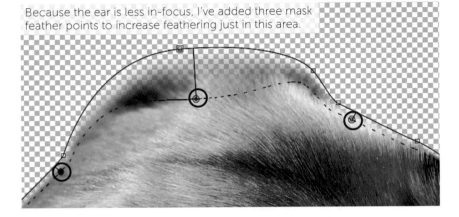

Because the ear is less in-focus, I've added three mask feather points to increase feathering just in this area.

You can read more about mask options in chapter 4 of the Compendium.

The Interface & Editing

Animation

Text

Shapes, Masks & Mattes

Effects

3D

Special Tools & Features

Expressions

Mattes

Let's now bring our masked Beemo into our other comp. The easiest way to do this is with copy/paste.

- Select the Beemo.jpeg layer.
- Copy it with ⌘–C/Ctrl–C or Edit > Copy.
- Double-click the Computer-Layers composition in the Project panel.
- Paste Beemo into it with ⌘–V/Ctrl–V or Edit > Paste.
- Reposition and scale Beemo so she's somewhat aligned in the frame of the computer screen.

Creating a Matte

What if I only want to see Beemo within the confines of the Screen layer? That's a job for a matte, not a mask. A matte is similar to a mask in that it's used to crop an image. However, a matte is a two-layer process. I'll use the transparency data (or alpha channel) of the Screen layer, and apply that to the Beemo layer.

First, a Note on Workspaces

You probably can't see the matte options at first. That's because After Effects defaults to viewing Switches in the timeline. We want to switch this to Modes.

- Click Toggle Switches/Modes at the bottom of the timeline.

⊙ ◑ ● 🔒	🏷	#	Layer Name	🐠 ✳ ↖ fx 🖽 ◎ ● ⬡	Parent & Link	
👁		1	📄 [Beemo.jpeg]	🐠 /	◎ None	⌄
👁		2	Screen	🐠 /	◎ None	⌄
		3	WebsiteBackground	🐠 /	◎ None	⌄
👁		4	Computer	🐠 /	◎ None	⌄

The timeline should now show these modes:

⊙ ◑ ● 🔒	🏷	#	Layer Name	Mode	T	TrkMat	Parent & Link	
👁		1	📄 [Beemo.jpeg]	Normal ⌄			◎ None	⌄
👁		2	Screen	Normal ⌄		None ⌄	◎ None	⌄
		3	WebsiteBackground	Normal ⌄		None ⌄	◎ None	⌄
👁		4	Computer	Normal ⌄		None ⌄	◎ None	⌄

Another option is to click on the **Modes pane** icon.

Setting Up Mattes

We'll be using the Screen layer as a matte for the Beemo layer. However, we also want to see the Screen layer. In this case, we'll want two instances of the Screen layer, so let's duplicate it.

- ➡ Select the Screen layer.
- ➡ Duplicate it with ⌘-D/Ctrl-D, or Edit > Duplicate.
- ➡ Move the new duplicate, Screen 2, directly atop the Beemo layer in the timeline.

#	Layer Name
1	Screen 2
2	[Beemo.jpeg]
3	Screen
4	WebsiteBackground
5	Computer

We do this because of a cardinal rule of mattes: the layer to be matted must sit directly under the matte layer.

On to the Matte-r at Hand

Now, let's tell After Effects we want Screen 2 to be the matte for Beemo.

- ➡ Find the column that says TrkMat.
- ➡ For the layer Beemo, click on None underneath the TrkMat column.
- ➡ Set this to Alpha Matte "Screen 2".

#	Layer Name	Mode	T	TrkMat	Parent & Link	
1	Screen 2	Normal ⌄				
2	[Beemo.jpeg]	Normal ⌄		None ⌄	● No Track Matte	
3	Screen	Normal ⌄		None		
4	WebsiteBackground	Normal ⌄		None	Alpha Matte "Screen 2"	
5	Computer	Normal ⌄		None	Alpha Inverted Matte "Screen 2"	

The Interface & Editing

Animation

Text

Shapes, Masks & Mattes

Effects

3D

Special Tools & Features

Expressions

The timeline should now look like this:

In the **Composition** panel, note that we can now see Beemo only within the boundaries of Screen 2.

This is helpful because the screen contents and the screen boundaries are separate layers. I could animate Beemo moving around, and we'd see her only in the area of the screen. Or, I could animate the screen matte to change Beemo's visibility. Or, parent them together to move them as one. Mattes are great tools for screens and windows.

Precomposing

Let's give our website a different background.

➡ Turn on visibility for the WebsiteBackground layer.
➡ In the timeline, move the layer just below the Beemo layer.

Here's the problem: I want WebsiteBackground to also be matted by Screen 2. However, I can only matte one layer to another. Basically, I want After Effects to treat both Beemo and the website background as a single layer. In other words, in this composition, I want a single layer for the website, even though it's made of multiple assets. We do that with **precomposing**.

Set Up the Precomp

➡ Select the Beemo.jpeg layer in the timeline.
➡ Hold down shift and select the Website-Background layer.
➡ Precompose them with ⌘-shift-C/Ctrl-Shift-C or Layer > Pre-compose.

You'll see the Pre-compose dialog.

Pre-compose

New composition name: `Pre-comp 1`

○ Leave all attributes in 'Computer_Layers'
Use this option to create a new intermediate composition with only 'Beemo.jpeg' in it. The new composition will become the source to the current layer. This option is not available because more than one layer is selected.

● Move all attributes into the new composition
Use this option to place the currently selected layers together into a new intermediate composition.

☐ Adjust composition duration to the time span of the selected layers

☐ Open New Composition

(Cancel)   (OK)

The Interface & Editing

Animation

Text

Shapes, Masks & Mattes

Effects

3D

Special Tools & Features

Expressions

#	Layer Name
1	Screen 2
2	[Website Precomp]
3	Screen
4	Computer

➲ Set the new composition name to Website Precomp.

➲ Click OK.

Now, check out the timeline.

We've folded Beemo and the website background into a single layer. That layer is a precomposition, often referred to as a precomp.

A precomp isn't really anything fancy. It's just a composition inside another composition. Our precomp lives in the Project panel just like our other comps.

It seems as if we must now redo our matte for the precomp.

➲ Under Website Precomp's TrkMat, set it to Alpha Matte "Screen 2".

Project ≡

Website Precomp ▼ , used 1 time
1920 x 1080 (1.00)
Δ 0;00;15;00, 59.94 fps

Name		Type	Siz
Beemo		Composition	
Beemo.jpeg		ImporterJPEG	1.
Computer_Layers		Composition	
› Computer_Layers Layers		Folder	
Website Precomp		Composition	

Working with Precomps

Precomps are great. Anytime you want to take something that normally affects only one layer—such as an effect, mask, or matte—but apply it to multiple layers, it's a good idea to precompose those layers into one. Precomps also function like regular assets, and can be reused throughout a project.

But now we have a slight problem. What if I want to edit the layers within my precomp? For that, we have to open the precomp and edit it.

Open a Precomp from the Project Panel

Since a precomp is really just a comp, we can double-click the Website Precomp in the Project panel to open it.

⮑ Open the Website Precomp from the Project panel.

We're now looking at the precomp, which contains Beemo and the website background. It looks like we also have a duplicate of the Screen 2 matte that came with us, which is probably no longer necessary. For now, we can just ignore it.

Any changes we make inside the precomp are reflected back in the top-level (Computer_Layers) composition.

⮑ Make a change to Beemo, such as moving or scaling the layer.

Quickly Navigating between Compositions

Since we might be moving back and forth between our precomp and top-level comp, let's look at a faster way to move between the two.

⮑ Tap the tab key.

This brings up the Composition Mini Flowchart wherever your cursor is, showing which

The Interface & Editing

Animation

Text

Shapes, Masks & Mattes

Effects

3D

Special Tools & Features

Expressions

composition you're in, which precomps (if any) are within this comp, and if this comp is inside another comp. We can also use it to navigate between comps easily.

➡ Click on Computer_Layers in the Composition Mini Flowchart.

And we're back in the top level! Note that the change we made within the precomp are now reflected in the top-level comp.

Viewing Multiple Compositions

Quickly navigating between a comp and a precomp is a great way to work efficiently. However, it can be difficult to edit a precomp without knowing exactly how it will look in the top-level comp. Luckily, there's a way we can look at both a comp and a precomp at the same time.

Normally, the Composition panel displays whichever timeline is currently open. We want to lock the Composition panel so the top-level comp is always displayed.

➡ At the top of the Composition panel tab, click the Lock icon.

➡ Open the Website Precomp by pressing tab, as described above.

The Composition panel for Website Precomp should appear next to the Computer_Layers Composition panel.

If yours isn't looking quite right, see Compendium chapter 1 for info on rearranging panels.

➡ Click the Lock icon on the Website Precomp Composition panel to keep this screen persistent.

Now, you should be able to edit the precomp while having a second view into how things are laid out in the top-level comp. This is helpful for making sure elements are aligned within the screen.

Note that the secondary Composition panel will update as soon as the mouse is released, and won't play back. After Effects can only play one composition at a time.

Animate It

Let's add some stuff!

Animating a Mask

Let's have the screen load by masking it, then animating it.

- ➡ Navigate to the Computer_Layers comp.
- ➡ Select Website Precomp.
- ➡ Select the Square Shape tool ▣ from the Toolbar (Q).

Just like how the Pen tool can make both shapes and masks, we can use our Shape tools to draw masks and shapes. Again, the difference is whether or not a layer is selected.

- ➡ Using the Square Shape tool, draw a mask around the screen big enough to include all of it.

   Let's animate this on, working backward.

- ➡ Navigate to 1 second in the timeline.

- ➡ Select the Website Precomp layer and tap M to reveal the Mask Path keyframes.
- ➡ Set a keyframe for Mask Path.
- ➡ Navigate to 0 seconds.
- ➡ Switch to the Selection tool.
- ➡ Double-click on a mask point in the Composition panel to show a bounding box around all mask points.

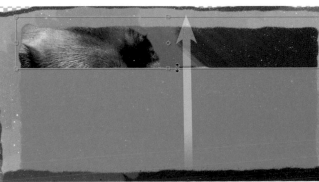

- ➡ Shrink the mask upward, until the layer is completely masked off and can't be seen.

The mask should now animate on, as if the screen is loading from the top to the bottom. This is a rare instance where a linear keyframe makes sense.

The Interface & Editing

Animation

Text

Shapes, Masks & Mattes

Effects

3D

Special Tools & Features

Expressions

Animating an Effect

There's a great effect to make this look like a loading webpage.

- Make sure Website Precomp is still selected.
- Navigate to Effects > Stylize > CC Block Load, and apply the effect to the layer.
- Open the Effect Controls panel if it's not already open. It should appear nested within the Project panel. If it doesn't, open it with Window > Effect Controls: Website Precomp.

- In the Effect Controls panel, deselect the CC Block Load option for Start Cleared.
- Set the timeline to 1 second.
- In the Effect Controls panel, enable keyframes for Completion.

While you can create keyframes in the Effect Controls panel, I prefer to switch to the timeline.

- With Website Precomp still selected in the timeline, tap U to hide the current keyframes.
- Tap U again to reveal all keyframes.

You should see the CC Block Load Completion keyframe we've set in the timeline.

- Navigate to 2 seconds.
- Set the Completion to 100.

The screen should look like it's loading in the way that old dial-up websites used to. Ah, nostalgia.

Timing Within a Precomp

What if I wanted to time out an animation in a precomp, but have it occur after animation in the top-level comp? Good news—the timeline playheads are synchronized between the two.

- In the Computer_Layers comp, navigate to 2 seconds, right when Block Load completes.
- Switch to Website Precomp.

Note that we're at 2 seconds in the precomp as well. So here's the takeaway: If I want to time animation between a comp and a precomp, I can find the spot I want animation to occur in the top-level comp, move my playhead to that time, and then switch to the precomp. After Effects will remember the position of my playhead between the two.

Now, let's add some text to the precomp.

- Create a new text layer with text that reads Beemo.com.
- Make it look good.
- Position it within the precomp, but use the ability to see both comps at the same time to place it in a good spot in the precomp.

➡ Apply the Typewriter animation preset, starting at 2 seconds.

Retiming

Now we have keyframes in two compositions. This can make retiming a challenge; if I want part of this animation to be slower, I need to now think about adjusting keyframes across multiple compositions. This issue gets compounded as your project increases in complexity.

There's a workaround I like to use that is sometimes simpler than adjusting keyframes. First, let's collapse Computer_Layers into single layer, in a new composition.

➡ In the Project panel, drag the Computer_Layers comp onto the Create New Composition icon.

This is kind of like precomping, except we've collapsed all the layers of a comp into a brand-new comp. You should see a new composition with a single layer that contains all of our animation.

We can retime this entire layer as one with a feature called Time Remapping. This lets us keyframe the timing of a layer.

➡ In the timeline, right-click Computer_Layers and select Time > Enable Time Remapping.

You should now see keyframes for Time Remap.

To use this feature, I like to first set keyframes where I know certain events have happened using the Add Keyframe button ◄ ◊ ►.

⮕ Navigate to 1 second and add a Time Remap keyframe.
⮕ Do the same for 2 seconds and 4.5 seconds.

You should now have your animation beats represented by keyframes.

| 0:00f | 00:15f | 01:00f | 01:15f | 02:00f | 02:15f | 03:00f | 03:15f | 04:00f | 04:15f |

Website mask   Website mask ends,   Block Load ends,   Text animation
starts   **Block Load** starts   text animation starts   ends

It's now much simpler to slide these keyframes around to change the timing of your entire animation.

⮕ Retime your animation by sliding around these keyframes—make certain parts slower or faster.

| 0:00f | 00:15f | 01:00f | 01:15f | 02:00f | 02:15f | 03:00f | 03:15f | 04:00f | 04:15f |

Website mask   Website mask ends,   Block Load ends,   Text animation
starts   **Block Load** starts   text animation starts ends

That's it for this lesson, but feel free to keep experimenting with masks, mattes, effects, and timing.

Moving On

Congratulations—you've completed what I consider to be the basics of After Effects. You now know how to import and arrange assets, animate with keyframes, use effects, and create text, shapes, masks, and mattes. This is the core of After Effects.

There are two lessons left that dive into more advanced features. While these lessons are useful and will lead to mastery of the software, they go beyond the core functions that every After Effects user must know.

So, take a moment. If you're feeling overwhelmed, or perhaps just a little whelmed, it's okay to go back and refresh these concepts. Don't move on unless you're feeling comfortable with the previous four chapters. Perhaps even take some time to practice on your own before jumping into the rest. Then, when you're ready to dive a little deeper, read on.

5 3D, Character Animation & Expressions

This chapter covers several advanced topics. First, we'll convert a scene into 3D. After Effects' 3D capabilities, although somewhat limited, can be a quick way to give your scene the illusion of depth.

From there, we'll touch on the Puppet tool as an introduction to character animation.

We'll look at Layer Styles, which are a different type of effect than what we've seen before.

Finally, we'll learn some basic expressions and how they can help your animation—even without keyframes.

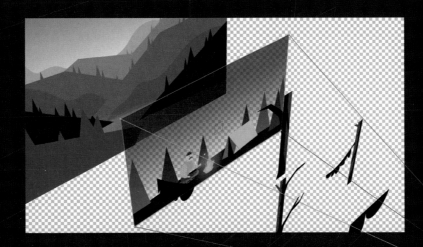

Set Up the Project

I hope you like setting up projects.

- ➡ Fire up a new After Effects project, either by clicking New Project from the splash screen, or with File > New Project.
- ➡ Save this project into Lesson 5 > 05_Project, naming it Lesson 5.
- ➡ Import Woods Campfire.ai from the Lesson 5 > 04_Stills folder. Make sure you import as a Composition – Retain Layer Sizes.
- ➡ Open up the Woods Campfire composition.

And here we have a lovely scene of a fella enjoying a campfire in the woods.

What Is (and Isn't) 3D

For some students, when they hear "3D" they immediately think that we're going to use After Effects exclusively to make the next Pixar film. Let's be clear—that's not happening. After Effects' 3D tools are mainly used to 3D-ify 2D assets. That often means rotating flat objects away from the camera (like flipping a postcard), or moving objects in Z-space (that is, away from the camera) to create the illusion of depth. We'll be doing the former in this lesson, and using a camera to move through the scene.

Some Quick Parenting

In just a minute, we'll be converting objects to 3D and pushing them toward and away from the camera. Objects in the foreground will be close to the camera, and background objects will be farther away.

I have five layers in this scene that ought to be kept at the same distance from the camera, as they're five objects that make up a single plane. Those layers are Tent, Fella, Fire Glow, Fire, and Foreground Trees. Let's parent these to a Null so we can move them as one.

➡ Create a new Null Object, with Layer > New > Null Object.

➡ Name the Null Midplane Mover and move it just above the Tent layer.

➡ Parent the Tent, Fella, Fire Glow, Fire, and Foreground Trees to the Null.

🏷	#	Layer Name			Parent & Link
	1	Front Branch			None
	2	Front Bttm Trees			None
	3	Back Bttm Trees			None
	4	Midplane Mover			None
	5	Tent			4. Midplane M
	6	Fella			4. Midplane M
	7	Fire Glow			4. Midplane M
	8	Fire			4. Midplane M
	9	Foreground Trees			4. Midplane M
	10	Backgro...Mountains			None
	11	Sky			None

The Interface & Editing

Animation

Text

Shapes, Masks & Mattes

Effects

3D

Special Tools & Features

Expressions

3D

In order to access 3D tools, we must first convert layers to 3D layers.

➦ Before moving on, make sure you're in the Switches interface by clicking **Toggle Switches and Modes** at the bottom of the timeline.

You should see the switches that are visible in the previous graphic.

Convert a Layer to a 3D Layer

Converting a layer to a 3D layer is simple.

➦ Click in the box underneath the 3D icon 🔯 for all layers.

Tip: You can click in the top Toggle 3D Layer box, hold the mouse down, and drag through all the boxes to quickly convert all layers.

The Gizmo

Off the bat, it seems like nothing's changed—and that's true. However, we now have the ability to move an object in 3D space. Let's take a look at that.

If you can't see these icons, remember to click on **Toggle Switches and Modes**.

➦ Select the layer Tent.

Now that this is a 3D layer, we can see the gizmo, an interface for moving objects in 3D space.

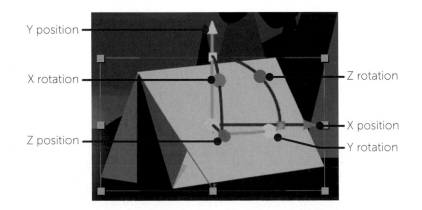

We now have three arrows to manipulate position—a red arrow for X, green for Y, and new to us, a blue arrow to move an object about the Z-axis, which is toward and away from the camera. There are also red, green, and blue balls on the gizmo that can be clicked to rotate the object about the X (bowing to and away from the camera), Y (twirling about the vertical axis), and Z (our classic rotation) axes.

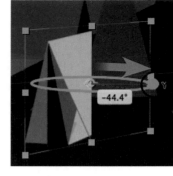

➡ Practice using each of the six gizmo handles to move the object in 3D.

In this example, I'm rotating the tent about the Y axis. Note that layers can now intersect. Think of 3D layers as being much more physical—I can't see the back of the tent because I've rotated it so it's behind other layers. As such, the stacking order of layers isn't as important to what's visible—it's now about where things are positioned within the composition.

➡ When you're done, hit Undo to reset the tent to its original position.

3D Views

In just a minute, we'll move some layers into various Z positions so some are closer to the camera, and others are farther away. But it's difficult to see 3D-ness on a 2D monitor. Let's change our interface so we can see from multiple views at once.

Note how in the bottom-right corner of the Composition panel, we now have 3D options. These only show up if you have at least one 3D layer in the composition.

➡ Select 1 View and change it to 2 Views.

You should now see two views of the scene, side-by-side in the Composition panel.

Each view can show a different angle of your scene. Note that the left-side view displays Active Camera in the top-left corner. Active Camera is what your composition looks like. The right side

The Interface & Editing

Shapes, Masks & Mattes

Special Tools & Features

says Default, which looks a whole heck of a lot like Active Camera. Let's make this an alternate view of the scene.

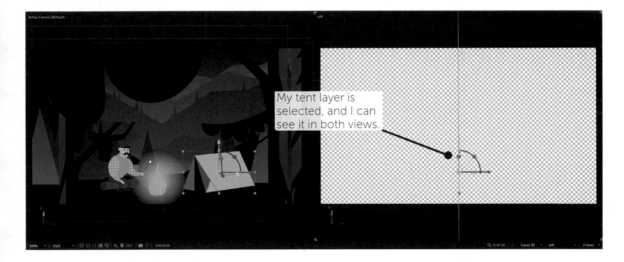

➡ Make sure the panel on the right is active, or selected. You should see blue triangles in the corner of the panel.

➡ Switch the panel view from Default to Left.

We can now see the same scene from two different angles at the same time—our Active Camera, which is what we'll ultimately edit and export, and the Left side view, which shows our 3D layers from the side. When we move our layers to and from the camera, seeing the scene laid out from the side will be a helpful way to judge depth.

Note that each view has its own controls—things like zooming and the Hand tool can be applied to each one.

Arranging 3D Layers

We're about to start mucking with the layers, but I don't want to deviate too far from the original look. Here's a trick to take a snapshot of our original layout.

➡ Click the camera icon 📷 at the bottom of the Composition panel.

This will come in handy shortly. Now, let's give this scene depth by moving our foreground objects closer to the camera, and background objects farther away in Z-space.

➡ Select the layer Front Branch.

➡ In the Left view, click and drag the blue Z-axis gizmo and move it to the right, or closer to the camera. I'll move mine to a Z position of about -1600.

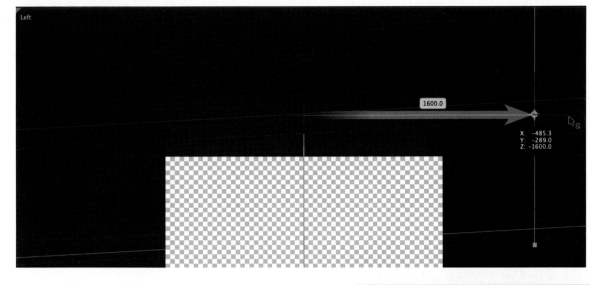

We can also tap P to reveal our 3D position coordinates in the timeline. We'll now see three numbers: one for X, Y, and Z.

#	Layer Name	
1	Front Branch	
	Position	-485.3,-289.0,-1600.0

We can also see that moving an object closer to the camera means *decreasing* its Z value. This might feel a little counterintuitive.

Compensate for Scale

While we want to create depth by moving objects closer to the camera, I don't want to mess up the original layout of this scene. So, the next step is to scale down Front Branch so it looks similar to where it started.

➡ Scale down Front Branch, either by clicking and dragging the corners in either view, or by tapping S in the timeline. Scale it down to about 40%.

➡ Position the layer so it's in the top-left corner of the Active Camera view.

This should now look very similar to how we started. Not totally sure if it does? Let's go back to the snapshot we took earlier.

Press and hold the View Snapshot button 🔘 at the bottom of the timeline to view our original layout.

➡ Adjust the Front Branch as necessary so it's fairly similar to the original scale and position. It's okay if it's not pixel perfect.

Wondering what's going on? We want to give our scene physical depth without changing what it looks like. Later, when we add a camera, we'll push into the scene, which will create beautiful parallax motion, showing off our 3D-ness. I promise, it'll be cool.

Now, Give Your Other Layers Depth

➡ Move Front Bttm Trees closer to the camera, but not as close as Front Branch.

The Interface & Editing

Animation

Text

Shapes, Masks & Mattes

Effects

3D

Special Tools & Features

Expressions

➡ Rescale and position it.

➡ Move Back Bttm Trees closer to the camera, but not as close as Front Bttm Trees.

➡ Rescale and position it.

➡ Let's leave Midplane Mover alone for now.

➡ Move Background Mountains away from the camera.

➡ Rescale and position it.

➡ Move Sky away from the camera, past Background Mountains.

➡ Rescale and position it.

When all is said and done, your Left view might look something like this:

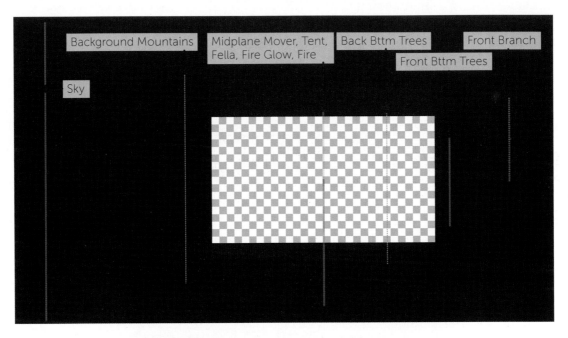

And the Active Camera should look pretty unchanged from where we started.

If you're lost or stuck, feel free to just copy my position and scale values.

The Course

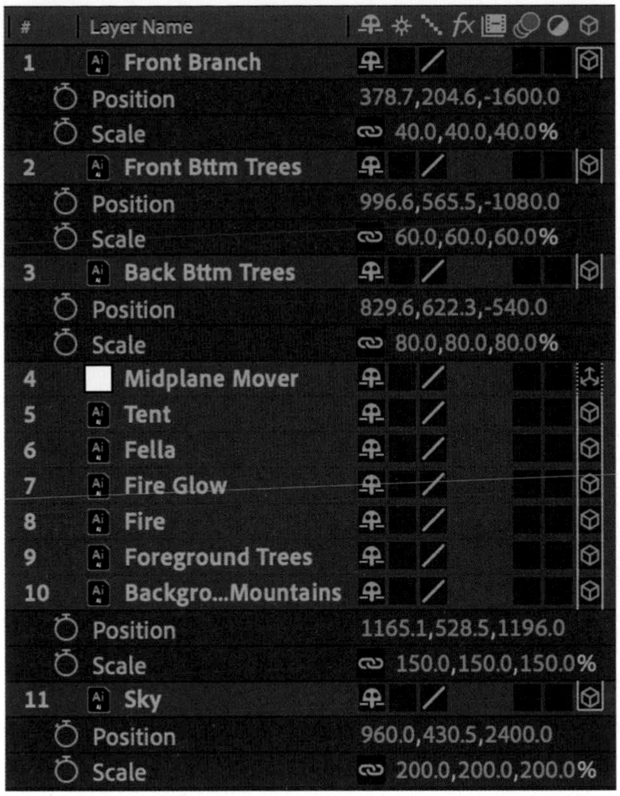

#	Layer Name							
1	Front Branch							
	Ō Position	378.7,204.6,-1600.0						
	Ō Scale	40.0,40.0,40.0%						
2	Front Bttm Trees							
	Ō Position	996.6,565.5,-1080.0						
	Ō Scale	60.0,60.0,60.0%						
3	Back Bttm Trees							
	Ō Position	829.6,622.3,-540.0						
	Ō Scale	80.0,80.0,80.0%						
4	Midplane Mover							
5	Tent							
6	Fella							
7	Fire Glow							
8	Fire							
9	Foreground Trees							
10	Backgro...Mountains							
	Ō Position	1165.1,528.5,1196.0						
	Ō Scale	150.0,150.0,150.0%						
11	Sky							
	Ō Position	960.0,430.5,2400.0						
	Ō Scale	200.0,200.0,200.0%						

The Interface & Editing

Animation

Text

Shapes, Masks & Mattes

Effects

3D

Special Tools & Features

Expressions

Cameras

Now that we've made a great 3D layout, we can add a camera to our composition. Cameras are optional, but they allow us to move through the scene and experience the 3D-ness of it all.

Creating a Camera

A camera is technically a layer, so we'll create it through the Layer menu.

➡ Select Layer > New > Camera. You'll see the Camera Settings dialog.

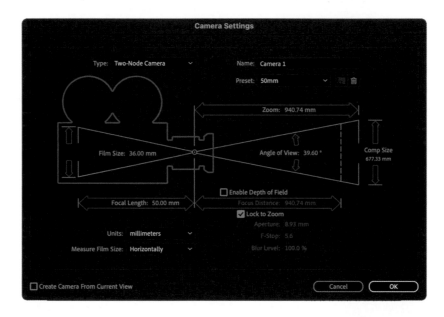

In the top-left corner of the interface, you'll see an option for camera Type. We want to make sure ours is set to One–Node Camera, which is simpler to set up and can move a little more freely.

➡ Set the camera Type to One–Node Camera.
➡ Click OK.

There is now a camera layer in the timeline. This means the Active Camera view is seeing whatever the camera is seeing.

Animating the Camera

The camera defaults to positioning itself where we started this scene. That's great; this will be our starting shot. We'll then move the camera closer to the action. Let's set a Position keyframe for the camera.

➡ Make sure the time is at 0 seconds.
➡ Select the Camera 1 layer.
➡ Tap P to show Position controls.
➡ Click the stopwatch to enable Position keyframes.

Now, let's jump to the end of this camera movement, and set a second keyframe.

➡ Move the playhead to 5 seconds.

Moving the Camera

There are several ways of moving the camera. We can manually dial in position values, or click the camera in Left view and move it around.

However, let's move the camera by using the Camera tools. Note them in the Toolbar—they're only there if a 3D layer is present in your scene.

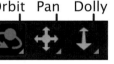

The camera, as seen from the **Left** view.

➡ Press C to switch to the Orbit tool.

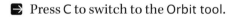

A single tap of C activates the first Camera tool, which is Orbit. This lets us point the camera in a different direction—which we don't want to do.

Orbit Pan Dolly

➡ Press C again to switch to the Pan tool.
➡ Press C a third time to switch to the Dolly tool.

The Dolly tool lets us move the camera about the Z-axis, and closer to our little fella. That's the one we want.

➡ Click and drag your mouse upward in the center of the composition until the camera is closer to the man, framing the scene nicely.

Now let's move the camera about the X and Y axes to frame this up a little better.

The Interface & Editing

Animation

Text

Shapes, Masks & Mattes

Effects

3D

Special Tools & Features

Expressions

➡ Press C twice, so you're on the Pan tool.
➡ Click and drag within the composition to move the camera into a nice spot.

My final camera position value is [927,784,-1346], but yours doesn't have to match.
Now let's do some housekeeping.

➡ Tap N to set the Work Area End to 5 seconds.
➡ Ease those keyframes!
➡ Watch and enjoy.

Notice the parallax as foreground objects move more than background objects. This obviously took much longer to set up than a 2D scene, but hopefully you see the merits.

Depth of Field

Let's give our camera a Depth of Field effect, which will place some objects out-of-focus, and enhance the 3D-ness of the scene.

➡ Unfurl Camera 1 > Camera Options.
➡ Find Depth of Field and click Off, which will switch it to On.

To make the effect less subtle, we can increase the Aperture.

➡ Increase the Aperture until you find a blurriness you like. I've set mine to around 500.

Now we must make sure the camera is keeping the right objects in focus.

➡ Hop to the beginning of the timeline.
➡ Set a keyframe on Focus Distance.
➡ If needed, play with Focus Distance until the Fella is in focus.

In my version, the foreground is already perfectly in focus, so I don't need to make any changes.

The Interface & Editing

Animation

Text

Shapes, Masks & Mattes

Effects

3D

Special Tools & Features

Expressions

◨ Go to the end of the animation.

◨ Change the Focus Distance until the Fella is in focus.

When viewing the scene from the Left view, you can see a pink plane that is the focus distance. Aligning it with the objects in the scene means your objects are in focus.

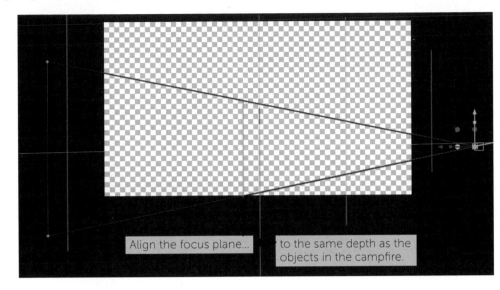

Align the focus plane... to the same depth as the objects in the campfire.

◨ Ease those keyframes.

Slow playback? Hit the Draft 3D button  in the lower right of the Composition panel to switch off Depth of Field and lower the overall quality of the scene.

That's it for our lesson on 3D, but there are many more features to discover in chapter 5 of the Compendium. For now, if you're happy with the layout and camera motion, you may now switch back to 1 View.

Character Animation

Let's make our character move a little. After Effects users have been creating all sorts of various plug-ins to help animate characters—DUIK, RubberHose, and Joysticks 'n Sliders to name a few. For now, let's focus on the tools that come with the software. The Puppet tool is a simple yet effective way to manipulate a precreated character. We can use it to make a rig, which lets us bend certain parts of the character. In this section, we'll have our Fella bend his arm up and down as he roasts his marshmallow.

It'll be easiest to work with the camera zoomed in a little, so I'll be working on this section at the 5-second mark in the timeline.

Setting Up the Puppet Tool

➡ Find the Puppet tool icon ✪ in the Toolbar.

➡ Click and hold on it to open the various Puppet tools.

➡ Select the Puppet Advanced Pin tool.

➡ Select the Fella layer.

➡ With the Puppet Advanced Pin tool selected, click on his left elbow.

By placing a Puppet Pin in his elbow, we can now rotate his elbow. However, if we attempted that right now, we would rotate the entire character. We have to use more pins to tell After Effects what we *don't* want to move. For that, I like to just use the Puppet Position Pin tool.

➡ In the Toolbar, switch back to the Puppet Position Pin tool ✪.

➡ Place pins in the man's head, left shoulder, stomach, and both sides of the log.

We probably won't need to touch these new yellow pins. They'll exist to make sure the rest of his body doesn't move as his arm does. Now, let's test the rig out.

- Click on the green Advanced Pin that we first created.
- Click and drag on the outer ring to rotate the pin, and his arm.

Hopefully his arm—and not much else—moves up and down as you rotate the pin. If you have extra body parts that are moving with the Advanced Pin, you may need to lock them down with other Position Pins.

Puppet Keyframes

Checking out the details of this effect in the timeline, you can see that Puppet Pins are automatically keyframes.

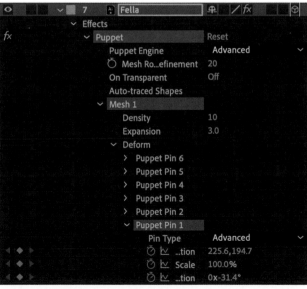

Puppet Pin keyframes are found under Effects > Puppet > Mesh 1 > Deform.

Our **Advanced Puppet Pin** is called **Puppet Pin 1**. Note keyframable **Position**, **Scale**, and **Rotation** attributes, which have already been **keyframed**.

We've been keyframing since chapter 1, and you can probably figure out how to add and manipulate keyframes to animate Puppet Pins. Let's look at a new way to animate with some randomness, without keyframes. Yes, I'm talking about…

The Interface & Editing

Animation

Text

Shapes, Masks & Mattes

Effects

3D

Special Tools & Features

Expressions

Expressions

Expressions are a powerful tool that use a coding language to unlock the full potential of After Effects. If that last sentence made you groan, fear not. There are many ways of making Expressions relatively painless. And if coding is your thing, then get ready for some excitement.

Enable Expressions

I want to add an Expression to the Rotation value of Puppet Pin 1, so it moves with some randomness and I don't have to keyframe it.

➡ If you haven't already, find Fella > Effects > Puppet > Mesh 1 > Deform > Puppet Pin 1 > Rotation in the timeline.

➡ Hold down opt/Alt and click the Rotation stopwatch.

Holding down opt/Alt and clicking a stopwatch opens the Expression Editor for that parameter.

Opt/Alt-click this stopwatch...   ...to open the **Expression Editor**.

Add a Wiggle Expression

We're now going to manually type in a little line of code to tell After Effects to wiggle this parameter. Wiggle is a preset that allows After Effects to generate random numbers within parameters you set.

➡ Click within the Expression Editor.

➡ Delete the text that's already there.

➡ Type in the following text, exactly:

```
wiggle(.5,20)
```

Frequency argument
Magnitude argument

Playing the scene back, you should see the pin's rotation wiggle.

How Does It Work?

The wiggle expression has two arguments, which are the numbers in the parenthesis separated by a comma. The first number (.5) is how many wiggles per second should be performed. A value of .5 means we'll see a wiggle every two seconds. The second number (20) is a limit to the range of the wiggle. A value of 20 means that every two seconds, you'll get a random number that's either 20 greater or less than your starting value.

Advanced Parenting

Another simple yet powerful way to use Expressions is to link parameters together. We already know we can use parenting to link Position, Scale, and Rotation between two layers. But with Expressions, you can link just about anything.

Add Another Wiggle

Let's make the fire appear to flicker, by having the Fire Glow layer wiggle in Opacity.

- Select the layer Fire Glow.
- Press T to bring up its Opacity attribute.
- Set its Opacity to 50%.
- Opt/Alt–click on the Opacity stopwatch.
- Enter the following wiggle Expression for Opacity:

```
wiggle(2,30)
```

The glow around the fire should now flicker twice per second, +/- 30.

Opt/Alt-click this stopwatch

Add a Layer Style

I want to add a glowing effect to the Fella, as if the fire is illuminating him. I'll do this with a Layer Style. Layer Styles are special types of effects that are applied *after* other effects and masks. This way, the style will be applied after the puppet distortion.

- Right-click the Fella Layer and select Layer Styles > Inner Shadow.
- Scroll down in the timeline to find Fella's Layer Styles, and unfurl Layer Styles > Inner Shadow.
- Set the Blend Mode to Lighten.
- Set the Color to orange (you can use the eyedropper to select the same color as the fire).
- Set the Angle to about -30.

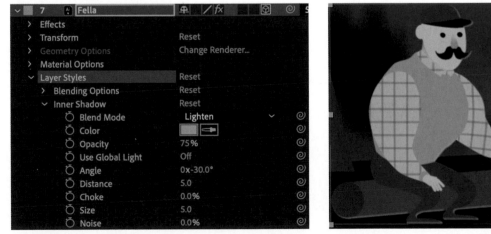

Linking Attributes

I now want to make the Opacity of the Layer Style linked to the wiggling Opacity of Fire Glow.

The Interface & Editing

Animation

Text

Shapes, Masks & Mattes

Effects

3D

Special Tools & Features

Expressions

This is where Advanced Parenting comes into play.

➡ Find the Pickwhip icon next to the Inner Shadow's Opacity.

➡ Click and drag from Inner Shadow's Opacity onto Fire Glow's Opacity.

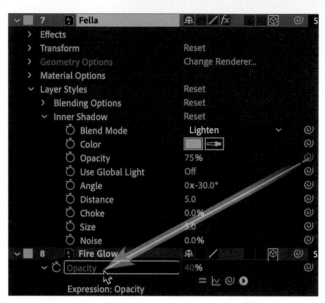

The Opacity of the Inner Shadow effect is now linked (basically, parented) to the Opacity of the Fire Glow layer. By pickwhipping attributes, we actually tell After Effects to write an expression for us, deriving the values of a parameter from another.

Clicking the triangle next to **Opacity** reveals its expression in the **Expression Editor**.

This automatically generated expression tells us that this value is being pulled from Fire Glow's **Opacity** parameter.

The Opacity of the Layer Style should now match the Opacity of the Fire Glow.

Linking and Modifying Attributes

Let's now link the size of the Layer Style effect to the Opacity of Fire Glow. The brighter the glow, the bigger the effect.

➡ Pickwhip Inner Shadow's Distance to Fire Glow's Opacity.

Just like before, the value of Fire Glow's Opacity is now the value of the Inner Shadow's Distance. A range of 20–80 makes sense

The Interface & Editing

Animation

Text

Shapes, Masks & Mattes

Effects

3D

Special Tools & Features

Expressions

for an Opacity value, but it's quite high for an Inner Shadow Distance value.

However, we can edit Expressions and perform some basic math functions to lower these ranges. That's right, it's math time!

➡ Unfurl the triangle next to Inner Shadow Distance to open the Expression Editor.

It should say:

```
thisComp.layer("Fire Glow").transform.opacity
```

➡ Append "/6" to the end of the Expression, so it reads:

```
thisComp.layer("Fire Glow").transform.opacity/6
```

Now the Expression reads: borrow the number from FireGlow's opacity, then **divide it by 6.** So a value of 20 becomes 3.33, and a value of 80 becomes 13.33. This feels like a much better range for this type of value.

Now the fire and the glow created by the fire should appear to flicker as one.

One Last Little Effect
Let's distort the flames of the fire, so they ripple.

➡ Select the Fire layer.
➡ Go to Effect > Distort > Wave Warp and add that effect.
➡ In the Effect Controls panel, set the Direction to 0°.
➡ Set the Pinning to Bottom Edge.
➡ If you wish, play with the Wave Height, Wave Width, and Speed.

You should be left with a very delightful campfire scene. Bravo!

6 Motion Tracking & Compositing

So far, this book has focused on design and motion graphics. But many people use After Effects for special effects and video production. I haven't forgotten those folks—this chapter is for them! While all previous features can be used for video (effects, masks, etc.), this chapter will focus on some video-only features. First, we'll cover motion tracking, which makes stuff stick to your footage. Then, we'll look at rotoscoping, the process of slicing certain elements out of video. Finally, a little bit of compositing, which is the art of realistically integrating digital effects.

Set Up the Project

One last time!

⮕ Fire up a new After Effects project, either by clicking New Project from the splash screen, or with File > New Project.

⮕ Save this project into Lesson 6 > 05_Projects, naming it Lesson 6.

⮕ This time, we're importing clips from the Lesson 6 > 02_Video folder. Import BeemoBoop.mov and MochaMe.mov.

The Footage Panel

Often, we don't need all of our footage to be brought into a composition. We can use the Footage panel to trim a clip before it even makes it into the comp.

Open a Clip in the Footage Panel

⮕ Double-click on MochaMe.mov from the Project panel to open it in the Footage panel.

Here we can see the footage that we'll be using. In just a moment, we'll replace the screen in this shot with something else.

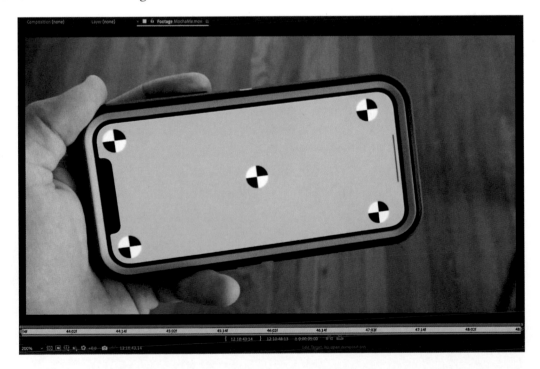

The Interface & Editing

Animation

Text

Shapes, Masks & Mattes

Effects

3D

Special Tools & Features

Expressions

This shot is a little longer than it needs to be. Let's trim it.

➥ Move the playhead to just after the finger leaves the frame—about 12:10:47:13 should do.

Note that the current timecode is found in the box at the bottom of the panel 12:10:43:14 . Also, video sometimes gives wacky timecodes. Don't be alarmed that it starts at 12 hours.

➥ Trim the clip's Out point, or where we want this clip to end, either by pressing opt-]/Alt-] or by pressing the Set Out Point To Current Time button ▮.

The teal bar now ends at the playhead, indicating that we'll only
be bringing in the first section of the video into the **comp**.

Now, Create a Comp

Let's turn MochaMe.mov into its own composition.

➥ In the Project panel, click and drag MochaMe.mov onto the composition icon ▣ at the bottom of the panel.

You should now have a composition called MochaMe, containing just the trimmed footage.

Motion Tracking with Mocha

If you haven't already guessed, we'll be placing the BeemoBoop movie into this phone, as if it's what's on-screen. This digital screen replacement is a common practice, since it's difficult to shoot video of a screen and have it look good in-camera.

Our first step is to track this phone screen. This process converts the movement of the phone into keyframes, so After Effects can then apply the phone's movement to another layer. For this, we'll use a plug-in that comes with After Effects, called Mocha AE. Although we'll have to learn a new piece of software, it's ultimately the simplest and most effective way to track a flat moving surface.

Open the Mocha AE Effect

To get started, we first have to apply Mocha AE as an effect to the layer.

- ➡ Make sure the MochaMe.mov layer is selected.
- ➡ Click on Effect > Boris FX Mocha > Mocha AE.
- ➡ In the Effect Controls panel, click on the big Launch Mocha AE button.

After you close the various registration prompts and messages, you should see the Mocha AE interface.

Create Rectangular X–Spline   Enable Planar Surface

If yours doesn't look like mine, make sure you're in the **Essentials Workspace**.

Track Forward

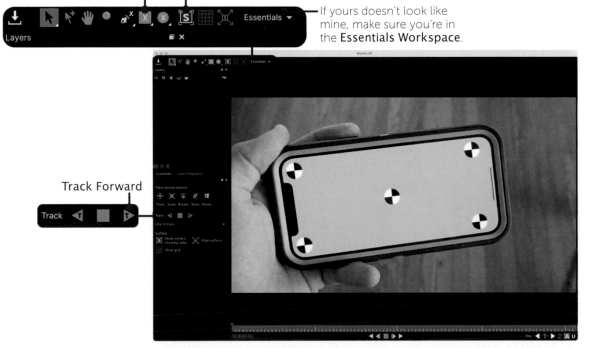

The Interface & Editing

Animation

Text

Shapes, Masks & Mattes

Effects

3D

Special Tools & Features

Expressions

Tracking a Flat Object

The first step is to tell Mocha what we want to track. Do we want to follow my hand? The floor? No, we want to follow the phone—and we have to tell Mocha so. We'll start by creating a rectangular spline layer. This is similar to a shape path, but it's used to tell Mocha the object we want to follow.

➡ Click on the Create Rectangular X–Spline Layer icon ▣ at the top of the interface.

➡ Draw a rectangular spline by clicking and dragging over the phone.

This will create a new layer called Layer 1, as seen in the Layers panel.

We can also see our spline in the playback window. The spline has spline points in the corners, and spline tangent handles projecting from the corners. We don't need to worry about the handles for this lesson.

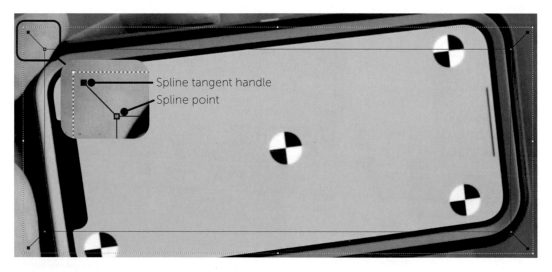

Positioning the Spline

We now need to move the spline points so they surround the phone itself.

➡ Click and drag each spline corner so the entirety of the phone is accurately contained within the spline. The red line should be exactly on the phone's edge.

When you're done, it should look like this:

Even though we can't see the top-left corner of the phone, we can guess where it would be by ensuring the red lines are flat against the phone.

Enable Planar Surface

While the phone is what's being tracked, we don't want to place our video where the corners of the splines are—that would look like a video covering up the entire phone, and not just the screen. The next step is to enable a planar surface, which is where our tracked object will eventually go.

➡ Click the Enable Planar Surface icon ⬛ in the Toolbar at the top of the screen.

You should now see a blue rectangle in the center of your spline. This is the planar surface.

The Interface & Editing

Animation

Text

Shapes, Masks & Mattes

Effects

3D

Special Tools & Features

Expressions

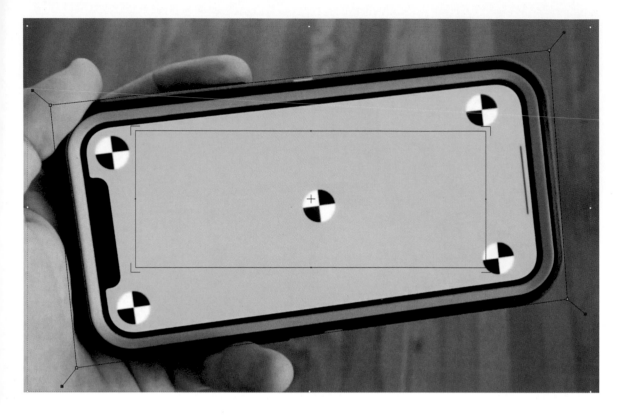

➡ Similar to how you positioned the spline points, position the corners of the planar surface so it perfectly hugs the interior of the phone screen.

Double-check that both your spline and planar surfaces are well-aligned before moving on.

Track It

Now that we've set it all up, we simply have to tell Mocha to track the object. Mocha should do the rest.

⮕ Click the Track Forward button ▶ in the Essentials panel on the left side of the interface.

Mocha should advance forward one frame at a time, and automatically track your spline to the phone, and place the planar surface on the screen. Neat!

⮕ Press the spacebar to preview the track.

If anything looks off, head back to the first frame, reposition the track points, and press Track Forward again.

Exit Mocha

⮕ Save your progress with ⌘–S/Ctrl–S or click the Save icon in the top-left corner.
⮕ Close or quit Mocha.

Apply the Track

Now the Mocha effect is holding our valuable data. We need to get it out of Mocha and into AE. First, let's place the object to which we want to apply the track into our composition.

⮕ Switch back to the Project panel.
⮕ Drag BeemoBoop.mov into the composition or timeline, as the top-most layer.

#	Source Name
1	BeemoBoop.mov
2	MochaMe.mov

The Interface
& Editing

Animation

Text

Shapes, Masks
& Mattes

Effects

3D

Special Tools
& Features

Expressions

The Mocha AE Effect

Now, let's paste the Mocha tracking data onto the Beemo footage.

- ⮕ Select the MochaMe layer.
- ⮕ Open the Effect Controls panel.
- ⮕ Unfurl the Tracking Data section.
- ⮕ Click on Create Track Data.

You'll then be prompted to select a Mocha layer. We should only have one layer, Layer 1.

- ⮕ Click OK.

The motion data should then populate the Tracking Data section.

- ⮕ Under Export Option, select Corner Pin (Support Motion Blur).
- ⮕ Under Layer Export To, select 1. BeemoBoop.mov.
- ⮕ Hit Apply Export.

And, bam.

Mocha AE then converts its data into points for the Corner Pin effect, which is applied to the targeted layer. The video should follow the phone quite accurately.

Need to fix anything? The Corner Pin effect has keyframes for all four corners, on every frame. You can select the effect in the Effect Controls panel and move a point, if needed. However, for a big change, it's likely easier to go back into Mocha, reconfigure your spline or surface plane, then repeat the subsequent steps.

Mocha is pretty cool, as it's smart about tracking flat objects, and setup is fairly simple. To learn more about what Mocha can do, as well as other ways to track your video footage, check out chapter 7 of the Compendium.

The Interface & Editing

Animation

Text

Shapes, Masks & Mattes

Effects

3D

Special Tools & Features

Expressions

Rotoscoping with the Roto Brush

There's a problem at the midpoint in this comp.

The hand that enters the frame goes underneath the composited image. We need to fix this. In order to do so, we need a layer with just the hand on it. Thinking back to chapter 4, we can isolate objects with masks. However, this is footage—we need a new mask shape on every frame.

Animating a mask to span multiple frames is called rotoscoping. Keyframing a mask path over a long video can be an incredibly tedious process. Luckily, After Effects has a tool that will make this much easier for us, called the Roto Brush tool.

First, a Little Setting Up

The hand needs to be its own layer. So, let's duplicate MochaMe.

- Select MochaMe in the timeline.
- Duplicate the layer, either with ⌘-D/Ctrl D, or Edit > Duplicate.
- Move the new, duplicated layer above BeemoBoop, so it's the topmost layer in the timeline.
- Rename this layer (by pressing return/Enter) to hand.

#	Layer Name
1	hand
2	[BeemoBoop.mov]
3	[MochaMe.mov]

Let's now trim the hand layer so it only contains frames where the finger is in front of the screen.

- Navigate to the first frame where the hand covers the screen, at 12:10:45:03.
- Trim the In point of the hand layer to this time, either by dragging the layer's edge to the playhead, or with opt-[/Alt-[.
- Navigate to the last frame where the hand covers the screen, at 12:10:46:03.
- Trim the Out point of the hand layer to this time, either by dragging the layer's edge to the playhead, or with opt-]/Alt-].

Now we're ready to roto.

Using the Roto Brush

This chapter lets you explore not one silly panel, but two! To use the Roto Brush tool, we need to bring our shot into the Layer panel.

➡ Double-click the hand layer in the timeline to open the clip in the Layer panel.

The **Layer panel** is good for viewing a layer on its own, and a single effect or mask.

➡ Then, select the Roto Brush tool from the Toolbar.
➡ It'll be easiest to use this effect starting from the middle of the clip, so move the playhead to around 12:10:45:10.

The Roto Brush tool lets us paint a vague shape on our footage, and After Effects will automatically select similar pixels. Photoshop users might find this akin to the Quick Select tool.

The key with the Roto Brush tool is to select a decent amount of your subject, without selecting any part of the background. You can easily change the brush size to just under finger-width, which will help us out. Here's how:

The Interface & Editing

Animation

Text

Shapes, Masks & Mattes

Effects

3D

Special Tools & Features

Expressions

➡ With the Roto Brush tool selected, hold down ⌘/Ctrl and drag the mouse upward or downward until the size of the brush circle is slightly smaller than the fingertip.

➡ Now, click and drag to paint a line down the middle of the fingertip.

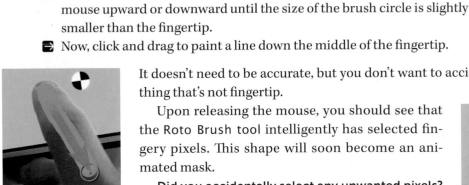

It doesn't need to be accurate, but you don't want to accidentally paint anything that's not fingertip.

Upon releasing the mouse, you should see that the Roto Brush tool intelligently has selected fingery pixels. This shape will soon become an animated mask.

Did you accidentally select any unwanted pixels?

Hold down opt/Alt while using the Roto Brush tool to remove pixels from your selection.

Take note of the timeline in the Layer panel.

The frame that we just painted on is stored as the main frame, indicated by a black diamond. After Effects will extrapolate rotoscoped frames from the data inputted by this frame.

Main frame

Now, Propagate!

The next step is to let After Effects attempt to automatically use data from our main frame to follow the finger. All you have to do is…

➡ Press the spacebar.

After Effects will go frame by frame and attempt to follow the finger. This one shouldn't require much attention, but if you see some extra pixels get included into the finger that don't belong, erase them with the Roto Brush tool and opt/Alt. It's better to catch these mistakes sooner rather than later.

Don't forget about the frames before the main frame.

Happily propagated and rendered frames

➡ Use ⌘–left arrow/Ctrl–left arrow or Page Up to roto brush frames before the main frame.

➡ Again, make sure to remove any errors as you go.

Freeze!

Happy with the roto? We have one more step to convert this into After Effects data.

➡ Press the Freeze button at the bottom of the Layer panel.

Yep, this might be the one time you actually want After Effects to freeze. This tells After Effects you're done with propagation, and it will reduce the resources required to process the effect. After it processes, playback on your roto-brushed footage will now be much faster. If you decide you need to go back and refine things, hit the Freeze button again to unfreeze.

➡ Switch back to the Composition panel by clicking on the corresponding tab.

Since the finger is on its own layer and masked out, we can now see it atop the phone. The finger has a bit of a hard edge to it; let's fix that.

➡ With the hand layer selected, head to the Effect Controls panel.
➡ Find the Roto Brush & Refine Edge effect and dial the Feather up to about 10.

We've still got an ugly green glow to the finger, due to the green light from the phone being cast on it. Luckily for us, since this is such a common problem with green screens, After Effects has an effect to fix it.

➡ Find Effect > Keying > Advanced Spill Suppressor and apply it to the hand layer.

Heck, we might as well apply that effect to the MochaMe layer while we're at it, since that's experiencing some green cast as well.

➡ In the Effect menu, note that your most recently used effect is listed at the top.
➡ Apply Advanced Spill Suppressor to MochaMe.

The Interface & Editing

Animation

Text

Shapes, Masks & Mattes

Effects

3D

Special Tools & Features

Expressions

A Few Final Tweaks

This is looking great, but there are a few last minute things we can do to really make it shine.

Mask the Phone Screen

This video has sharp corners, but the phone screen has rounded corners. We can easily fix this with a mask. However, combining a mask with a distortion effect such as Corner Pin can yield unpredictable results. It's a good idea to use precompositions in a case such as this.

- Select the BeemoBoop layer.
- Precompose it with Layer > Precompose or ⌘–shift–C/Ctrl–Shift–C.
- Name the new precomp BeemoPrecomp.
- Select Leave all attributes in MochaMe.

We want to leave the Corner Pin effect in the top-level comp, so the precomp becomes just a video.

- Select Open New Composition.
- Hit OK.

You should now be in a precomp with just the video footage, and no effects.

- Use the Rounded Rectangle tool to draw a mask with soft corners around the entire video.

This isn't quite the right shape. It will be much easier to adjust this if we can see both the pre-comp and top-level comp at the same time.

- Using our technique from chapter 4, lock the Composition panels and arrange both the MochaMe and BeemoPrecomp Composition panels side by side.

➡ Now, adjust the mask in the precomp so the image fits within the phone screen.

You may now reset your workspace if you wish.

➡ Head back to the MochaMe comp.

Compositing

In the world of VFX, compositing refers to the realistic integration of effects onto footage. Let's explore some of that now and make this screen look more like a screen.

First off, remember that phone screens emit light. Screens rarely display very dark pixels. So let's brighten the screen.

➡ Apply Effect > Color Correction > Brightness and Contrast to BeemoPrecomp.
➡ Increase the Brightness—somewhere between 50 and 100 ought to do it.

The Interface & Editing

Animation

Text

Shapes, Masks & Mattes

Effects

3D

Special Tools & Features

Expressions

Another point about the phone emitting light—the light should spill into the surrounding edges.

➡ Apply Effect > Stylize > Glow.
➡ Increase the Glow Threshold to 95%, the Glow Radius to 16, and the Glow Intensity to 0.5.

It's subtle, but now the brighter pixels emit a faint glow into the surrounding phone case.

Glowy Finger

Now that we've brightened the image, it doesn't quite look like the finger is receiving light from the phone screen. The best effect for this is the Inner Glow Layer Style—but that's also going to cause some problems. Nothing we can't manage!

➡ Duplicate the hand layer with ⌘-D/Ctrl-D or Edit > Duplicate.
➡ Rename the duplicated hand layer to hand glow.
➡ Right-click on hand glow and select Layer Styles > Inner Glow.
➡ In the timeline, find hand glow > Layer Styles > Inner Glow and unfurl it.
➡ Increase the Size to 40.

➡ Lower the Opacity to 50%.

Remember, Layer Styles affect the entire layer, so we're seeing a glow inside the entire roto-scoped edge. Even if we were to matte this, the glow would still appear on the edge of the matte. We can fix this problem by precomping the layer, and moving the Layer Style into the precomp.

➡ Precompose hand glow.
➡ Name it hand glow precomp.
➡ This time, we want to select Move all attributes into the new composition.
➡ You may deselect Open New Composition.
➡ Click OK.

The only way to truly tame a Layer Style is to move the Layer Style into a precomp. Now, this layer itself has no effects—they all live within the precomp.

The next step is to matte the effect, so we see it only inside the confines of the phone screen. We'll use a duplicate of BeemoPrecomp as the matte.

➡ Select BeemoPrecomp.
➡ Duplicate the layer with ⌘-D/Ctrl-D or Edit > Duplicate.
➡ Rename the newly duplicated layer glow matte.
➡ Move glow matte above hand glow precomp in the timeline.
➡ Click Toggle Switches/Modes at the bottom of the timeline.
➡ Set hand glow precomp's TrkMat to Alpha Matte "[BeemoPrecomp]".

⊙ ♦ ● 🔒	🏷	#	Layer Name	Mode		T	TrkMat	
	› ■	1	🔲 glow matte	Normal	⌄			
⊙	› ■	2	🔲 [hand glow precomp]	Normal	⌄		Alpha	⌄
⊙	› ■	3	🔲 hand	Normal	⌄		None	⌄
⊙	› ■	4	🔲 [BeemoPrecomp]	Normal	⌄		None	⌄
⊙	› ■	5	🔲 [MochaMe.mov]	Normal	⌄		None	⌄
🗖 🗗 🗗 🗗	Frame Render Time **8ms**			Toggle Switches / Modes				

Now, we just need to blur the matte so we don't see the hard edge.

➡ Select glow matte.

The Interface & Editing

Animation

Text

Shapes, Masks & Mattes

Effects

3D

Special Tools & Features

Expressions

➦ Select Effect > Blur and Sharpen > Gaussian Blur.
➦ Increase the Blur to 80.

Now, the edge of the finger glows, but the effect is only visible inside the screen area.

Looks pretty convincing to me!

What's Next?

You've done it—you've completed six chapters of complex software. Give yourself a pat on the back, pour an appropriate beverage, and take a break.

Believe it or not, you know how After Effects works. It's deceptively simple—clips are added to timelines, and then have keyframes, masks, mattes, effects, Layer Styles, and Expressions applied. It's the combination of these elements that makes After Effects a truly endless learning experience. I've been using it for over a decade, and I still learn new things quite frequently.

If you've found a lesson that seems right up your alley, check out the corresponding Compendium chapter to learn all the bells and whistles for that feature. You just might find something that speeds up your workflow, or inspires a wacky new idea. I also recommend reading through the first two chapters of the Compendium, as there may be some core concepts that will benefit the way you work.

There are endless resources out there to help you with your next steps. Want to learn a specific effect? Google it. There's probably a tutorial out there. If not, there are several online communities, such as the After Effects community forum and After Effects Reddit, which are full of people who once knew nothing about this software and are willing to help other newbies. The motion graphics community is a good one, so take advantage of it.

Good luck, and happy animating.

THE
COMPENDIUM

1 The Interface & Editing

In this chapter, we'll look at how After Effects works—where things live, how to set up and optimize projects, and how to begin creating and working in compositions. We'll also jump to the end and cover the essentials of exporting videos.

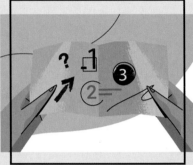

Before You Get Started

Instead of truly importing a file, After Effects makes a reference to where the file lives on your computer. This allows users to keep their project files small, which is easier for sharing and backup. Because of this feature, it's crucial that your assets live in a dependable, consistent spot in your computer, and ideally stay there for the duration of your project.

Organizing Your Files

It's best to keep a regular file structure for all your projects. You may want to create a template folder structure that you copy for each project before you begin editing. It could look something like this:

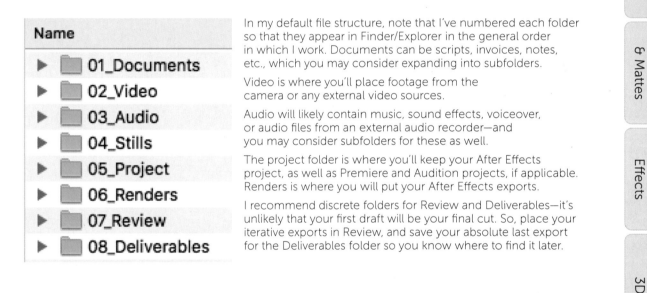

In my default file structure, note that I've numbered each folder so that they appear in Finder/Explorer in the general order in which I work. Documents can be scripts, invoices, notes, etc., which you may consider expanding into subfolders.

Video is where you'll place footage from the camera or any external video sources.

Audio will likely contain music, sound effects, voiceover, or audio files from an external audio recorder—and you may consider subfolders for these as well.

The project folder is where you'll keep your After Effects project, as well as Premiere and Audition projects, if applicable. Renders is where you will put your After Effects exports.

I recommend discrete folders for Review and Deliverables—it's unlikely that your first draft will be your final cut. So, place your iterative exports in Review, and save your absolute last export for the Deliverables folder so you know where to find it later.

Be sure to name the parent folder something descriptive, perhaps not just the name of the client, but the name of the project as well.

The Interface & Editing

Animation

Text

Shapes, Masks & Mattes

Effects

3D

Special Tools & Features

Expressions

The Interface

After Effects has a myriad of panels. Some, like the Project panel and timeline, are essential; others, you may never need.

Workspaces

The arrangement of panels is called the workspace. Any workspace can display any panel; however, the preset workspaces will highlight panels that you may need in the moment, and hide unnecessary ones. The workspaces are fully customizable to your liking, and you can create your own entirely new ones.

Change your workspace in Window > Workspace, or in the Toolbar at the top of the screen. For the majority of the Compendium, I will be working in the Default Workspace.

Resizing and Rearranging Panels

To resize a panel, move the cursor between any two panels until it changes to a symbol. Click and drag your mouse to expand or shrink the panel.

When it comes to rearranging panels, you have several options:

- You can divide a panel in half, so the original space is split between the original panel and the new one.
- You can nest a panel, so it appears as a tab.
- You can split the whole screen, so that a panel runs across the side, top, or bottom of your interface.
- You can completely detach a panel.
- You can make a panel full screen by hovering your cursor over it and pressing the ` key. Press the ` key again to return.

Arranging panels with the split function

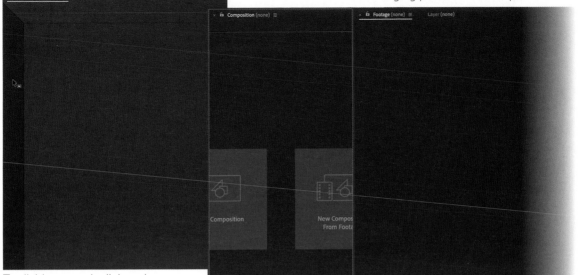

To divide a panel, click and drag on the panel name.
Drag it to a space occupied by another panel (above). If you hover over the edges of the new panel, you'll see purple trapezoids appear on the top, bottom, left, or right edges of the original panel. Release your mouse to have the new panel share the space of the original panel (above right).

Arranging panels with the nest function

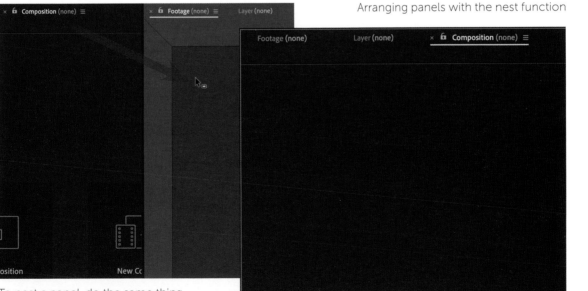

To nest a panel, do the same thing, but release the panel into the center of another panel (a purple square will appear in the middle of the panel).

Your new panel will now be a tab nested into the original one. This is called a group.

Arranging panels with the
screen split function.

To split the whole screen,
drag your panel to the edge
of the interface. You'll see
a green bar appear (left).

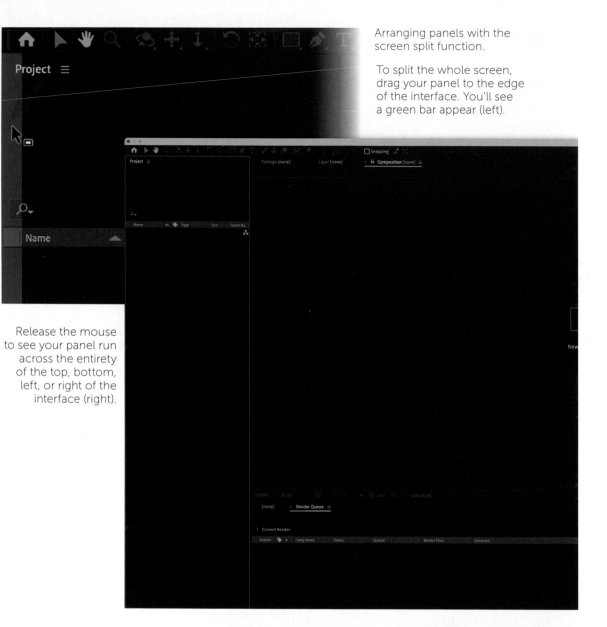

Release the mouse
to see your panel run
across the entirety
of the top, bottom,
left, or right of the
interface (right).

Finally, if you drag a panel
to just outside the After
Effects interface, you
will detach it, allowing
you to move a panel
to a second monitor.

Panels and Custom Workspaces

If you're happy with the layout, you can save your custom setup by selecting Window > Work-spaces > Save as New Workspace. You'll then be prompted to name your workspace layout. You can view and edit your workspaces by selecting Window > Workspaces > Edit Workspaces. Here you can customize which workspaces appear in the Workspaces panel, or delete workspaces altogether.

If you get lost in your panels, select Window > Workspaces > Reset to Saved Layout, which will reset the workspace either to the state it was in when it was saved, or to the default settings.

Speaking of the Window menu, any panel that exists in After Effects can be found here. Occasionally panels get closed or deeply hidden, so there's no need to panic if you can't find one. Simply select it from the Window menu to reopen it.

What follows is a list of each panel in After Effects, some of which will be covered in more detail in a later chapter.

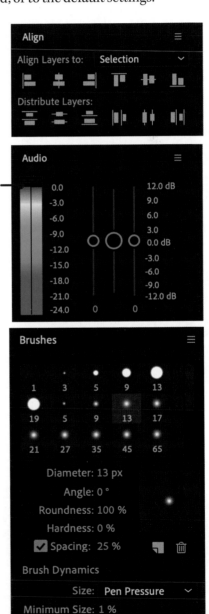

Peak indicator

Align Panel

An essential panel for design, the Align panel lets you align and distribute layers, either to the composition, or relative to other layers.

With Align Layers to, you can choose to align your layers to your composition, or with at least two layers selected, you can align the layers to one another. Choose between align left, horizontal center, right, top, vertical center, or bottom. With three or more layers selected, you can evenly distribute the layers relative to one another, typically using the horizontal or vertical options.

Audio Panel

If your composition has audio, you can monitor the output levels in the Audio panel. If the peak indicator turns red during playback, your audio is exceeding the maximum output value, and will contain undesirable distortion. You can also adjust the volume of your selected clip using the sliders, either using the center slider for both speakers, or the left and right sliders to control the respective speakers individually.

Brushes Panel

Here you'll find controls for the Brush, Clone Stamp, and Eraser tools. These will be covered in more detail in chapter 7 of the Compendium.

Animation

Text

Shapes, Masks & Mattes

Effects

3D

Special Tools & Features

Expressions

Character Panel

Control text created by the Type tool in the Character panel. More detail on this in chapter 3 of the Compendium.

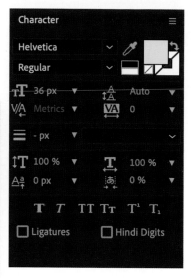

Content-Aware Fill Panel

Automatically remove unwanted surfaces and textures with this panel. This will be covered in more detail in chapter 7 of the Compendium.

Effects & Presets Panel

While the Effects portion of this panel is a copy of the Effects menu, this panel is the exclusive way to access presets, which are animations and backgrounds created by the nice folks at Adobe. Find them at the top, labeled * Animation Presets. Effects will be covered in chapter 4 of the Compendium.

Essential Graphics Panel

Want to edit your After Effects compositions in Premiere? This panel allows you to create mogrts, which are Motion Graphic Templates exported out of After Effects that can be read and edited inside Premiere. You can also choose which parameters are brought into Premiere for editing. This allows you to lock attributes that you know should not be touched, and create a less daunting interface for the Premiere user. Let's walk through making a lower-third title.

- First, create the composition as you would normally.
- Open the Essential Graphics panel.
- Under Primary, select your composition.

- You can select Solo Supported Properties to see all the attributes that Premiere can edit. Note that not everything inside After Effects is listed here.
- To add a parameter into your Motion Graphic Template, drag it from the Timeline panel into the Essential Graphics panel.

Some supported properties for a text and shape layer. If it's listed here, it can be edited in Premiere.

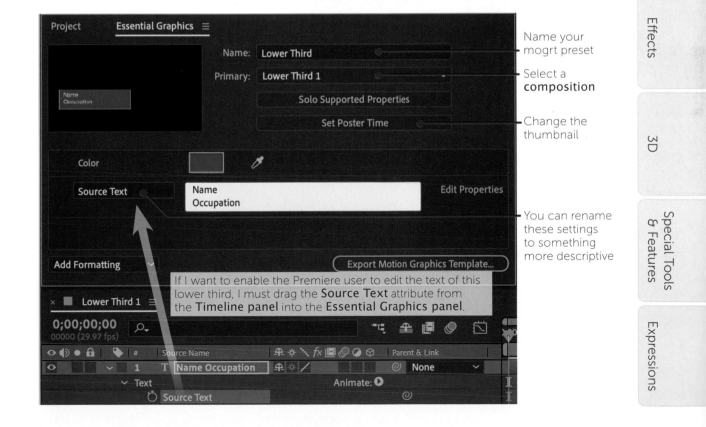

The Interface & Editing

Animation

Text

Shapes, Masks & Mattes

Effects

3D

Special Tools & Features

Expressions

When you're all done, save your mogrt with the Export Motion Graphics Template button.

In Premiere your mogrt template should appear in the Essential Graphics panel. After you add it to a timeline, you can use the same panel to edit the parameters you added to After Effects' Essential Graphics panel.

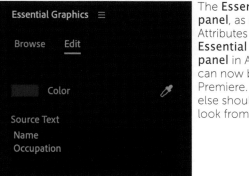

The **Essential Graphics panel**, as seen in Premiere. Attributes added to the **Essential Graphics panel** in After Effects can now be edited in Premiere. Everything else should retain its look from After Effects.

Want to learn more about mogrts? Check out:
https://helpx.adobe.com/content/dam/help/en/stock/contributor/Making_MOGRTs.pdf.

Info Panel

The Info panel displays the RGB and Alpha value of wherever your cursor is inside a Composition, Layer, or Footage panel. You can change the color space displayed by clicking on the hamburger menu (three stacked, horizontal lines) in the upper-right corner of this panel. This panel also displays the X and Y coordinates of your cursor. With a layer selected, the Info panel displays the layer's name, Duration, and In and Out point timing. During playback, the Info panel tells you your playback speed, and whether or not After Effects is successfully playing the frame rate of your composition.

Learn Panel

Displays tutorials on learning After Effects, which you obviously won't need.

Libraries Panel

If you're using Adobe Stock to create libraries to browse and organize stock assets, those assets can appear directly inside this panel. You can even drag assets from this panel into your compositions, and license them directly from the panel.

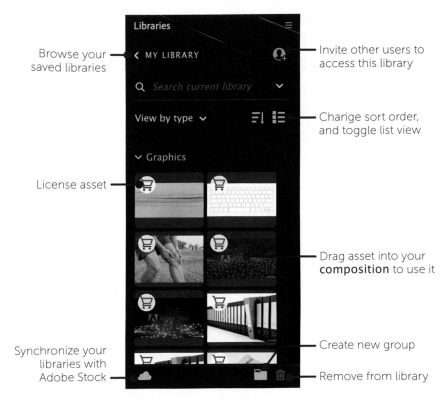

Browse your saved libraries

Invite other users to access this library

Change sort order, and toggle list view

License asset

Drag asset into your **composition** to use it

Synchronize your libraries with Adobe Stock

Create new group

Remove from library

Lumetri Scopes Panel

This panel displays a scope called Waveform (RGB). This scope reads your image from left to right and plots each pixel vertically onto this graph. Bright pixels land on the top of the scope, with darker pixels toward the bottom. You can also see your red, green, and blue pixels separated. Comparing the left and right sides of your scope to your image, you can generally identify which scope points are connected to which elements in the frame.

The Interface & Editing

Animation

Text

Shapes, Masks & Mattes

Effects

3D

Special Tools & Features

Expressions

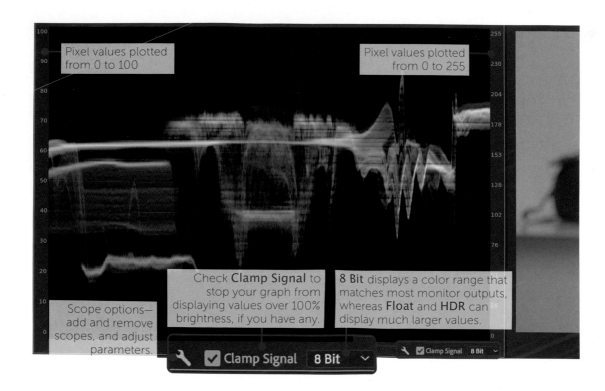

Pixel values plotted from 0 to 100

Pixel values plotted from 0 to 255

Scope options—add and remove scopes, and adjust parameters.

Check **Clamp Signal** to stop your graph from displaying values over 100% brightness, if you have any.

8 Bit displays a color range that matches most monitor outputs, whereas **Float** and **HDR** can display much larger values.

These brighter pixels represent the subject's sweater. Would you have otherwise known the sweater is brighter than the background?

On the side of the frame is some sort of seamless background paper. According to the scopes, it's slightly blue.

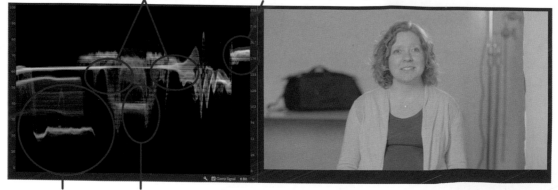

These dark pixels must be the bag.

Slightly darker pixels with much more blue than green and red likely represent the subject's blouse.

I highly recommend keeping your scopes visible while modifying color. Between monitor calibration and your eyes playing tricks on you, it's difficult to see objective truth with colors. Plus, scopes let you see the limits of your color range—since this example is a low-contrast shot, I'm able to see how much more contrast I can introduce before I start clipping my blacks and whites.

While Waveform (RGB) is a great way to see contrast, let's look at some other scopes available to us by clicking on the wrench at the bottom of the Lumetri Scopes panel. Selecting a new scope

Panels and Custom Workspaces   Lumetri Scopes Panel   **153**

The Interface
& Editing

Animation

Text

Shapes, Masks
& Mattes

Effects

3D

Special Tools
& Features

Expressions

adds it to the panel; you can then deselect scopes you don't wish to see.

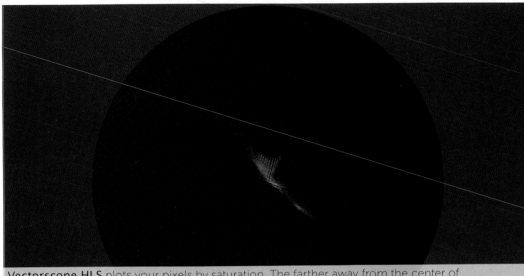

Vectorscope HLS plots your pixels by saturation. The farther away from the center of the scope, the more saturated the color. Notice the faint rainbow in a circle on the edge indicating the hue of the pixel. While **Waveform (RGB)** is a great way to see the contrast of your whole image, it's difficult to tell the level of saturation by the discrepancy of red, green, and blue lines. **Vectorscope HLS** is a great way to see not only how saturated your image is, but also the overall level of saturation available to you. Just for fun, try dropping in some stills of movie frames and even paintings with interesting color palates to see where they lie in the **Vectorscope**—and see if you can get your footage to match! Clamp Signal   8 Bit ⌄

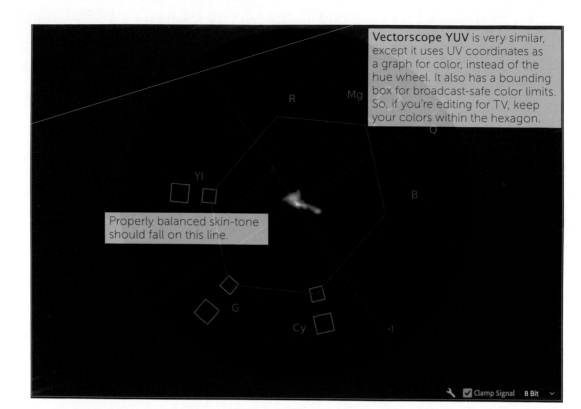

Vectorscope YUV is very similar, except it uses UV coordinates as a graph for color, instead of the hue wheel. It also has a bounding box for broadcast-safe color limits. So, if you're editing for TV, keep your colors within the hexagon.

Properly balanced skin-tone should fall on this line.

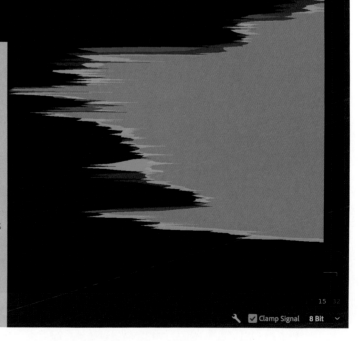

The next scope on our list is **Histogram**. Photoshop users may be familiar with this one. It's similar to **Waveform** in that it plots the pixels on your screen, but instead of organizing them left-to-right based on screen placement, it gathers every pixel and places them from bottom-to-top based on brightness (bottom are dark pixels, top are bright pixels). We'll get an overlay of our red, green, and blue pixels, but overlapping pixels appear as gray, which makes this a less-than-ideal color-grading tool. **Histogram** will, however, display the topmost and bottommost values of each red, green, and blue channel, even if it's just a single pixel.

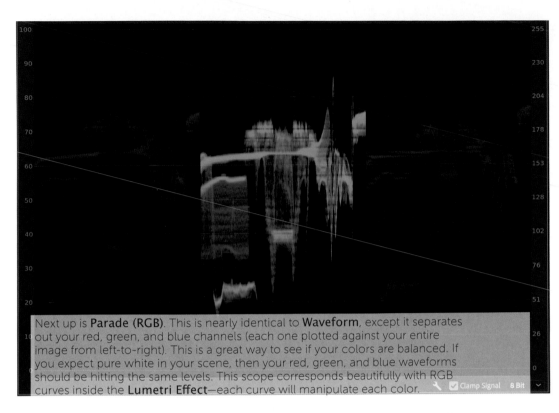

Next up is **Parade (RGB)**. This is nearly identical to **Waveform**, except it separates out your red, green, and blue channels (each one plotted against your entire image from left-to-right). This is a great way to see if your colors are balanced. If you expect pure white in your scene, then your red, green, and blue waveforms should be hitting the same levels. This scope corresponds beautifully with RGB curves inside the **Lumetri Effect**—each curve will manipulate each color.

I usually work with both Waveform RGB and Vectorscope YUV open. Under the Presets section of the wrench, you'll find some custom layouts.

We also have options for what our Parade and Waveform scopes show. Both list (RGB) after their names, but that data set can also be changed in the wrench. Parade Type affects the Parade scope. Instead of RGB, you can set it to YUV, which will separate out the luminance channel (Y) from the color channels (U and V). Or, view either RGB or YUV as black-and-white graphs with the –White option.

Instead of the RGB Waveform Type, we can display Luma, which displays only the brightness of our scene and does away with the colored overlays. YC separates out luminance (the green data) and chroma, or color pixels (the blue data). Finally, YC no Chroma is nearly identical to Luma.

You can then change the Colorspace that the scopes display. It's best if these match your footage, so Automatic is probably fine. Rec. 601 was the standard for SD footage, 709 is the new standard for HD footage, and 2020 is for HDR. Note that this is just for setting up the scopes panel and will not affect your output.

Finally, choose the Brightness of your scopes. Again, this affects only your scopes display, and not your video output.

Mask Interpolation Panel

When a mask changes shape, it can be difficult to control how it animates from shape A to shape B. This panel writes keyframes from one point to the next, and adds vertices to your mask, giving

The Interface & Editing

you a little more control on how it gets there.

- First, select at least two Mask Path keyframes.

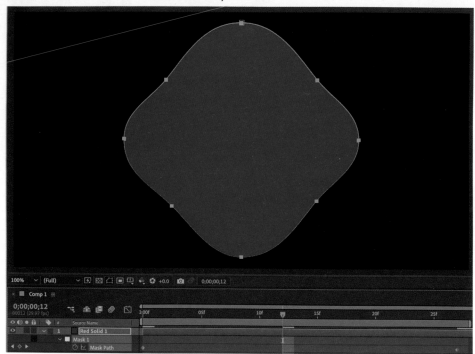

- Choose the desired settings within the Mask Interpolation panel.

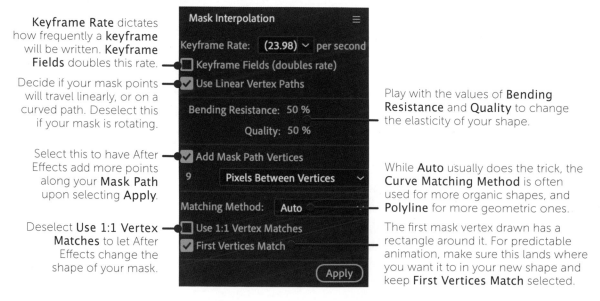

Keyframe Rate dictates how frequently a **keyframe** will be written. **Keyframe Fields** doubles this rate.

Decide if your mask points will travel linearly, or on a curved path. Deselect this if your mask is rotating.

Select this to have After Effects add more points along your **Mask Path** upon selecting **Apply**.

Deselect **Use 1:1 Vertex Matches** to let After Effects change the shape of your mask.

Play with the values of **Bending Resistance** and **Quality** to change the elasticity of your shape.

While **Auto** usually does the trick, the **Curve Matching Method** is often used for more organic shapes, and **Polyline** for more geometric ones.

The first mask vertex drawn has a rectangle around it. For predictable animation, make sure this lands where you want it to in your new shape and keep **First Vertices Match** selected.

- Click Apply.

After Effects will write a keyframe between the ones you selected, containing your settings. Depending on your settings, it may also add more points along your mask.

The Interface & Editing

Animation

Text

Shapes, Masks & Mattes

Effects

3D

Special Tools & Features

Expressions

Media Browser Panel

Use the Media Browser panel to find files on your computer. Drag files from the Media Browser into the Project panel to import them into your project. You can even select an After Effects or Premiere project to bring in compositions and sequences from other projects.

Use the file tree to browse your drives and folders   Filter by file type   Filter by directory type   Search

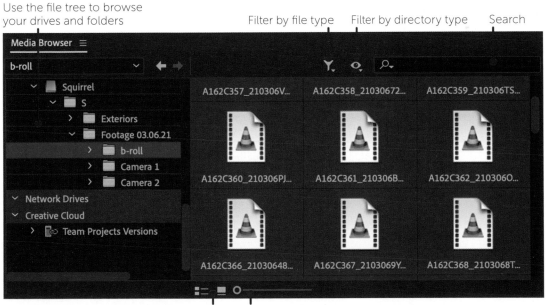

Toggle between list view and icon view   Change view size

Metadata Panel

View and edit data on your assets. This can be helpful to create search terms that will filter information when you're searching in the Project panel.

Motion Sketch Panel

Use your mouse to draw Position keyframes.

- Select a layer.
- Customize your settings.
- Click Start Capture.
- Drag your mouse in the composition window to write keyframes.

100% **Capture speed** writes **keyframes** in real-time. 50% plays time at half speed, resulting in faster **keyframes**, and 200% plays time at double speed, resulting in slower **keyframes**.

Motion Sketch ≡

Capture speed at: 100 %
Smoothing: 1
Show: ☑ Wireframe
☐ Background
Start: 0;00;00;00
Duration: 0;00;30;00
(Start Capture)

Increasing the **Smoothing** converts your spatial **keyframes** into Bezier curves.

Choose whether or not to show the **Wireframe** (bounding box) of your object, and the **Background** as you draw.

Paint ≡

Opacity: 100 %
Flow: 100 %   13

Mode: Normal   ∨
Channels: RGBA   ∨
Duration: Constant   ∨ 1 f
Erase: Layer Source & Paint   ∨

Clone Options
Preset:

Source: Current Layer   ∨
☐ Aligned   ☐ Lock Source Time
Offset: 0 ,   0
Source Time Shift: 0 f

☐ Clone Source Overlay: 50 %

Paint Panel

This panel contains controls for the Brush, Clone Stamp, and Eraser tools. These will be covered in more detail in chapter 7 of the Compendium.

Paragraph Panel

Control text created by the Type tool in the Paragraph panel. More detail on this in chapter 3 of the Compendium.

Paragraph ≡

+≣ 0 px   +≣ 0 px   +≣ 0 px
≣← 0 px   ≣ 0 px   ▶¶ ¶◀

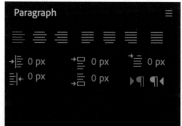

Preview Panel

Playback options. See "Playback" (page 190).

Progress Panel

This panel displays the progress of Content-Aware Fill.

Properties Panel

Coming soon! If the Properties panel shows up when you

The Interface & Editing

Animation

Text

Shapes, Masks & Mattes

Effects

3D

Special Tools & Features

Expressions

start adding keyframes, rejoice. This new panel is a mirror of your timeline properties and parameters—it's just a place to show them in a more accessible location. No more digging through your timeline to find that small shape layer attribute. If you're seeing the Properties panel as you work through these lessons, feel free to use it.

Review with Frame.io Panel

After Effects now lets you upload videos directly to Frame.io, which enables you to quickly share with collaborators and get time-based feedback, all without leaving After Effects.

Select a Project   Add Collaborator   Reload, Notifications, Help, My Account

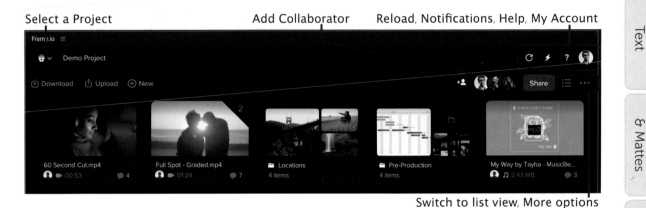

Switch to list view, More options

You can switch between projects or create a new project with the Select a Project button. Having multiple projects helps with organization, and you can share entire projects with collaborators so they can see all versions.

Add your active composition, comps in the Render Queue, an entire folder, or an entire project to your Frame.io project with the Upload button. You'll then see some upload options.

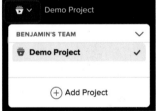

You can then share the entire project with the Share button, or click on video options to share individual videos with collaborators.

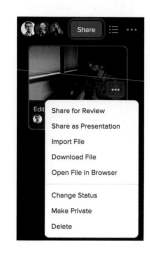

Collaborators will view the video through a web browser, where they can annotate and add comments. What's really neat is the comments appear directly inside the Frame.io panel! Clicking on a comment takes you to the corresponding timecode of your sequence.

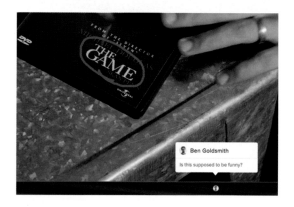

Your Creative Cloud plan comes with 100GB of Frame.io storage and the ability to create five projects. You can upgrade your plan at http://frame.io/pricing.

Smoother Panel

This allows you to smooth out keyframes, which is helpful if you have many messy keyframes, such as when using Motion Sketch. The higher the Tolerance, the more liberties this effect uses when reducing keyframes.

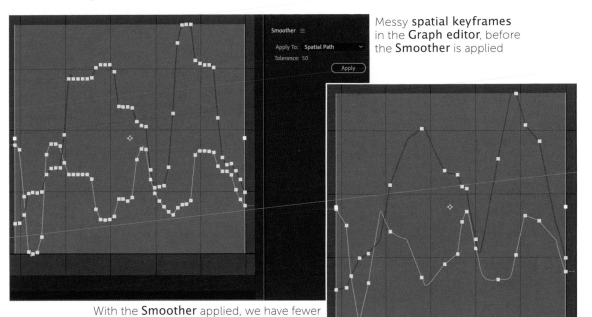

Messy **spatial keyframes** in the **Graph editor**, before the **Smoother** is applied

With the **Smoother** applied, we have fewer **keyframes** and smoother motion

Toolbar

Choose a tool or change your workspace here. Note that the Tools panel is contextual, meaning it will display different tools depending on what's selected.

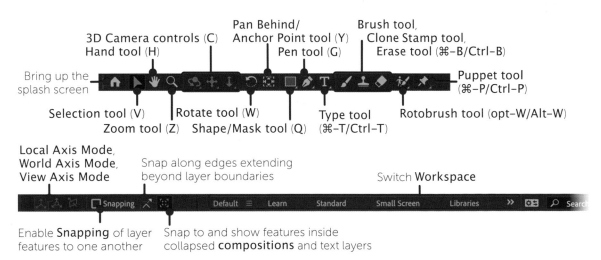

3D Camera controls (C)
Hand tool (H)

Pan Behind/
Anchor Point tool (Y)
Pen tool (G)

Brush tool,
Clone Stamp tool,
Erase tool (⌘–B/Ctrl–B)

Bring up the splash screen

Puppet tool
(⌘–P/Ctrl–P)

Selection tool (V)
Zoom tool (Z)

Rotate tool (W)
Shape/Mask tool (Q)

Type tool
(⌘–T/Ctrl–T)

Rotobrush tool (opt-W/Alt-W)

Local Axis Mode,
World Axis Mode,
View Axis Mode

Snap along edges extending beyond layer boundaries

Switch **Workspace**

Enable **Snapping** of layer features to one another

Snap to and show features inside collapsed **compositions** and text layers

Animation

Text

Shapes, Masks & Mattes

Effects

3D

Special Tools & Features

Expressions

Tracker Panel

This panel calls the Track Camera, Track Motion, Warp Stabilizer, and Stabilize Motion functions. Track Camera, Track Motion, and Stabilize Motion will be covered in chapter 7 of the Compendium. Warp Stabilizer calls the effect of the same name, which is covered in chapter 4 of the Compendium.

Wiggler Panel

Use this to add random keyframes.

- Select at least two keyframes.
- Set the desired parameters in the Wiggler panel.
- Select Apply.

Keyframes will be added between the selected ones.

Note that while the Wiggler panel has its uses, I recommend adding randomness with the Wiggle expression, detailed in chapter 8 of the Compendium.

Create a **Spatial Path** for Position keyframes, otherwise choose **Temporal Graph**.

For a **Spatial Path**, choose the dimensions on which you'd like to operate. You can make your X and Y axes wiggle independently or together, or operate exclusively on one axis.

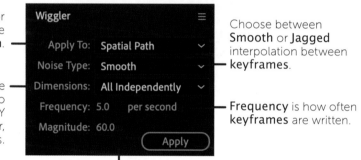

Choose between **Smooth** or **Jagged** interpolation between keyframes.

Frequency is how often keyframes are written.

Magnitude is the maximum random value the **Wiggler** will deviate from its starting value, using both positive and negative values.

Effect Controls Panel

If a layer has an effect applied to it, control the effect's parameters in the Effect Controls panel.

Flowchart Panel

The flowchart is a map of your composition, revealing the contents of precomps, and the usage of assets throughout your project. With a composition open, reveal its flowchart with Composition > Composition Flowchart.

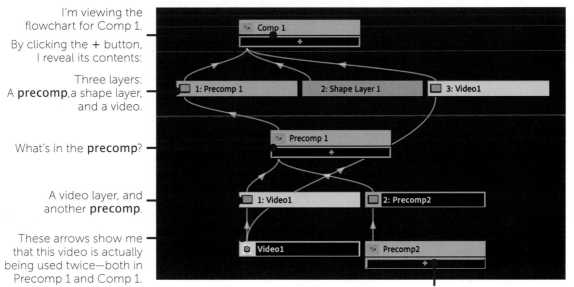

I'm viewing the flowchart for Comp 1.

By clicking the + button, I reveal its contents:

Three layers: A **precomp**, a shape layer, and a video.

What's in the **precomp**?

A video layer, and another **precomp**.

These arrows show me that this video is actually being used twice—both in Precomp 1 and Comp 1.

What's in Precomp2? I don't care, so I'll collapse it with the + button.

Right-clicking the Flowchart panel tab reveals helpful display options. In this example, I changed the view to Bottom to Top.

The other panels are all worthy of their own sections, so let's get to those.

The Interface & Editing

Animation

Text

Shapes, Masks & Mattes

Effects

3D

Special Tools & Features

Expressions

The Project Panel

Everything in After Effects starts in the Project panel. It's where you'll import and organize your assets, store your compositions, and view data on your items.

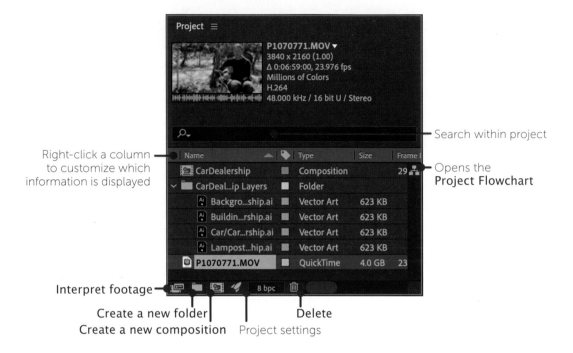

Right-click a column to customize which information is displayed

Search within project

Opens the **Project Flowchart**

Interpret footage

Create a new folder

Create a new composition   Project settings

Delete

Importing Files

Before we start working, we have to bring the asset into After Effects. There are several ways to go about this:

- Drag and drop from Finder/Explorer into the Project panel.
- Select File > Import > File (⌘–I/Ctrl–I).
- Double-click an empty area inside the Project panel.
- Use the "Media Browser Panel" (page 157).

Importing Layered PSD and AI files

When importing a layered Photoshop or Illustrator file, After Effects can preserve the document's layers. This way, you can select and modify elements within the artwork, opening up many possibilities.

If you import one of these files, you have three options. Note that you'll see a different interface depending on whether or not you import via dragging or the File menu. The terminology is slightly inconsistent between these interfaces, but the concepts are the same.

- Import as Footage: This will flatten the document and treat it as a single layer. You can choose to merge your layers, or import a single layer.
- Import as Composition – Retain Layer Size/Footage Dimensions: Layer Size: Imports with layers, and each layer is the size of the object within it.
- Import as Composition/Footage Dimensions: Document Size: Imports with layers, and each layer is the size of the entire canvas/artboard.

Top, a layer imported with the footage dimensions set to **Layer Size**. Bottom, the footage dimensions set to **Document Size**. I find the former easier to work with in most cases.

Warning: Importing multiple layered PSD or AI files will not prompt this option, and will default to importing as footage. Import layered PSD and AI files one at a time.

Importing Image Sequences

An image sequence is a series of still images that make up the frames of a video. If you want After Effects to read your stills as a video, import using the File menu, and make sure to select Image Sequence in the dialog box. Conversely, if After Effects is erroneously interpreting stills as frames of a video, make sure that Image Sequence is deselected.

Asset Options

Right-click an object in the Project panel to discover some options. The availability of options depends on what type of object you've selected.

Composition Settings

See "Composition Settings" (page 175).

Open in Essential Graphics

See "Essential Graphics Panel" (page 148).

New Comp from Selection

Creates a new composition based on the frame size, frame rate, and duration of the selected object.

Replace with Precomp

Replaces all instances of the asset with a precomp of the asset.

Create Proxy

If your footage is sluggish, you may consider replacing it with a proxy while you work. A proxy is a low-resolution duplicate of your footage.

The Interface & Editing

Animation

Text

Shapes, Masks & Mattes

Effects

3D

Special Tools & Features

Expressions

Guides and Rulers

These work best together, so enable them both. Rulers show the X and Y coordinates of your image. You can click and drag from a ruler to create a guide, which is a straight vertical or horizontal line that sits on your image while you work. Guides can be helpful for ensuring that all your titles are placed in the same place, for example. You can have objects snap to guides with View > Snap to Guides. You can also right-click a guide to type in an exact position value. Want it in the vertical center of your 1080 comp? You can type 1080/2 and have After Effects perform the math for you.

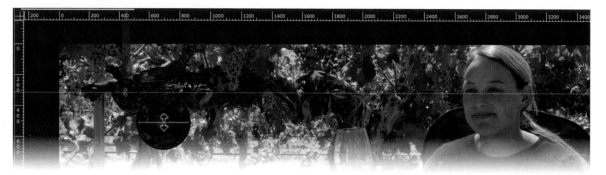

Channel and Color Management

Digital images are made of a combined red, green, blue, and sometimes alpha (transparency) value. By selecting one of these settings, you can see a black-and-white image displaying exactly how much data is in each channel. The brighter the pixel, the higher the value (therefore, on the alpha channel, black is transparent and white is opaque).

If you've enabled Color Management in your project , you can temporarily switch color management off and on with this feature. See "Color" (page 168).

Under View > Simulate Output, you can see what your image might look like when viewed on monitors with varying color profiles. Then, you can easily toggle this view off and on using the Color Management icon.

Adjust Exposure

Drag these values to temporarily brighten or darken the image within this panel. This won't affect your output—it's just a means of making things easier on your eyes. Click the iris icon to reset.

Take/Reveal Snapshot

Click the camera to take a snapshot of your image—and brace yourself for a fantastically retro sound effect. At any point, you can click and hold the Reveal Snapshot icon to show the image that was captured. This can be helpful for comparing one shot to another.

Playback in the Footage Panel

Press the spacebar to play your footage. It may play slowly at first—we'll cover that shortly. You can jump to the start of your footage with the home key, or to the end with the end key. Advance a single frame forward with ⌘–right arrow/Ctrl–right arrow, and backward with ⌘–left arrow/Ctrl–left arrow. Or, achieve the same results with page down and page up.

The playhead indicates where in the timeline you're viewing. You can click and drag it to zip through your footage, or simply click in the timeline to jump to a new time. You can zoom into the timeline with = and zoom out with –, or drag the timeline navigator handles inward.

You can zoom into your image with the Magnification Ratio setting, your mouse's scroll wheel, or ⌘–=/Ctrl–= to zoom in and ⌘––/Ctrl–– to zoom out. You can also click the Zoom tool in the toolbar 🔍 (hotkey Z) and click on your image to zoom in. Opt/Alt-click zooms out.

You can move the image around the panel by clicking and dragging while holding the spacebar, or switching to the Hand tool ✋ (hotkey H) in the Toolbar and dragging.

Setting In and Out Points

If the Footage panel is viewing raw camera footage, it's unlikely that you'll want all of the footage in your composition. In this panel, you can set In and Out points to trim your clip so you're only bringing in what you need.

To set an In point, navigate your playhead to where you want to start your footage. Then, either press the Set In point button ▐ or use the hotkey opt-[/Alt-[.

To set an Out point, navigate your playhead to where you want to end your footage. Then, either press the Set Out point button ▌ or use the hotkey opt-]/Alt-].

Timecode

Take note of how After Effects is displaying the current time and the time settings of your In and Out points. This format is called timecode, and it's displayed in Hours:Minutes:Seconds:Frames.

Adding Footage to a Composition

You can click and drag your footage from the Project panel into a preexisting composition, or use it to create a new composition by dragging it to the New Composition button 🖼.

If you have a composition already open, you can also add footage to it by using the Ripple Insert Edit 🔳 and Overlay Edit 🔲 buttons in the Footage panel.

Adding a clip to a **comp** with **Overlay Edit** simply drops in the shot wherever your playhead is.

Adding a clip to a **comp** with **Insert Ripple Edit** pushes everything to
the right of that clip over, so the clip makes room for itself.

The Interface
& Editing

Animation

Text

Shapes, Masks
& Mattes

Effects

3D

Special Tools
& Features

Expressions

The Timeline Panel

The timeline is where we control what's on-screen, when.

Timecode. Click and drag to change.
Click with ⌘/Ctrl to switch to frame count

Toggle track
visibility, mute,
solo, and lock   **Comp** search bar

Timeline navigator handles

Composition Mini–Flowchart,
Shy Layers, Frame Blending,
Motion Blur, Graph Editor   Playhead   Work area

Add Marker

Labels   Layers   The switches   Parent and Link

Timeline zoom   **Comp** button

Expand/collapse other panes

I came here to push buttons and chew bubblegum, and I'm all out of bubblegum.

Toggle Track Visibility, Mute, Solo, and Lock

Click the eyeball 👁 to turn off the visibility of a track. If a track has audio, click the speaker 🔊 to silence the track. Click the box underneath the solo icon to turn off visibility of all layers except for that one. Finally, click the box underneath the lock icon 🔒 to prevent selection of that layer. Locking layers is helpful for foreground or background layers that you keep selecting by accident.

Labels

Labels are simply the color of your layers, and the bounding box visible around selected layers. You can change label colors to better organize the way your timeline looks.

Layers

Hey, here are your layers! The order of your layers matters; the layers on top will appear above the layers on the bottom (unless they're 3D layers). You can easily change the selected layer with ⌘-up arrow/Ctrl-up arrow to select the layer above, and ⌘-down arrow/Ctrl-down arrow to select the layer below. You can rearrange layers by clicking and dragging, or by selecting a layer and pressing ⌘-]/Ctrl-] to move it up, and ⌘-[/Ctrl-[to move it down.

Selecting a layer and pressing return/Enter allows you to rename the layer in the Timeline panel. This also switches the panel view from displaying the Source Name to the Layer Name, indicated by text above your layers. Clicking that text while holding down the ⌘/Ctrl key switches it back.

The Switches

On each layer, you may be able to enable one of the seven switches, each of which is wildly unique. If you cannot see these switches, chances are you're looking at the modes, which will be covered in chapter 5 of the Compendium. If this is the case, be sure to select Toggle Switches/ Modes at the bottom of this panel.

Toggle Shy Layer

The character you used to doodle in your notebooks makes an appearance, but he's shy. Shy layers are a means of cleaning up your timeline and hiding layers you might not need frequent access to. This is different from clicking the eyeball to turn off track visibility—shy layers will still be visible in the composition, but not in the Timeline panel.

Clicking the Toggle Shy Layer icon tells After Effects that you'd like the layer to be shy. Then you can show or hide your shy layers by selecting the Show/Hide Shy Layers button 🌐 at the top of the Timeline panel.

A **timeline** with shy layers hidden. Note the index (that is, layer numbers) is missing a few, and the **Show/Hide Shy Layers** button is active.

Continuously Rasterize/Collapse Transformations

One button, two functions, and an icon that doesn't really look like anything. What's not to love?

The Continuously Rasterize feature is what's called when you select this switch on a vector layer—generally, this is an Illustrator or EPS format. This enables you to scale the layer past 100% without losing quality. Otherwise, the image will be rasterized, and will show pixelization when enlarged. Note that enabling this feature is more processing-intensive.

The Interface & Editing

Animation

Text

Shapes, Masks & Mattes

Effects

3D

Special Tools & Features

Expressions

Left, an Illustrator layer scaled up 3000% without **Continuous Rasterization**. Right, with. Crispy!

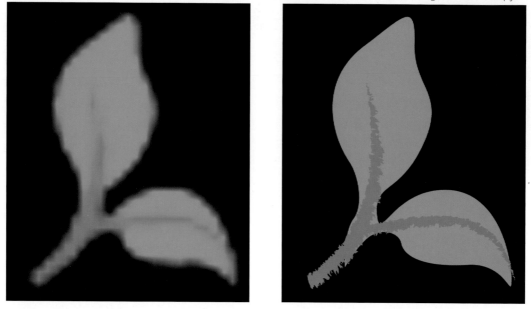

Selecting this button on a precomposed layer (see "Pre-Composing," page 192) changes the way After Effects reads the layer. Normally, a precomp layer is like a flattened version of several layers. While there may be some complex stuff happening inside the precomp, in the parent comp, it's just a postcard of everything inside the precomp.

However, with Collapse Transformations selected on a precomp layer, the precomp acts more like a folder containing your layers. Basically, layers, plus their effects and transforms, act as through they're inside the parent comp, not the precomp.

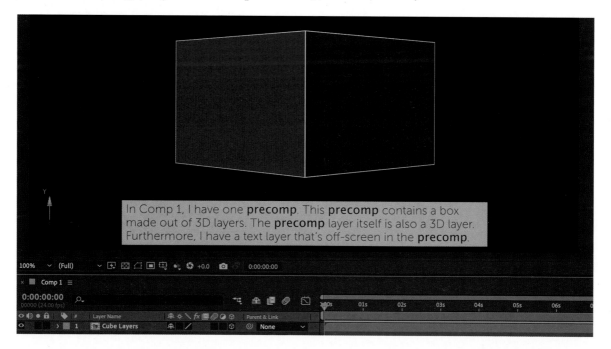

In Comp 1, I have one **precomp**. This **precomp** contains a box made out of 3D layers. The **precomp** layer itself is also a 3D layer. Furthermore, I have a text layer that's off-screen in the **precomp**.

The Interface
& Editing

Animation

Text

Shapes, Masks
& Mattes

Effects

3D

Special Tools
& Features

Expressions

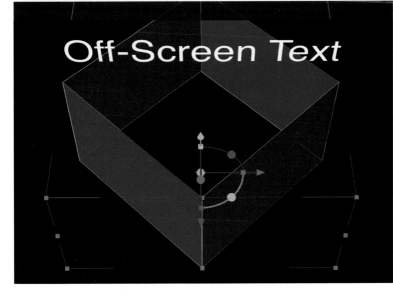

Without **Collapse Transformations**, moving the camera around this box is like moving a camera around a postcard. Even though the **precomp** is full of 3D stuff, by default, **precomps** are treated as flattened layers.

Turning on **Collapse Transformations** essentially brings the transformation data from my **precomp** into Comp 1. Instead of Comp 1 reading the **precomp** as a flattened postcard, it thinks of it as a folder containing each discrete layer. I can now see the 3D-ness of my layers coming through my top-level **comp**. Plus, text that was off-screen in the **precomp** is now visible.

Quality and Sampling

Toggle between various quality preferences on your layer. By default, layers are set to ▨, which is standard quality. With this preference, scaling up a raster image or video uses an algorithm called bilinear to determine how to draw new pixels. Click the Quality and Sampling button again to change to ◩, which introduces a higher-quality sampling method for scaling up images called bicubic. You might notice slightly sharper edges, at the expense of a little processing time. A third click gives you draft quality ◪, which looks the worst but renders the fastest.

Effects

Turns off all effects for that layer.

Frame Sampling

When slowing down a video file, the default method for introducing new frames is called Frame Sampling, in which the nearest frame is "borrowed" and duplicated. This can sometimes produce a stuttery video. After Effects offers two other methods for a smoother look. Click the switch once to enable Frame Blending ▥, in which new frames are generated by crossfading from one to the next. Click the switch again to enable Optical Flow , in which your pixels are analyzed, and brand-new frames are drawn. You might guess that this is A, the coolest, B, the most processing-intensive, and C, the most prone to gooey pixelated catastrophic failure.

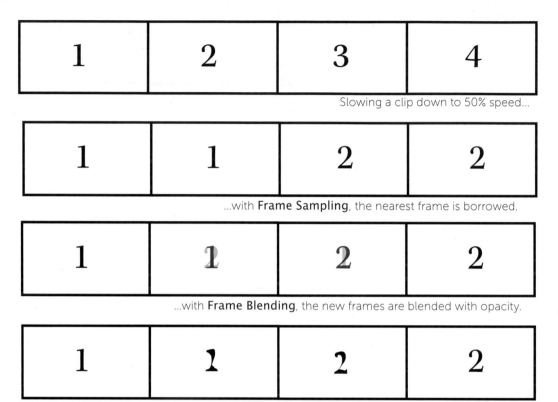

Slowing a clip down to 50% speed...

...with **Frame Sampling**, the nearest frame is borrowed.

...with **Frame Blending**, the new frames are blended with opacity.

...with **Optical Flow**, brand-new frames are drawn.

Note that using either Frame Blending or Optical Flow can slow After Effects down, so it may not be necessary to preview these effects in the Composition panel. You can toggle the display of these effects with the big Enable Frame Blending button at the top of the Timeline panel.

If you're exporting from the Render Queue with Best Settings, this button will automatically be switched on for you upon export. **Warning**: If you're exporting with Media Encoder, you must manually switch this button on before export to see your results.

Motion Blur

Is it weird to have a favorite switch? Motion Blur is essential. We humans like to talk a big game about how cool it is that series of still images can be perceived as motion, but that concept only goes so far. In truth, our brains process motion best when there's a little bit of consistency between frames. Pause a movie during an action scene—you'll notice fast motion contains blur. Cinematographers shoot with low shutter speeds to intentionally capture this motion blur onto the frames; it's just easier to follow movement.

This same principle applies to animation. Luckily, it's very easy to hit this switch and automatically apply motion blur to your assets, which renders a motion trail as objects move. Plus, it's legal in all fifty states.

Although slightly emphasized for effect, this motion trail is much easier on the eyes when the red ball is zipping through the frame.

How does it work? After Effects looks at the position of your asset in the frames before and after, then subdivides the movement X number of times (16 by default), then renders on the screen with increasing opacity.

You can customize the look of your motion blur by going to Composition > Composition Settings, then clicking on the Advanced tab. The Shutter Angle dictates how big your streaks are—the higher the angle, the bigger the streaks. Shutter Phase allows you to favor a certain part of the movement, with a lower phase displaying the earlier half, and a higher, the later. Samples Per Frame increases the quality of the blur by drawing more frames, but will dramatically increase render times. Adaptive Sample Limit sets a maximum for the total number of blur frames rendered at once in your composition.

Note that using Motion Blur can slow After Effects down, so it may not be necessary to preview these effects in the Composition panel. You can toggle the display of this effect with the big Enable Motion Blur button ⊘ at the top of the Timeline panel.

If you're exporting from the Render Queue with Best Settings, this button will automatically be switched on for you upon export. **Warning**: If you're exporting with Media Encoder, you must manually switch this button on before export to see your results.

Adjustment Layer
No, it's not a black-and-white cookie. Click this button to convert a layer into an Adjustment Layer. Adjustment Layers take their effects and apply them to all layers below.

3D Layer
Converts the layer to a 3D layer. At their simplest, 3D layers allow you to move and rotate an object in 3D space. At their most complex, 3D layers are an entire chapter's worth of lights, cameras, materials, reflections, and geometry. See chapter 6 of the Compendium for all that.

The Interface & Editing

Animation

Text

Shapes, Masks & Mattes

Effects

3D

Special Tools & Features

Expressions

Parent & Link

Use this section to parent layers, either by dragging the Pickwhip 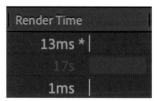 from the child to the parent layer, or by using the drop-down menu. For the rules on parenting, see chapter 2 of the Compendium.

Expand/Collapse Other Panes

There's more to the Timeline panel than what we see out of the box. In the lower-left corner of this panel, we can display any combination of the switches, modes, the In/Out/Duration/Stretch pane, and the Render Time pane. The Timeline panel doesn't have to be pane-ful.

In	Out	Duration	Stretch
0:00:00:00	0:00:02:08	0:00:02:09	100.0%
0:00:00:08	0:00:02:07	0:00:02:00	100.0%
0:00:00:05	0:00:02:03	0:00:01:23	100.0%

The **In/Out/Duration/Stretch pane** displays helpful information about where layers live in the **timeline**. You can also drag the blue numbers to edit these parameters.

The **Render Time pane** tells you which layers are taking a long time to render. If your previews are slow, try toggling off any layers in the red. An asterisk indicates the layer is cached, and should play quickly.

Render Time
13ms *
17s
1ms

Comp Search Bar

Got a large composition? Not only can you search for layers, but you can even search attributes. It takes several clicks to find the Line Cap setting on a shape layer, but it's very quick to type it into the search bar. The magnifying glass drop-down shows recently edited attributes.

Timeline Buttons

Some of the buttons at the top of the Timeline panel relate to the previous sections, some are brand-new.

The Composition Mini-Flowchart shows the relationship of comps to precomps. You can use it to quickly navigate from a precomp to a top-level comp, or vise versa, by clicking on the comp within the Mini-Flowchart. The Mini-Flowchart is also activated by pressing the Tab key.

Clicking the Hide Shy Layers button hides all layers for which the Shy switch is activated. If a layer has frame blending or motion blur, you can choose to display that feature in the Composition panel by toggling the corresponding button. Lastly, the Graph Editor button displays the Graph Editor, which will be discussed in the next chapter.

Work Area

If your composition is two minutes long, it's unlikely that you'll need to keep track of all two minutes at once—you're much more likely to focus on smaller segments at a time. The work area is helpful for this, as it works nicely with many playback functions. See "Playback" (page 190).

You can set your work area by clicking and dragging the work area handles, or set the start of the work area to your current playhead with B, and set the end of the work area to your current playhead with N.

Setting a **work area** allows for playback options that let you focus on a small section of your **comp**.

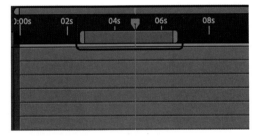

To reset your work area to the span of your entire timeline, double-click within the work area.

You can use the work area to trim the duration of your composition. With a work area set, right-click between the work area boundaries and select Trim Comp to Work Area.

Editing

The Timeline panel also allows you to trim and edit your clips. The textured colored strip indicates when your layer is visible.

Retiming Clips

You can click and drag the center of clips to change their position in the timeline. Press [to align a clip's In point to your current playhead. Press] to align a clip's Out point to your current playhead.

You can click and drag the end of a clip to trim it. Press opt-[/Alt-[to trim a clip's In point to your current playhead. Press opt-]/Alt-] to trim a clip's Out point to your current playhead.

Click and drag a clip to move it, or align its **In point** to your current time with **[**.

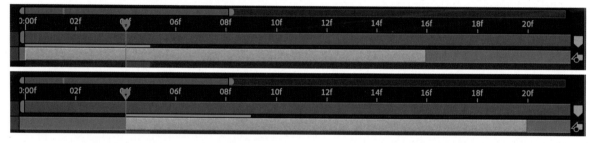

Click and drag the end of a clip to trim it, or trim its **In point** to your current time with **opt-[/Alt-[**

For video clips, you can change which section of the video clip is displayed. This is basically moving its In and Out points simultaneously, while retaining its original duration. Premiere users might recognize this as the function of the Slip tool. Just like in Premiere, call this function with the hotkey Y, then drag click and drag a video clip.

Duplicate a clip with ⌘-D/Ctrl-D. Split a clip at the playhead time with ⌘-shift-D/Ctrl-Shift-D. Both commands can also be called from the Edit menu.

A clip is split into two, each becoming its own layer.

Changing Clip Speed

There are several ways to change the speed of your footage.

Time Stretch

The simplest way is to right-click a clip and select Time > Time Stretch. This will bring up the dialog to the right.

Decreasing Stretch Factor speeds up your footage, and increasing it slows it down. A Stretch Factor of 50% is double speed, 200% is half. (And for you Premiere users, yes, this does feel backward!) Or, you can type in the duration you'd like your clip to be and it will speed up or slow down accordingly.

Hold in Place is like an anchor point on the timeline—deciding what *doesn't* move when the clip is stretched.

When slowing footage down, you might consider "Frame Sampling" (page 181).

Time Remapping

You can also obtain complete manual control over the speed of your clip. To do so, right-click a clip and select Time > Enable Time Remapping. This brings up the Time Remap attribute in the timeline. Here, you can keyframe the timing of your source clip.

Even though I'm on frame 0 of my **composition**, I've time remapped my footage with a **keyframe** so it's actually displaying 36 seconds into the footage's source timecode. I could duplicate this **keyframe** to hold on this frame.

You can even use time remapping to retime entire compositions. Just drag the composition from the Project panel onto the New Composition icon, so your comp is now just a single layer in a brand-new comp. Then, time remap it. This might be a faster way to tweak timing, especially if your animation has lots of keyframes and precomps. Even if you're using time remapping to slow down keyframed animation, After Effects will reinterpret your keyframes to keep your animation smooth. No frame blending needed.

Putting a **comp** into another **comp** and time remapping it is a great way to retime complex animation.

The Interface & Editing

Animation

Text

Shapes, Masks & Mattes

Effects

3D

Special Tools & Features

Expressions

Other Time Options

Right-clicking a layer and hovering over Time reveals two more helpful options: Time-Reverse Layer (plays footage backward), Freeze Frame (enables a Time Remap with a Hold keyframe on your current frame), and Freeze on Last Frame (does the same as Freeze Frame, but on your last frame).

Responsive Design

Consider this animation: A spaceship takes two seconds to fly into the frame, stays still for some time, then takes two seconds to leave the frame. Riveting, I know. Now, let's say I want to drop this ship animation as a precomp inside another comp. That's great, but now I can tell the animation is too short. I could slow it down with Time Stretch, but that will slow down the whole animation—the entrance and exit speed would be affected. What if I could make it so my intro and outro speed remains constant, and only my idle portion gets retimed? There's a way! It's called Responsive Design.

Responsive Design works by having you set Protected Regions—regions unaffected by time squish. In this case, I want my intro and outro to always be two seconds, so I'll make those first and last two seconds Protected Regions. The middle part of the animation will be squishy.

In this case, I'll head to Composition > Responsive Design — Time > Create Intro and Create Outro. One can also use the work area to define a Protected Region. Doing so places blue markers on the timeline. Set the markers so that they "freeze" the parts of the animation you don't want to change.

The stuff between these blue markers will not be affected by a time stretch. Everything not within these markers will be squished. By protecting the intro and outro, I can ensure that they remain two seconds long each, even when the **comp's** timing changes.

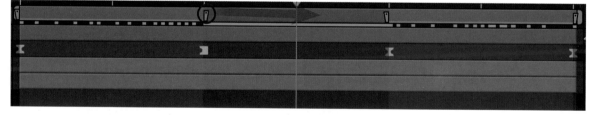

The next step is to drag this comp into a new comp. If it's already in a comp, you must right-click the layer and select Markers > Update Markers from Source, otherwise the Protected Regions won't be recognized. A precomp with Protected Regions looks like this:

Typically, clicking and dragging the ends of a clip will trim it. Not the case with a precomp with Protected Regions. Now, simply dragging the end of the clip will shorten or lengthen it, but it will only squash or stretch portions of the clip that are *not* Protected Regions.

The Interface
& Editing

Animation

Text

Shapes, Masks
& Mattes

Effects

3D

Special Tools
& Features

Expressions

Behold, as we trim the clip, we speed up only the squishy section unaffected by **Protected Regions**. Our clip is now like an inverse Hot Pocket: molten lead interior, sub-zero exterior.

Is Essential Graphics your thing? This is a great way to create a lower-thirds template for Premiere. Premiere speaks Protected Regions, so you can retime a lower third in Premiere that uses this attribute without worrying about speeding up your intro or outro animation.

Scene Edit Detection

If you've imported an edited clip that contains cuts, Scene Edit Detection can automatically detect whenever your clip has a cut. To use it, right-click a shot in the timeline and select Scene Edit Detection, or find the same option in the Layer menu. You can either add markers whenever there's a cut, or split up the layer.

Turn a single clip with edits...

...into a clip with markers denoting edits...

...or split it into multiple clips.

Playback

Pressing the spacebar plays from your currently selected panel. You may notice playback is sluggish on first viewing, but faster on subsequent views. This is because on playback, After Effects calculates what your frames look like, and stores that information in your computer's RAM, or random access memory. The next time you play that section, After Effects can recall what those frames look like, and display them much faster. If a frame is stored in RAM, you'll see a green bar above it in the timeline.

This is all to say that After Effects is a resource-intensive piece of software, and the more RAM your machine has, the more frames can be stored in RAM, and the more responsive the software will be. Don't forget about the various tips on speeding up the software—lowering adaptive resolution, turning off Color Management, turning off Motion Blur and Frame Blending, and disabling Continuous Rasterization, to name a few.

The Preview Panel

Let's explore different options for previewing our footage.

At the top of the panel, notice your transport controls. These can all be achieved with hotkeys—see "Playback in the Footage Panel" (page 172).

The Shortcut section says this: When you press (this button), apply the below settings. The default is spacebar—therefore, we're looking at the options for what happens when you press the spacebar. There are many more key combinations available to use, or customize. For example, you could designate shift-spacebar to play your work area full screen at full quality.

Include designates what is displayed in playback. You have toggle options for Video, Audio, and Overlays and Controls 🔲 (bounding boxes and mattes, which generally aren't displayed in playback). Clicking the Loop button 🔁 toggles between looping, or just playing once.

Range dictates what is played, and often references the "Work Area" (page 185).

- Work Area Extended by Current Time plays from your playhead and stops and the end of your work area.
- Work Area will play within the duration of your work area, regardless of where the playhead is.
- Entire Range ignores the work area.

Play From dictates where playback begins—either the current time or start of Range. Frame Rate allows you to play at a different frame rate than your comp—I don't recommend changing this. If your render times are egregious, you can elect to Skip frames upon render, which is slightly more elegant than lowering the frame rate. I generally set my Resolution to Auto, which will preview at the same resolution as the settings in your comp's resolution. Note that this can be changed. Finally, note the Full Screen option.

The Layer Panel

Double-click a layer from the Composition panel to open it in the Layer panel. This panel is very similar to the Footage panel, but note that changes in the Layer panel affect layers currently in your comps, whereas changes in the Footage panel must then be imported into a composition.

The Layer Panel Interface

I'm not going to lie to you—the Layer panel isn't that exciting. There are a few small differences in the functionality of this panel compared to the Footage panel.

For one, note the View drop-down. It is possible to view masks and effects on a layer from this panel. Don't all clap at once.

Finally, note that some functions, such as the Tracker, Rotobrush, and Paint tools must operate within the Layer panel. We'll cover those in chapter 7 of the Compendium.

The Interface & Editing

Animation

Text

Shapes, Masks & Mattes

Effects

3D

Special Tools & Features

Expressions

changes inside your precomp, and seeing the effects inside the top-level comp.

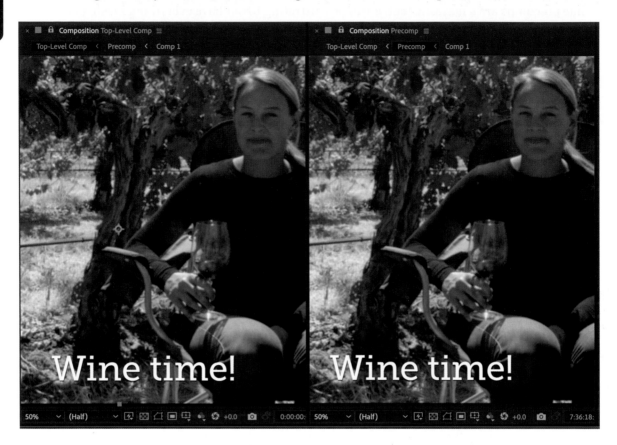

Note that you can only view real-time playback in one comp at a time.

Rendering and Encoding

We're going to jump ahead to the end and talk about how to save your videos as standalone files.

What's the Difference?

The main way After Effects creates a video is through a process called rendering, in which After Effects writes each frame to the disk. Typically, this results in a large, high-quality file that is excellent for importing into Premiere, or archiving. The most common render format is a QuickTime file, writing in a codec called ProRes (a codec is a language that a computer uses to write a media file, and the QuickTime wrapper supports several different codecs).

When we talk about encoding, it's a more complicated process that can look at the entire video file, and throw away data that isn't necessary. Typically, this results in a small, lower-quality file that is excellent for sharing or uploading to the web. The most common encoding format is H.264, which gives you a smaller .mp4 file.

After Effects' renderer can't encode—it can only render. If you wish to encode your renders, you must either first render and then bring that file into Adobe Media Encoder, or utilize Adobe Media Encoder to handle your export, instead of After Effects' Render Queue. Let's look at methods for rendering, rendering then encoding, and direct encoding.

Render with the Render Queue

When you're ready to render a composition, you must send the comp to After Effects' Render Queue, which is where you'll decide on your export settings. With a composition opened, add it to the Render Queue with Composition > Add to Render Queue, or drag it from the Project panel into the Render Queue. If the Render Queue isn't open, you can do so from the Window menu. You can add as many compositions as you'd like to the Render Queue.

Render Settings

Click on the blue text that reads Best Settings to check out what this setting does by default.

Animation

Text

Shapes, Masks
& Mattes

Effects

3D

Special Tools
& Features

Expressions

The Adobe Media Encoder Interface

Adobe Media Encoder is a powerful tool to convert video and audio files into many formats. Like the Render Queue, it allows you to import multiple videos, adjust their settings, and batch-export them at once.

Whether or not you dragged a video file into AME's Queue panel, or selected an Add to AME option, you should see something like this:

We'll want to choose a format and preset, and then choose our destination and file name.

Under Format, note the multitude of options. For a small file for web delivery, you'll want H.264.

There are many options under Preset. Generally, I use one of the Match Source options to ensure that I'm not reformatting my video. Choose from high-, medium-, and low-quality options.

Under Output File, select the blue text and decide where to save your file, then name it.

When you're ready to export your queue, either click the play button ▶ or hit return/Enter.

2 Animation

Most attributes in After Effects are represented by a number. The basic principle of animation is changing that number over time. Animation in After Effects is handled by keyframes, which are pieces of data that hold values at specific times. After Effects automatically changes these values between your set keyframes, which creates animation. And almost anything in After Effects can be animated.

Anchor Points

Let's pause for a minute to discuss how objects transform. Position, and more dramatically, scale and rotation, all occur about an object's Anchor Point. We can see the Anchor Point of a selected object—it's the little crosshair that defaults to the dead-center of an object.

It's easiest to visualize the importance of an Anchor Point when thinking about rotation. Picture a pen sticking into a piece of paper that you spin around. The paper spins around the point that the pen is stuck into. Similarly, our spaceship is spinning around the center axis. It's also scaling from the center, and once we begin to animate position, we'll see that position is measured from the Anchor Point.

For still photo editing, this is unimportant—we can simply rotate and scale however we want to. For animation, however, it's crucial to decide where you want these translations to occur. For example, if you want to zoom in on a person's face, the Anchor Point should be positioned on said face, so a single Scale control will set the image to where you want it to land. For our spaceship, think about how it might move if it were to rotate as it flies around.

Changing an object's Anchor Point after you've animated can be a hassle, and can cause unexpected issues. I always recommend setting an object's Anchor Point before you begin animating. I'll say it again for the people in the back: **Set an object's Anchor Point before you begin animating.**

The Pan Behind/Anchor Point Tool

So, how do we change an Anchor Point? With this oddly named tool , which can also be called with the hotkey Y. Yes, that's the same hotkey that lets us slip a video clip's In and Out points. With the Anchor Point tool selected, simply click and drag the crosshair in the middle of the image.

I'm no physicist, but it makes sense to me that the spaceship would rotate about the center of the ship.

You can reset your Anchor Point to an object's center by right-clicking the object or layer and selecting Transform > Center Anchor Point in Layer Content. While we're here, take note of a few helpful shortcuts, such as Flip, Center In View, Fit to Comp, and Reset.

Warning: When you move an object's Anchor Point with the Anchor Point tool, you're also changing the object's position—you just can't tell. There's some fancy math involved when this tool is used, but it's not apparent. This matters if you have keyframes enabled on an object's position—you might be writing more keyframes that you don't intend to. The takeaway? I guess I'll just say it one more time: **Set an object's Anchor Point before you begin animating.**

Animation

Text

Shapes, Masks & Mattes

Effects

3D

Special Tools & Features

Expressions

Keyframing

Now that we've accessed our Transform controls in the Timeline panel, we'll use keyframes to change these values over time. Almost anything in After Effects can be keyframed, and understanding them is essential to the core of this software.

Enabling Keyframes

To enable keyframes on a parameter, simply click the stopwatch next to the parameter you'd like to animate.

A few things have happened in this example. With my playhead at 00:00:00:00, I've turned on keyframes for Rotation. This creates a keyframe at 00:00:00:00, and this keyframe holds the Rotation value of 0°. The stopwatch is now blue, indicating that keyframes are enabled for this parameter. This means that any change I make to Rotation will write a new keyframe wherever my playhead is.

In order for animation to happen, we need at least two keyframes at two different times holding two different values. I'll move my playhead to 00:00:01:00 and change my Rotation value, either by dragging the blue numbers, or with the Rotate tool.

I now have two keyframes at two different times holding two different values; the keyframe at 00:00:01:00 holds a Rotation value of 24°. Animation will now occur—the object will rotate from 0° to 24° over the course of a second. We can predict the Rotation value at each time, since at 24 frames per second, it will be rotating one degree per frame.

Basic Keyframe Editing

Note the widget on the left of the timeline ◀ ◆ ▶ . This is the keyframe controller, or as at least one After Effects developer calls it, the KFC. If the diamond in the center of the KFC is blue, that means your playhead is currently on a keyframe. Changing that parameter's value will edit your current keyframe. That said, your playhead must be directly on the keyframe for that to happen—it's not enough to simply select the keyframe. That's where the left and right arrows come in handy. Click the KFC's left arrow to jump to your previous keyframe in the timeline, and the right arrow to jump to the next. This can also be achieved with the hotkeys J and K. If your playhead is not on a keyframe, you can click the center diamond of the KFC to add a new keyframe.

Note that keyframes can be copied and pasted, with good ol' ⌘–C/Ctrl–C and ⌘–V/Ctrl–V. This is helpful if you want an object to animate, stop, and then animate again. Recall that animation occurs when the values between two keyframes differ. Two identical keyframes will "hold" the value in place.

Unfortunately, you can only copy and paste keyframes on one layer at a time. If that's a pain, consider purchasing this script: https://aescripts.com/paste-multiple-keyframes/.

Click and drag keyframes to change the speed of your animation—positioning keyframes closer together produces faster animation, and positioning keyframes further apart creates slower animation. You can scale multiple keyframes at once to shrink or expand a series of keyframes. With multiple keyframes selected, click and drag on either the first or last keyframe while holding opt/Alt. Note that this may place keyframes between your frames.

To reverse the placement of your keyframes, select the keyframes you'd like to reverse, right-click on any of them, and select Keyframe Assistant > Time–Reverse Keyframes.

To quickly bring up keyframed parameters in the timeline, select a layer and press U. To view all edited properties of a layer, keyframed or otherwise, press U twice, like a double-click.

Keyframe Labels

Coming soon! Keyframe labels allow you to change the color of keyframes in the timeline. This is a great organizational tool so you can keep note of which keyframes do what. If this feature is available at the time you're reading this, use it by right-clicking a keyframe or keyframes and selecting Label, then choosing a color. Select Label Group will select all keyframes with the same label.

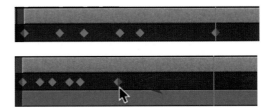

Note that when this feature is released, your **keyframe** selection may look different than the images printed in the rest of this book. Instead of **keyframes** turning blue to indicate selection, **keyframes** may be outlined, so you can see their label color.

Fancy Keyframe Interpolation

The default value of keyframes is linear—they move evenly from one value to the next. However, very few things in the real world move this way. Objects have momentum—they start off moving slowly, pick up speed, and unless they're a puppy charging headfirst into a dresser, often slow down as they reach their goal.

Keyframe interpolation refers to how keyframes get from value 1 to value 2, and it's often a good idea to give your objects a little bit of this inertia in their interpolation. While it may not seem like a big deal, even the default method of easing into your values bumps your animation up a notch.

Easy Ease

No, not the rapper. Easy Ease is the quickest way to apply just a bit of that inertia with a nice, default value.

To apply Easy Ease to your keyframes, select them, and either right-click any of them and select Keyframe Assistant > Easy Ease, or hit F9. (Note that often on Mac computers, F9 defaults to skipping your current song. You can either hit F9 along with the fn key, or if you don't like pressing that fn key, you can switch the defaults in System Preferences.)

This will change your keyframe from a diamond to an hourglass. The default Easy Ease eases your animation as a keyframe is approached, and eases your animation as a keyframe is exited.

In some instances, you may want a keyframe to be linear as it approaches and eased on its way out, or vice versa. For those moments, you can choose Keyframe Assistant > Easy Ease In or Easy Ease Out. To set an eased keyframe back to linear, click on it while holding ⌘/Ctrl.

Easy Ease	Easy Ease In	Easy Ease Out
eased in eased out	eased in linear out	linear in eased out

Keyframe Velocity

While the default Easy Ease has a great look, there may be times you want something a little snappier. With keyframes selected, you can right-click any of them and select Keyframe Velocity. In the following dialog, you can choose Influence, which dictates the curve of the interpolation. A value of 0.01% means easing is off, and 33.3% is the default value for Easy Ease. Increasing this percentage increases the snappiness of the curve—basically, starting slower, ending slower, and making up for that time with a faster in-between. Play with the percentage to find a value that suits you. We'll get a little bit more control over this when we get to the Graph Editor, but this is certainly faster.

Hold Keyframes

Hold keyframes are when you want a value to change, but not interpolate at all. Hold keyframes jump instantaneously from one value to the next. To change keyframes to hold keyframes, right-click and select Toggle Hold Keyframe.

The Graph Editor

Want even more control over your keyframes? With the Graph Editor, your keyframe values are plotted onto a graph to visualize how they're interpolating. Furthermore, you can edit keyframe values and curve shapes within the Graph Editor, unlocking more options than we've previously encountered.

The Graph Editor Interface

Switch to the Graph Editor by clicking the Graph Editor button 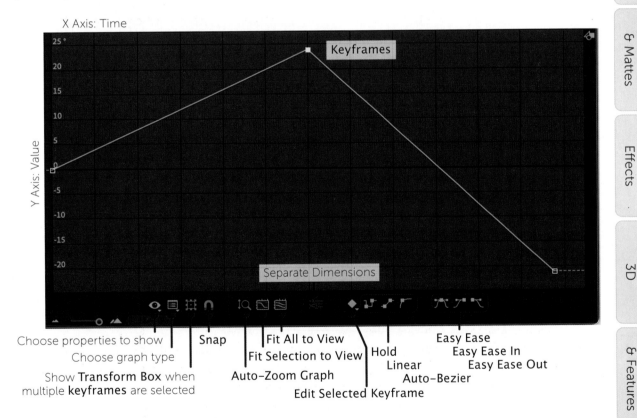 at the top of the Timeline panel. Display values by selecting a keyframed attribute from the timeline.

Off the bat, this is pretty cool. I can see my actual keyframe values (now represented by yellow squares) at certain times, and visualize their interpolation.

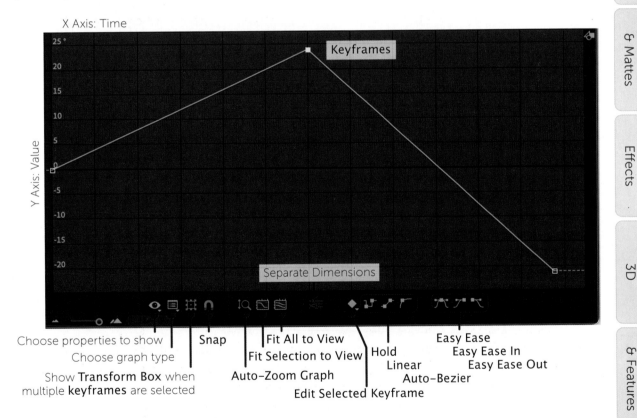

Choose Which Properties Are Shown

By default, you must select a property in the timeline for it to display in the Graph Editor. By clicking on the eyeball at the bottom of the Graph Editor, you'll discover other options: Show Selected Properties, Show Animated Properties (automatically displaying all keyframed properties), and Show Graph Editor Set.

That final one works a little differently. Notice a tiny Graph Editor icon 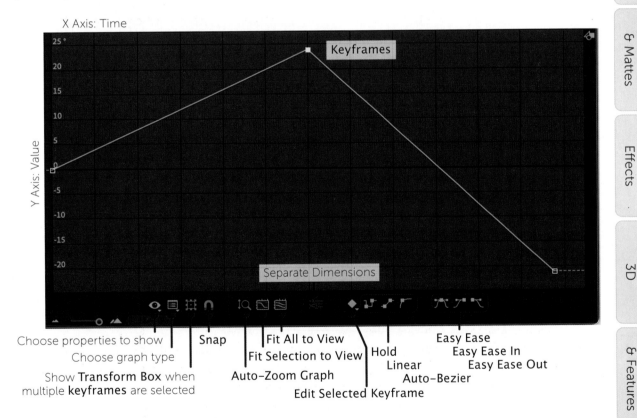 next to the

Animation · Text · Shapes, Masks & Mattes · Effects · 3D · Special Tools & Features · Expressions

The Interface & Editing

Animation

stopwatch. Selecting that adds it to the Graph Editor Set. This creates a little showcase of graphs that will be displayed as long as the layer is selected and Show Graph Editor Set is selected, saving you the time of manually selecting attributes that you frequently wish to view together.

Choose Graph Type and Options

By default, the Graph Editor displays the Value Graph, which is very intuitive. With this panel, we can view another type of graph.

The Speed Graph displays the speed at which an object is changing, measured in value per second.

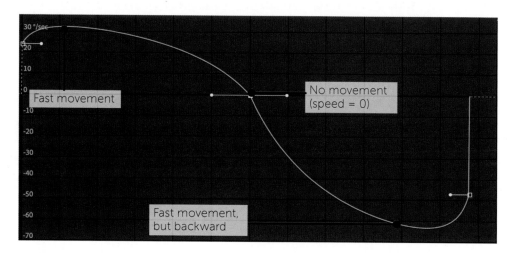

In this example, I'm viewing the speed of an object's rotation (not the same one as the previous example). Measured in degrees per second, I can see the object is rotating more quickly at the beginning, but slows down as it approaches the second keyframe. In the Speed Graph, a value of 0 means an object isn't moving. The further you get from zero—in either a positive or negative direction—the faster the movement. The image above shows another example of easing—the curve of the graph gently slopes down as the speed of the object approaches zero. Linear keyframes are straight lines on this graph (constant speed = straight lines).

We will discuss editing these graphs momentarily, but keep in mind that you can edit a Speed Graph in the same way as a Value Graph.

With Show Reference Graph selected, showing either graph displays the opposite one in the same window.

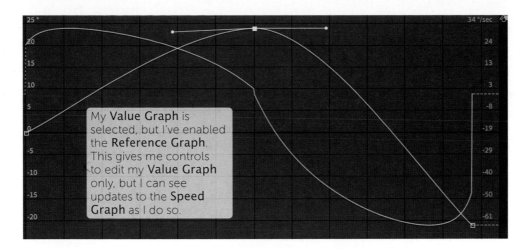

In the same window, note some self-explanatory and helpful display options: Show Audio Waveforms, Show Layer In/Out Points, Show Layer Markers, Show Graph Tool Tips, and Show Expression Editor. Finally, note an option to Allow Keyframes Between Frames.

With multiple keyframes selected, a bounding box is displayed around them. This bounding box functions very similarly to the one around a layer, in that you can drag the corners to scale your graph. Turn off this feature with the Show Transform Box When Multiple Keyframes Are Selected button.

Editing Graphs

We can very easily change keyframe values and timing in the Graph Editor by just clicking them and moving them around. We can also perform our previous functions (Velocity, Hold, etc.) in the Graph Editor—right-clicking a keyframe reveals options, and note the quick buttons for interpolation methods in the lower-right corner.

There's not a lot we can do with linear keyframes other than move them around. However, by converting a keyframe to non-linear, we unlock many ways to manipulate its curves. Change the type of keyframe with one of the buttons in the lower-right corner of the Graph Editor. Easy Ease or Auto–Bezier will do the trick, but note that their default values do look different.

Animation

Text

Shapes, Masks & Mattes

Effects

3D

Special Tools & Features

Expressions

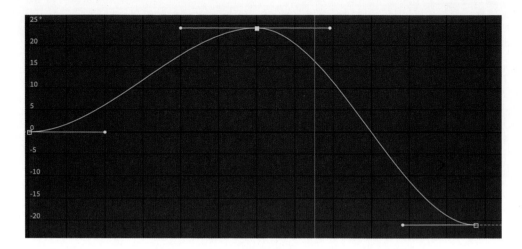

Here's a graph with Easy Ease enabled. Turning on Easy Ease does two things—it switches the graph type to Continuous Bezier, and then applies a nice default value.

Bezier (named after a French dude, so pronounced BEH-zee-ay) is a term that will come up several times throughout this book. It's way to manipulate a curve. Curves with Bezier handles—that is, the yellow knobs protruding from the keyframes—allow for great control of the shape of the curve.

Control the shape of the curve by changing the angle around the keyframe, and the distance of the handle to the keyframe.

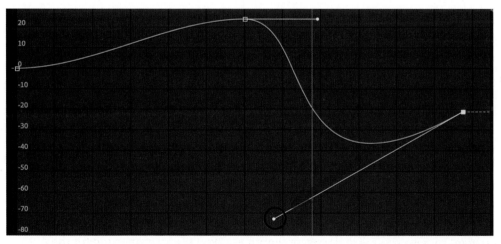

In this example, I've moved the Bezier handle so the Rotation value actually goes lower than the value of my final keyframe. This will cause an overshoot animation, in which the object goes a little further than it should, then snaps back. This is a fantastic way to simply add some playful cartoonishness to your animations.

Moving a Bezier handles while holding shift constrains the handle so it doesn't change its angle.

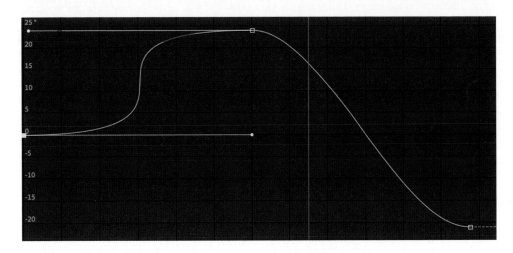

Remember our Keyframe Velocity? I've just achieved the same effect. Higher Keyframe Velocity = steeper S-curve in the Graph Editor.

While manipulating my center Bezier curve, changing the angle of one handle also changes the angle of the other—the handle seems to want to stay straight, so incoming and outgoing angles are the same. This is called Continuous Bezier. You can disable this by selecting a handle, then holding down opt/Alt while moving it. This will "break" the handle, allowing you to have more control over your curve shape.

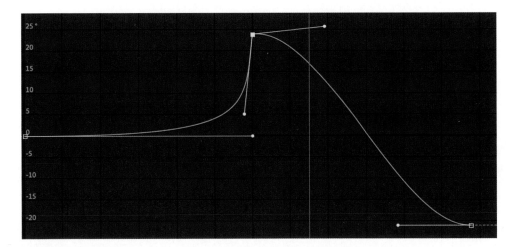

If you want to rejoin your broken Bezier handles, select the keyframe and hit the Auto–Bezier button ◢.

Keyframe Interpolation

You can also designate exactly which type of curve you'd like a keyframe to have by right-clicking on it and selecting Keyframe Interpolation.

- Linear sets it to linear.

Animation

Text

Shapes, Masks & Mattes

Effects

3D

Special Tools & Features

Expressions

- Bezier is a curve with broken Bezier handles that can be manipulated individually.
- Continuous Bezier is a curve with linked Bezier handles.
- Auto Bezier sets Continuous Bezier handles, but arranges them so it's a smooth input and output.
- Hold set keyframes to hold (no interpolation).

Scale Graphs

If your Scale function has Constrain Proportions turned on, the graph will be represented by a single curve. With Constrain Proportions turned off, the graph will have two curves: a red one for X and a green one for Y. Note that the X curve sits atop the Y curve, so you might need to move the handles around to grab the Y curve.

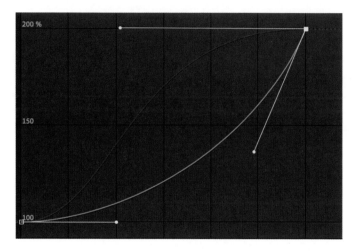

Spatial Interpolation

The pages above have all referred to a keyframe's temporal interpolation—how it moves throughout time. This property can be applied to all keyframes. However, Position keyframes have another parameter: spatial interpolation, or how they move throughout space. This gives us more options and control over how an object moves.

Position Keyframes in the Comp Panel

You can see an object's motion path in the Composition panel. Just like in the Graph Editor, you can click and drag keyframes (represented by squares) to change the points an object hits as it moves.

    With multiple position keyframes selected in the timeline, you can click and drag a single keyframe in the Composition panel to move all the keyframes together. This is a great way to preserve relative motion, but change where an object lands.

Animation

Text

Shapes, Masks & Mattes

Effects

3D

Special Tools & Features

Expressions

The Interface & Editing

Animation

By default, Position keyframes have Auto Bezier spatial interpolation. This means objects move along a curved path. These paths also have Bezier handles, allowing you to shape the curvature of an object's path, right in the Composition panel.

Just like in the previous section, you can change the interpolation of these keyframes by selecting them, right-clicking, and selecting Keyframe Interpolation. Note that you will now see options to change not only temporal interpolation, but also spatial.

You can change the default nature of spatial keyframes from Auto Bezier to Linear. Find that in Preferences > General > Default Spatial Interpolation to Linear. While we're here, note an option to change the Path Point and Handle Size, plus options on how the motion path is displayed under the Display section.

Position Keyframes in the Graph Editor

Like Scale keyframes, Position keyframes in the Graph Editor are represented by a red curve for X and a green curve for Y. You cannot edit these curves unless Separate Dimensions is selected. The nice folks at Adobe placed a button in the Graph Editor that achieves this.

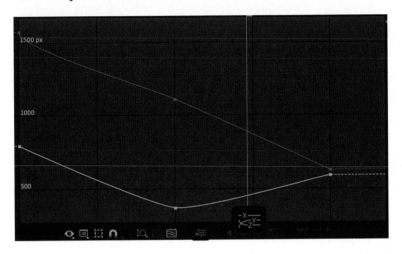

Rove Across Time

With multiple Position keyframes, it can be difficult to have an object move evenly from one spot to the next. Rove Across Time does this for you, by automatically changing the timing of your Position keyframes so movement is consistent.

Select at least three Position keyframes in the timeline, right-click any, and select Rove Across Time.

becomes...

What happened here? Well, our first and last keyframes remain the same. The keyframes between the two are shifted in time. This way, bigger movements get more frames to get from point A to B, and smaller movements get fewer. You no longer have control of the where the middle keyframes fall in the timeline; instead, After Effects will automatically shift them around for you.

In the Composition panel, you can still move keyframes around so your object hits certain points; the timing of your keyframes will automatically be adjusted.

In the timeline, while you can't change the timing of keyframes in the middle, you can click and drag your start or end keyframes to change the timing of your entire animation. The keyframes between will be shifted accordingly.

Animation

Text

Shapes, Masks & Mattes

Effects

3D

Special Tools & Features

Expressions

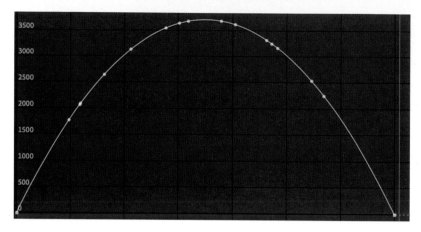

This feature doesn't have to result in linear keyframes. You can add Easy Ease to your roved keyframes, which will result in the entire animation starting off slow, speeding up, then ending slow. This is wonderfully visualized with the Speed Graph in the Graph Editor.

By default, **Rove Across Time** produces even movement, which would render the **Speed Graph** as a straight line. By adding **Easy Ease** to this, the speed graph is rendered as a perfect curve, with each **keyframe** plotted along it. The animation has inertia, and hits each position along the way.

Auto-Orient

While we're getting fancy with Position keyframes, we'd be remiss to not touch on Auto-Orient, a feature which has an object point in the direction it's traveling on its position path. Think of it as automatic rotation so the object is always aligned with its path.

To enable this, right-click an object and select Transform > Auto-Orient. In the following dialog, you can switch it on with Orient Along Path, or turn this feature off.

Parenting

Parenting is a fundamental concept to animation in After Effects. It can link the movement of one layer to another, so that controlling one layer (the parent) affects multiple layers (the children). Furthermore, child layers can also have their own movement in addition to inheriting movement from their parent layers. It's a rare occurrence where parenting actually makes your life easier.

Setting Up Parent/Child Relationships

After Effects' adoption process is much simpler than in real life. To define a layer as the child of a parent, drag the Pickwhip icon in the timeline ⌾ from the child to the parent layer.

You can also choose a parent layer with the Parent & Link drop-down, but that's way less fun.

In this example, the layer Ship becomes the parent to the layer Beam. Now, if I change the Position, Scale, or Rotation of Ship, I will also change it for Beam—basically, the Beam is coming with the Ship. Note that these transforms occur around the parent layer's Anchor Point. Also take note that Opacity is not part of the parenting action.

Children can have their own animation as well. Picture a bouncing ball on a moving platform. The bouncing ball is the child, with its own position animation. The platform is the parent, which can float around space, bringing the child with it.

You can hold shift while pickwhipping to move the child to the same position as the parent. Also take note that parenting will change the values of your layer's transforms, as they're now listed relative to the parent. Pickwhipping while holding down opt/Alt causes the layer to retain its Transform values. Said values will still be relative to the parent, so the layer might move.

You can have as many layers of parenting as you'd like, establishing a giant family tree with great-great-grandparents and fourth cousins whose names you're supposed to remember. The Parent & Link category of the Timeline panel is a great way to visualize whose kid is whose. You can also right-click a layer and hit Select Children.

Animation

Text

Shapes, Masks & Mattes

Effects

3D

Special Tools & Features

Expressions

Null Objects

Parenting is a great way to have several objects slide into a scene at once. But what if each layer needs its own animation? You wouldn't want any of those layers to be the parent (also, are they *really* ready?). In those cases, it may be helpful to create a Null Object. A Null Object is an empty layer that doesn't show up in your renders. At first this may seem like After Effects' most useless feature. However, animating groups of things together by parenting them to a Null Object is a fantastic way to build arbitrary controllers that are used to manipulate groups of layers. The Null Object then exists to serve as a parent controller. Think of it as a legal guardian for your layers.

Create a new Null Object with Layer > New > Null Object (don't forget to name it). Null Objects look like empty red bounding boxes. That box is just there as a visual reference for the layer's Transform properties, and it's something to click on. It won't appear in your renders, but you can always toggle the layer visibility if you wish.

Beam is parented to Ship, and Ship and Background are parented to a **Null Object** called Scene Mover. I can animate this **Null** to act like a camera, moving around everything in my scene.

👁 🔊 ● 🔒	🏷	#	Layer Name	🏵 ✳ ↘ *fx* 🎬 ⬭ ◗ ◔	Parent & Link
👁		›	1	⬜ Scene Mover	🏵 /	⟲ None ⌄
👁		› ⬛	2	Ship	🏵 /	⟲ 1. Scene Move ⌄
👁		› ⬛	3	Beam	🏵 /	⟲ 2. Ship ⌄
👁		› ⬛	4	Background	🏵 /	⟲ 1. Scene Move ⌄

3 Text

Text is a key way to display information in a motion graphic. While text can be animated like any other layer, it can also be animated per character, word, or line, without having dozens of layers.

SNAKE

The Interface
& Editing

Animation

Text

The Type Tool

Using the Type tool creates a text layer, in which you can type whatever you want (and in this chapter, I'll be typing *Lorem Ipsum*, which is placeholder gobbledygook). Text layers function like any other layer, but they don't exist in the Project panel. Access the Type tool from the Toolbar ▣ or with ⌘–T/Ctrl–T.

   Once a text layer has been created, the Text tool is what you'll used to edit the contents of the layer.

Point Text

With the Text tool selected, click anywhere in the Composition panel to create point text. Point text is free-form text that's perfect for titles or small chunks of information. After clicking, simply type to add

Lorem ipsum

whatever text you want. When you're done, you can hit escape, click in the timeline, or click on a different tool in the Toolbar.

   Just like any other layer, we can change the position, rotation, and scale of point text with our tools, or from the Timeline panel with PARTS. Text is a vector, so we can scale it infinitely without losing quality.

Paragraph Text

With the Text tool selected, clicking and dragging a box in the Composition panel creates paragraph text. Paragraph text is a rectangular text box. Unlike point text, resizing paragraph text changes the shape the text fits into. This makes it good for, you guessed it, paragraphs. Paragraph text also unlocks paragraph justification, by which words can be spread evenly through the box.

Step one: Draw the box.
Step two: Put your text in the box. It's text in a box!

Lorem ipsum dolor sit amet, consectetur adipiscing elit, sed do eiusmod tempor incididunt ut labore et dolore magna aliqua.

With the Selection tool, you can scale this layer like any other. However, scaling the box with the Text tool resizes the paragraph boundaries, changing the shape of your paragraph. Make sure that you're editing the text by clicking within the paragraph to reveal the bounding-box handles.

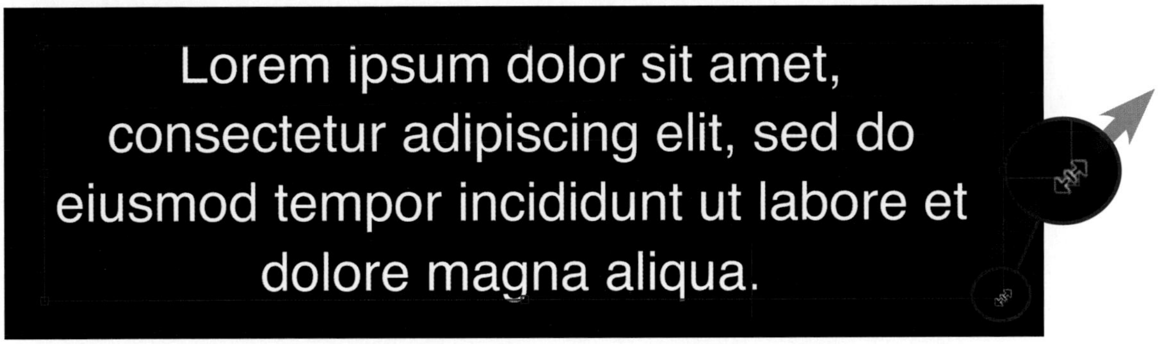

Lorem ipsum dolor sit amet, consectetur adipiscing elit, sed do eiusmod tempor incididunt ut labore et dolore magna aliqua.

You can convert point text to paragraph text, and vice versa. With the Text tool selected, right-click the text layer and select either Convert to Point Text or Convert to Paragraph Text.

The Vertical Type Tool

Clicking and holding on the Type tool icon reveals a secondary option, the Vertical Type tool, which is also accessed by pressing ⌘–T/Ctrl–T a second time. This writes text vertically, which is helpful for some Asian languages, or if you're the motion designer for *The Matrix*.

Lorem ipsum

Text

Shapes, Masks & Mattes

Effects

3D

Special Tools & Features

Expressions

The Character Panel

The Character panel is how we edit our text's appearance. Here's the rule of thumb with editing text: If the whole layer is selected, changing anything in this panel affects the entire layer. With text selected with the Type tool, this panel affects only the selected text.

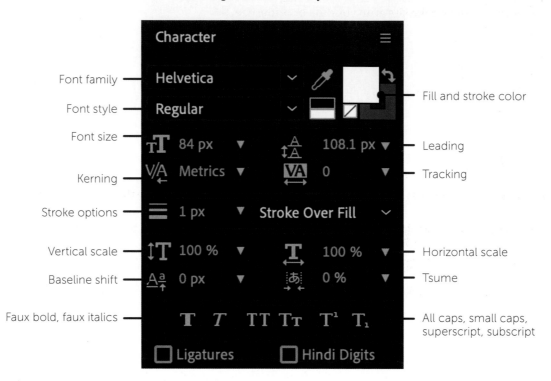

Font

Choose from the fonts installed on your system. Note that a subscription to Adobe Creative Cloud gives you unlimited access to Adobe Fonts. Head to https://fonts.adobe.com and browse thousands of fonts. Plus, these fonts sync with your Adobe account, so if you log into a new machine, your fonts will be automatically installed on your system.

Font Style

Choose from the available styles, typically bold, italic, etc. Note that different fonts have different styles, and basics like bold may not exist.

Fill and Stroke

Fill is the main color of your text. Clicking on the top solid square brings up the Color Picker, allowing

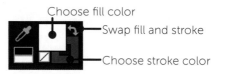

you to choose your text color. You can also use the eyedropper ![icon] to select a color on your screen, or quickly access black or white with the icons underneath the eyedropper ![icon]. Click the white box with a red stripe ![icon] to turn off fill. Clicking on the bottom outlined square allows you to add or change stroke, which is outline around text. You can also click on the arrows ![icon] to quickly swap your stroke and fill colors.

The stroke options section of this panel allows you to change the thickness of your stroke, and decide if the stroke sits atop your fill, or underneath.

Font Size

Choose the size of your font, in pixels. Sometimes it makes sense to change it here rather than scaling a layer.

Leading

Leading is the space between lines of text. This is one I often adjust, since the default feels a little

too spaced out for me. Fun fact: Leading derives its name from the age of the printing press,

where different-sized lead bars were used to create spaces between lines. Oh, and the leading

on this paragraph has been increased.

Kerning

Kerning is the space between two individual letters. You must set your cursor between two letters to adjust the kerning. Bad kerning is a wf ul to read.

Tracking

Tracking is the space between all letters. T h i s   i s   w h a t   i n c r e a s e d   t r a c k i n g   l o o k s   l i k e .

Vertical and Horizontal Scale

Make letters taller or **wider**.

Baseline Shift

By selecting individual letters, you can shift them ^{up} or _{down}.

Text

Shapes, Masks & Mattes

Effects

3D

Special Tools & Features

Expressions

Tsume

Think of Tsume as tracking with vertical text. This is useful only if you're using the Vertical Type tool. When confronted about this near-useless feature, Adobe said, "tsume."

Faux Bold and Faux Italic

If your font doesn't have a bold or italic style, Premiere can emulate what those might look like by using Faux Bold and Faux Italic.

All Caps

PERFECT FOR YOUR NEXT CONSPIRACY VIDEO.

Small Caps

LIKE YELLING, BUT FANCIER.

Superscript and Subscript

Great for math^2 and $C_6He_2mI_{52}S_{16}trY_{39}$.

Ligatures

The difference between fi and fi is within the ligature settings—this changes the way letters connect.

Hindi Digits

You know, for when you're typing digits in Hindi. Hindi Digits, new band name, I'm calling it.

The Paragraph Panel

Choose how text is laid out. Note that most of these features are applied only to paragraph text.

Alignment ——

Left and right indents ——

Add space before/after paragraph

—— Justification

—— Indent first line

—— Text direction

Alignment

Align left, center, or right. This text is left-aligned.

This text is center-aligned.

This text is right-aligned.

If I'm creating point text that I intend to be in the center of my comp, I center-align it—otherwise, if the text changes, I'll have to reposition it.

Justification

Paragraph text only. With justification turned on, words are spaced so that the text fills the entirety of the paragraph box, just like they are here.

In this paragraph, justification has been turned off, so text does not fill the entirety of the space. Note also that we have four options for what to do with the last line of text: align left, center, right, or justify to fill the space.

Indent Left/Right Margins

With the Type tool's cursor in a line, you can indent the left margin, or the right margin if a line is right-aligned or justified.

This is a great way to indent a second paragraph, such as this one.

Add Space Before/After Paragraph

Similar to leading, but increases space between line breaks.

Indent First Line

    This book does not believe in indenting the first line, but you may choose to do so, just as is done in this sentence.

Text Direction

Ostensibly changes the alignment.

Text

Shapes, Masks & Mattes

Effects

3D

Special Tools & Features

Expressions

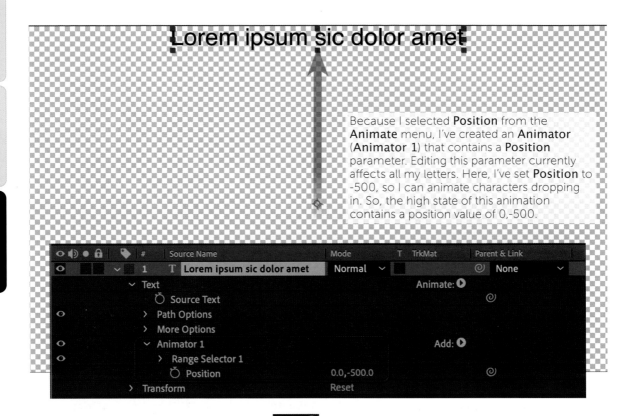

Because I selected **Position** from the **Animate** menu, I've created an **Animator** (**Animator 1**) that contains a **Position** parameter. Editing this parameter currently affects all my letters. Here, I've set **Position** to -500, so I can animate characters dropping in. So, the high state of this animation contains a position value of 0,-500.

By clicking the triangle next to Add Add: ◯, you can have a single Animator manipulate more than one parameter.

Animator 1 now states: "Everything within the **Range Selector** is moved vertically 500 pixels, and made red."

Manipulate the Range Selector

The Range Selector is used to select a range of characters. By default, all characters are within the Range Selector. Characters within the Range Selector are in the high state—that is, the Animator is on, and the defined parameters are applied to the letters. By manipulating the Range Selector, we exclude characters from it, setting them to the low state, in which the Animator is off and our text looks the same as it did before the Animator was added.

To summarize, if text is within the boundaries of the Range Selector, the properties defined in the Animator are applied to it. Text animation usually happens by animating the boundaries of the Range Selector.

The Range Selector is visible in the Composition panel, and you can move the ends around with the Selection tool.

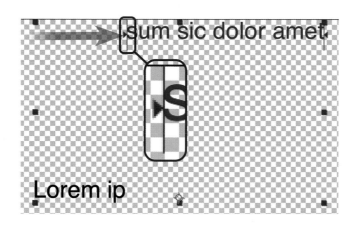

More commonly, the Range Selector will be manipulated in the Timeline panel, where you can also keyframe it.

A common way of animating letters is to animate the Range Selector's Start from 0% to 100%. So, with the Start at 0%, the entirety of the text is selected and in the high state. As Start moves to 100%, characters are excluded from the Range Selector and animated toward the low state. With a Start and End both at 100%, none of the characters are selected and the text is entirely in the low state.

If you want the high state to travel through your letters, you may wish to set the Start and End to include a few letters, then animate the Range Selector's Offset. Doing so basically moves the Start and End together.

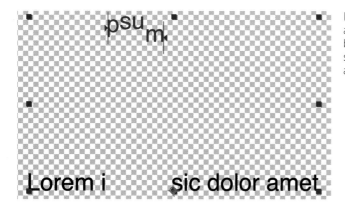

If I want the **Range Selector** to always select four characters, but change which characters are selected, I can move the **Start** and **End** together with **Offset**.

Advanced Range Selector Options

Unfurl the Advanced section of the Range Selector to reveal many more options.

Units

Choose between the Range Selector Start and End operating on units of Percentage or Index.

Text

Shapes, Masks & Mattes

Effects

3D

Special Tools & Features

Expressions

The Interface & Editing

Animation

Text

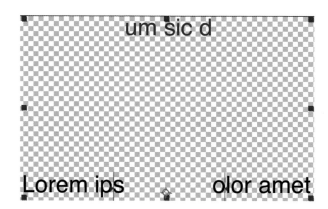

With a **Smoothness** of 0%, characters partially selected by the **Square**-shaped **Range Selector** are firmly in either the high or low state, with no in-between.

Ease High and Ease Low

Use these sliders to determine how characters transition from their high and low states.

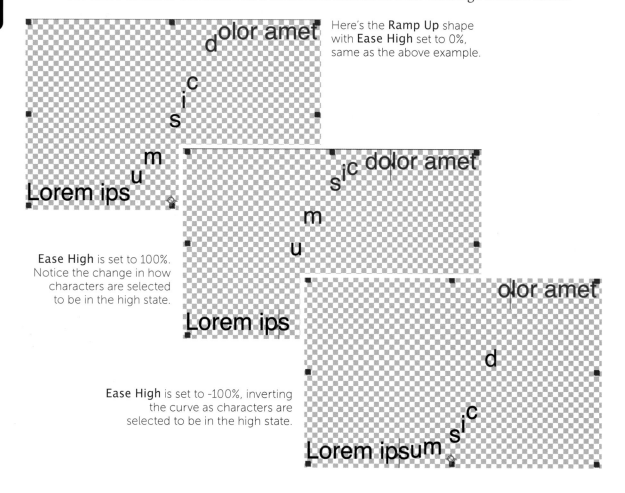

Here's the **Ramp Up** shape with **Ease High** set to 0%, same as the above example.

Ease High is set to 100%. Notice the change in how characters are selected to be in the high state.

Ease High is set to -100%, inverting the curve as characters are selected to be in the high state.

Randomize Order

For the chaotically inclined, switching Randomize Order to On has characters randomly selected to enter the high state, instead of going in order from start to finish. You can then adjust the Random Seed to find a randomness that appeals to your sick, twisted sense of style.

Wiggly Selector

The Range Selector isn't the only way to select characters. We can also use the Wiggly Selector, which randomizes which characters are selected and continually animates.

To apply a Wiggly Selector, select the Add triangle next to the Animator and select Selector > Wiggly.

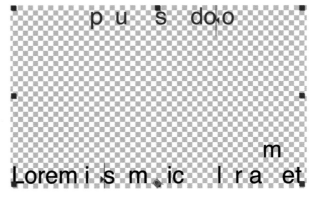

You might want to also delete the current Range Selector, but you can certainly operate with both. By having a Range Selector listed above a Wiggly Selector, the Wiggly Selector will only operate within the confines of the Range Selector.

We're now looking at some intense chaos where characters wiggle back and forth between the high and low state randomly. Let's look at the parameters available to us to control this madness.

Mode

If you're using both a Range Selector and a Wiggly Selector, the Mode here should be set to Intersect, saying "apply this Animator to characters that intersect both selectors."

Max and Min Amount

Note that by default, characters are animating toward -100% of the Animator value. Set the Min Amount to 0% to avoid this.

Text

Shapes, Masks & Mattes

Effects

3D

Special Tools & Features

Expressions

Wiggles/Second

Control the speed of the wiggles. If you wish for a wiggle to occur every two seconds, the value here would be 0.5.

Correlation

This controls the separation of the characters. A Correlation of 100% wiggles all characters together.

Temporal and Spatial Phase

Use these sliders to move through the wiggle. With a wiggle speed of 0, one could use these sliders to manually animate the wiggle.

Lock Dimensions

This is for when you have text moving about both X and Y axes. With Lock Dimensions on, X and Y are synced and your characters will travel diagonally between the two values. With Lock Dimensions off, your characters will oscillate between X and Y randomly.

Expression Selector

The final type of selector allows you to use an expression to select text. Expressions will be covered in chapter 8 of the Compendium.

Text Along a Path

This feature allows you to create text that sits on a curved path.

Create a Path

Creating paths will be detailed in the next chapter. The gist here is I'll use the Pen tool with a text layer selected, and draw some points to create a curved path. (By not closing the shape, a path is created rather than a mask.)

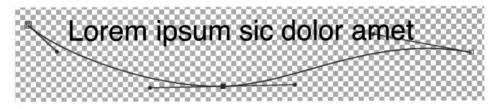

Putting Text on the Path

Open the text layer's triangle and select Text > Path Options > Path. From the drop-down, choose the layer's Path you'd like to use.

Bam! Your text is now aligned to the path. Updating and even animating the path is simple, as the text will stick to it.

Note that point text sits atop the line, and paragraph text sits underneath it.

The Interface
& Editing

Animation

Text

Path Options
We've got some customization available to us.

Reverse Path
Flips the text over the path.

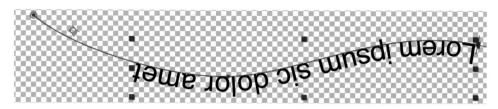

Perpendicular to Path
By default, a text path affects a character's position and rotation. Switch this off so it only affects the position.

Force Alignment
Turning this on adjusts the text's tracking so the letters fill the path.

First and Last Margin
First Margin adjusts where the text sits along the path. You can even move text off the path, and it will follow the trajectory. Animating this parameter allows your text to move through your path, like a roller coaster. Note that Last Margin will only work if Force Alignment is on.

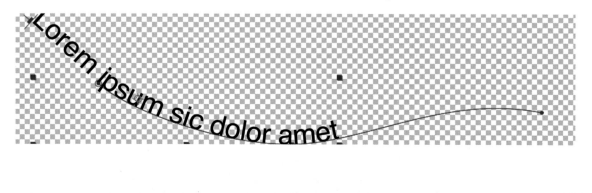

4 Shapes, Masks & Mattes

Shape layers are powerful tools that let you easily build assets, such as graphics and even characters, all within After Effects. This grants you total control over the look and animation of a graphic. And there's a lot these layers can do.

Masks are a means of cropping out parts of an image. Mattes use a layer to define the transparency of another layer.

Furthermore, this section will explore the Modes section of the timeline, with several other ways of setting transparency, plus Blend Modes.

The Interface & Editing

Animation

Text

Shapes, Masks & Mattes

Creating Shape Layers

Shape layers are first defined by a path—that is, the position of the vectors that make up the shape's outline. Then, a fill and/or a stroke is added, followed by a Transform control, plus any other effects.

There are two ways of creating shape layer paths—either by using preset shapes with the Shape tool, or by drawing your own with the Pen tool. We'll start with the former.

Creating Shapes with the Shape Tool

Find the Shape tool in the Toolbar. By default, it looks like a Rectangle, but clicking and holding on the icon reveals presets for Rounded Rectangle, Ellipse, Polygon, and Star. The tool can also be accessed with the hotkey Q. Multiple presses of Q cycles through the different shapes.

With the Shape tool active and no layer selected, click and drag in the Composition panel to create a new shape layer and draw a shape. **Note:** If a non-shape layer is selected, the Shape tool will instead add a mask to the layer. If a shape layer is selected, the Shape tool will add another shape to the same layer.

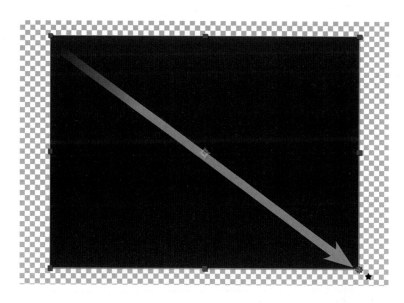

While clicking and dragging to create a shape, you can hold down shift to create a shape that's X and Y proportional, such as a perfect square or circle. Holding down opt/Alt while creating a layer scales the layer from where you clicked, instead of drawing from one corner to the opposite. You can also double-click the Shape tool icon in the Toolbar to drop a shape into your composition that fills the view, or do so while holding shift for a perfect square or circle.

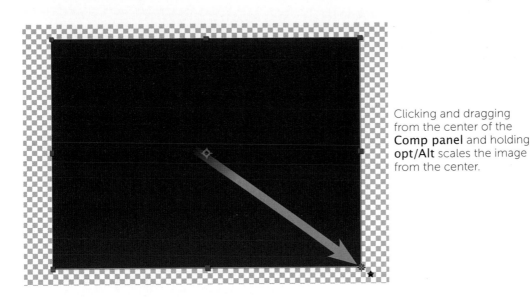

Clicking and dragging from the center of the **Comp panel** and holding **opt/Alt** scales the image from the center.

Once the shape is created, you have several options to change how the path points draw the shape.

Rectangle Path

Upon creating a rectangle or rounded rectangle, navigate to the shape layer's triangle and unfurl Contents > Rectangle 1 > Rectangle Path 1, and you'll see some options that are exclusive to rectangles: Size, Position, and Roundness.

Roundness allows you to control the curve of all four corners at once, which means the difference between a rectangle and rounded rectangle lies solely in this setting.

A rectangle can easily become a rounded rectangle, and vice versa.

Keep in mind: Editing the Size and Position in these categories edits the Size and Position of

Shapes, Masks & Mattes

Effects

3D

Special Tools & Features

Expressions

The Interface
& Editing

Animation

Text

**Shapes, Masks
& Mattes**

the **path points**, *before* fill and stroke are added. The Transform control at the bottom of the shape's contents control transforms *after* the fill and stroke are added. While Transform might distort things such as the stroke width, these path controls will not.

Ellipse Path

If you've drawn an ellipse (fancy name for an oval), your options here are Size and Position. An ellipse with equal X and Y sizes is a circle. Learning shapes is fun!

Polygon Path

A polygon is a shape with a variable number of sides. By default, this tool creates a pentagon, or five-sided shape.

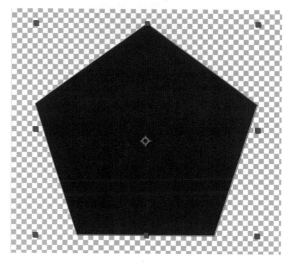

The parameters of a polygon are found under a category called Polystar Path. Under Type, you can switch between a polygon and a star. You can choose the number of points your shape has, thereby changing it from a pentagon to a triangle, octagon, or what have you. You'll find our familiar Position and Rotation controls here as well. Outer Radius is akin to scale, and Outer Roundness is similar to our rectangle roundness, controlling the shape of all vertices.

Star Path

A star is similar to a polygon, but for each outside vertex, it has an inside vertex as well, creating spokes.

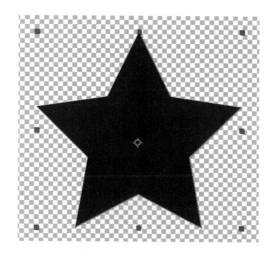

This shape is also edited under Polystar Path. Here, you can convert it to a polygon under Type. Just like with a polygon, we have controls for number of points, Position, Rotation, Outer Radius, and Outer Roundness. We can also control our Inner Radius and Inner Roundness. Playing with these values yields fun results. Roundness values can even go negative, flipping the vertices and creating loopy curves.

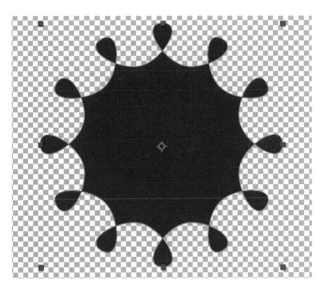

Creating Shapes with the Pen Tool

The above shapes are great, because they offer uniform controls for all vertices simultaneously, allowing great control of symmetrical shapes. In some instances, however, you want more control, with customizable shapes. For this, we will create shapes with the Pen tool that are customizable Bezier paths.

Note that by doing this, we lose our nice controls, such as Roundness, Number of Points, Inner and Outer Radius, etc. Basically, Bezier paths are manual mode, and if we want to recreate those nice shapes, we have to do it ourselves.

First, select the Pen tool 🖋 from the Toolbar, or activate it with the hotkey G. To create a brand-new shape layer, ensure that no other layer is selected. **Note again:** If a non-shape layer is selected, the Pen tool will instead add a mask to the layer. If a shape layer is selected, the Pen tool will add another shape to the same layer.

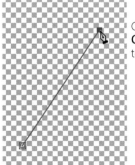

Click within the **Composition panel** to add vertices.

Clicking to create a point and then dragging creates a Bezier curve, allowing for a curved line. Holding down **shift** while doing so creates perpendicular curve handles.

Shapes, Masks & Mattes

Effects

3D

Special Tools & Features

Expressions

The Interface
& Editing

Animation

Text

**Shapes, Masks
& Mattes**

Unless you're creating a shape layer that's just a stroke (that is, a line graphic), you would typically finish your shape and close it by clicking on the point that you first drew, which has an extra square around it ⊡. The Pen tool displays a small circle 🖋₀ when hovering over this point.

Editing Bezier Paths

Assume the Pen tool is selected for the following section. Depending on what is selected, some of the following features can be edited with the Selection tool, but that selection is less important if the Pen tool is selected.

Clicking and dragging a vertex moves it. If the vertex is a Bezier curve, you can manipulate its Bezier handles to change the shape of the curve by adjusting the angle around the point and the distance from the point.

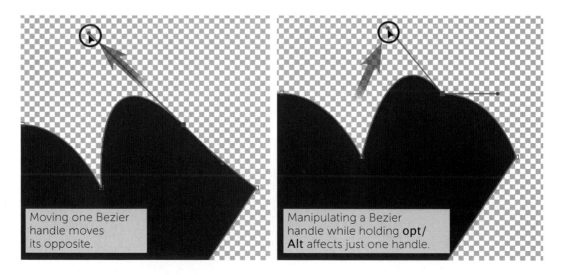

Moving one Bezier handle moves its opposite.

Manipulating a Bezier handle while holding **opt/ Alt** affects just one handle.

Clicking on a vertex while holding opt/Alt switches it from a hard edge to a Bezier curve, and vice versa. Or, achieve the same effect by clicking and holding on the Pen tool icon in the Toolbar and selecting the Convert Vertex tool, then selecting a vertex.

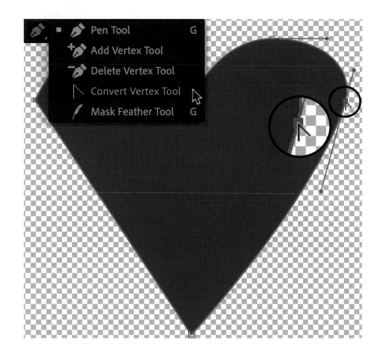

Add a new point along a path by simply clicking on the path.

Shapes, Masks & Mattes

Effects

3D

Special Tools & Features

Expressions

Change a Solid Fill's Color

With Solid Fill selected (as it is by default), click on the colored box next to Fill in the Toolbar.

Doing so brings up the Color Picker, After Effects' tool to choose any color.

The Color Picker

The default (and most intuitive) view of the Color Picker is HSB, which stands for hue, saturation, and brightness. Hue is also selected by default. This means that hue (or color) is adjusted via the color slider in the middle of the interface. The other two attributes, saturation and brightness, are selected in the color field. Dragging the color selector about the X-axis of the color field changes a color's saturation, or intensity. The Y-axis changes the color's brightness.

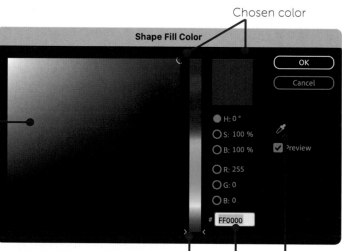

Chosen color

Color field: Adjusts the attributes that correspond to the selected color. Since hue (**H**) is selected, the field shows saturation (left-to-right) and brightness (top-to-bottom). If red (**R**) were selected, the field would be for choosing green and blue.

Color slider: Adjusts the value of the selected attribute; here, that would be **H**, for hue.

Hex code   Eyedropper

Hexadecimal

As you play around with colors, you'll notice a six-digit code made up of letters and numbers in the box at the bottom of the Color Picker dialog. This is the color's hexadecimal value, also known as a hex code. It's far more concise to write "496999" than it is to write "H:215, S:52, B:60," plus it dismisses the issue of varying color spaces. Often, companies specify colors they want used, and you can then find those colors written in hex code in a style guide. Simply type in the code to get the desired color.

Finally, select the eyedropper, then click a pixel within the Composition panel to use that exact color. When you're all done, select OK.

Editing Gradients

Both the Linear and Radial Gradients work similarly in that they transition a fill from one color (and/or opacity value) to another.

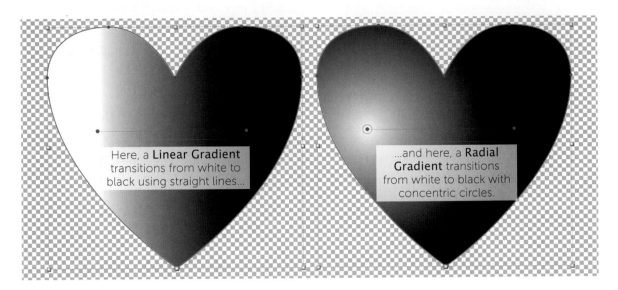

Here, a **Linear Gradient** transitions from white to black using straight lines...

...and here, a **Radial Gradient** transitions from white to black with concentric circles.

After choosing either gradient option, you can edit them in a similar fashion to a Solid Fill—first by selecting the gradiated box next to the word Fill. The difference in the next interface is the Gradient Editor.

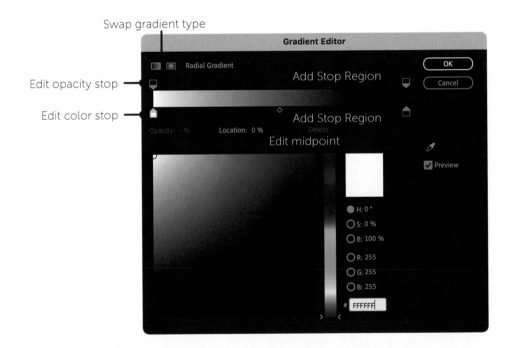

Swap gradient type

Edit opacity stop

Edit color stop

Gradients are composed of at least two stops. By setting colors for each stop, After Effects automatically transitions from one to the next—kind of like a keyframe, except not at all!

Gradients also have two sections—a top one to edit opacity, and a bottom one for color. Let's start with color. To edit a color stop, first select the color stop box. Then, choose a color using the Color Picker.

Shapes, Masks & Mattes

Effects

3D

Special Tools & Features

Expressions

The Interface & Editing

Animation

Text

Shapes, Masks & Mattes

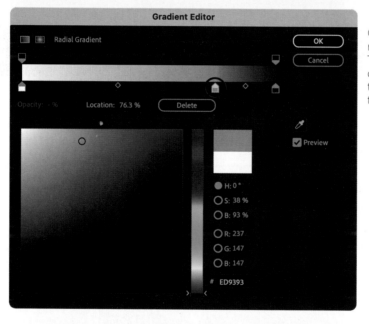

With the rightmost color stop selected, I can edit its color.

Gradients can also hold more than two colors. To add a new color stop, click anywhere between the existing color stops in the Add Stop Region.

Gradients don't need to go evenly from one color to the next. Between each is a midpoint controller, so you can favor one color versus another—kind of like **keyframe velocity**, but absolutely different.

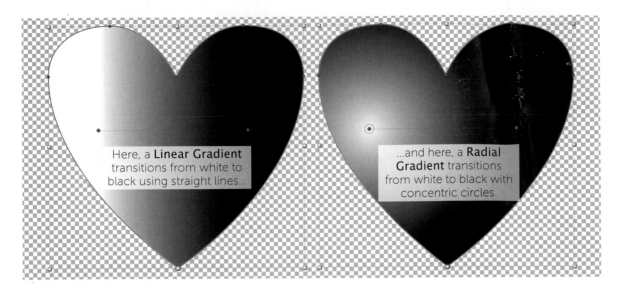

Here, a **Linear Gradient** transitions from white to black using straight lines...

...and here, a **Radial Gradient** transitions from white to black with concentric circles.

After choosing either gradient option, you can edit them in a similar fashion to a Solid Fill—first by selecting the gradiated box next to the word Fill. The difference in the next interface is the Gradient Editor.

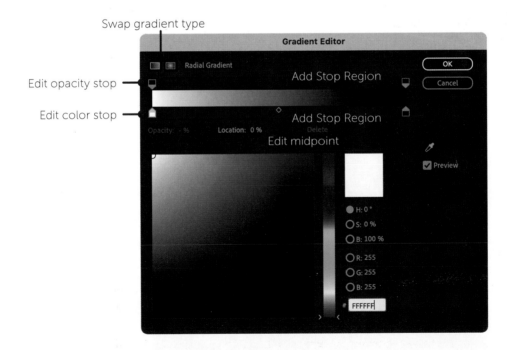

Swap gradient type

Edit opacity stop

Edit color stop

Add Stop Region

Edit midpoint

Gradients are composed of at least two stops. By setting colors for each stop, After Effects automatically transitions from one to the next—kind of like a keyframe, except not at all!

Gradients also have two sections—a top one to edit opacity, and a bottom one for color. Let's start with color. To edit a color stop, first select the color stop box. Then, choose a color using the Color Picker.

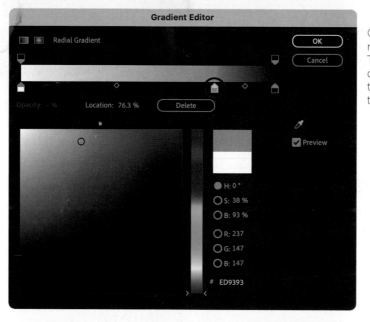

With the rightmost color stop selected, I can edit its color.

Gradients can also hold more than two colors. To add a new color stop, click anywhere between the existing color stops in the Add Stop Region.

Gradients don't need to go evenly from one color to the next. Between each is a midpoint controller, so you can favor one color versus another—kind of like **keyframe velocity**, but absolutely different.

The Interface & Editing

Animation

Text

Shapes, Masks & Mattes

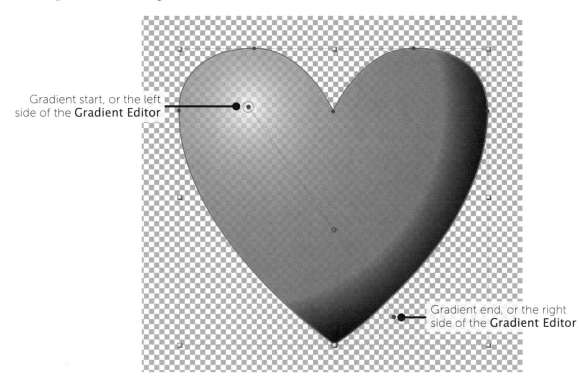

Opacity stops work similarly, except their values are edited by the **Opacity** slider in the interface. Transparency is represented by the checkered background of the **Gradient Editor**.

When you're ready to go, click OK.

In the Composition panel, you'll be able to see the controls for the gradient's placement on your shape as long as the Selection tool is selected. You can also move those points around to edit the placement of the gradient.

Gradient start, or the left side of the **Gradient Editor**

Gradient end, or the right side of the **Gradient Editor**

Shapes, Masks & Mattes

Effects

3D

Special Tools & Features

Expressions

254 **Editing Shape Layers** Edit a Shape's Fill

The Interface
& Editing

Animation

Text

Shapes, Masks
& Mattes

Fill Options in the Timeline

Heading to a shape layer's triangle and choosing Contents > Shape Name > Gradient Fill/Fill in the timeline reveals more options.

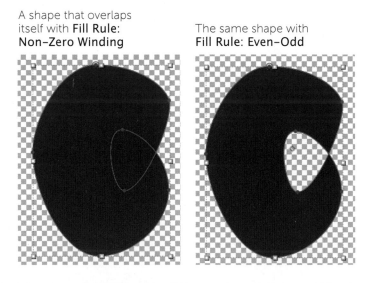

The word Normal next to your fill allows you to click on a drop-down menu to change the Blend Mode of the fill. See "Blend Modes" (page 277).

Composite gives you two options: Below or Above Previous in Same Group. Switching this to Above places the fill atop the stroke.

Fill Rule gives two options for shapes that self-intersect: Non–Zero Winding and Even–Odd.

A shape that overlaps itself with **Fill Rule: Non–Zero Winding**

The same shape with **Fill Rule: Even–Odd**

Finally, you'll find the controls for editing a fill living down here as well (such as gradient position and opacity), plus keyframe options.

Editing a Shape's Stroke

Editing a stroke, or outline around a path, functions identically to the options above, in which you can set a stroke to None, Solid, or even the two gradient options. Additionally, you can adjust the width of a stroke in the Toolbar.

Stroke options
Stroke color/gradient
Stroke width

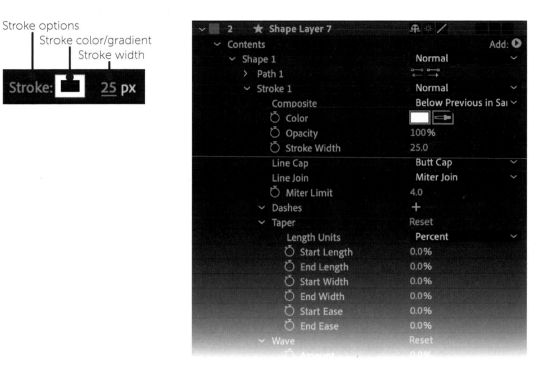

However, editing stroke options in the timeline unlocks some really cool features. Find them by unfurling a shape layer's triangle and then choosing Contents > Shape Name > Stroke.

Some of these features have already been touched upon. Let's look at some new ones.

Line Cap

Choose from Butt Cap, Round Cap, or Projecting Cap.

Butt Cap, in which the end of the stroke is flat and the author refrains from making a joke about Captain America's butt.

Round Cap, in which the end of the stroke is round.

Projecting Cap, in which the end of the stroke is flat but extends just beyond the end of the stroke.

Shapes, Masks & Mattes

Effects

3D

Special Tools & Features

Expressions

Wiggle Transform

This is very similar to the previous effect, only instead of randomly animating path points, this randomness is applied to whatever parameter you set in the Transform setting of this effect. This allows you to add random motion to the Anchor Point, Position, Scale, or Rotation.

Zig Zag

Not quite Wave, not quite Wiggle Paths, Zig Zag has its own look. Control the height of the zigs with Size, the width of the zags with Ridges per Segment, and choose between spiky zigs with Points set to Corner, or smooth zags with Points set to Smooth.

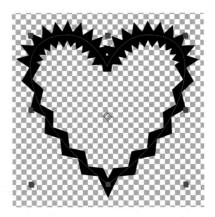

Masks

Masks are a simple means of cropping an asset. Unlike mattes, masks obey an asset's Transform controls, so they move where the asset goes.

Creating a Mask

With a video or image selected, you can either use the Shape tool to draw a mask in a preset shape, or use the Pen tool to draw your own mask, using same rules as outlined in "Creating Shapes with the Pen Tool" (page 245). Masks paths are always Bezier curves, even if you use the Shape tool.

Want to mask a shape layer? On a shape layer, the Shape and Pen tools normally add another shape. You can have them draw a mask instead by selecting this icon in the Toolbar ▨ before you draw.

You can toggle the visibility of masks in the Composition panel by selecting this icon from the bottom of the panel: ▣.

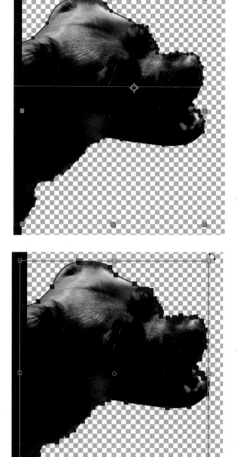

Editing a Mask

Masks follow the same rules as covered in "Editing Bezier Paths" (page 246). Here's the sometimes-confusing rule of thumb about editing mask points: With the layer selected in the timeline, you can use the Selection tool to move individual mask points. With the mask selected in the timeline, the Selection tool allows you to move the entire mask at once. In addition to editing individual mask points, you can also double-click on a mask point to show a bounding box around your points, allowing you to move, scale, and rotate your entire mask at once. Or, select multiple points and double-click on them to show the bounding box on just those points.

With a masked layer selected in the timeline, tapping M brings up basic mask controls. Tapping M twice, like a double-click, brings up all mask controls.

By default, a mask shows the interior of its path. Selecting Inverted hides the interior and shows the exterior.

1	📄 **This Majestic Creature**	⚘	╱			
⌄	Mask 1			Add	⌄	Inverted
	⏱ Mask Path			Shape…		
	⏱ Mask Feather			∞ 0.0,0.0 pixels		
	⏱ Mask Opacity			100%		
	⏱ Mask Expansion			0.0 pixels		

Shapes, Masks & Mattes

Effects

3D

Special Tools & Features

Expressions

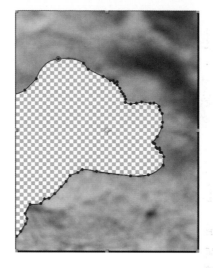

Mask Modes

The drop-down that defaults to Add works best if you have multiple masks on a layer. If your top mask is set to Add, a mask underneath it set to Subtract will use the second mask to remove contents within the top layer.

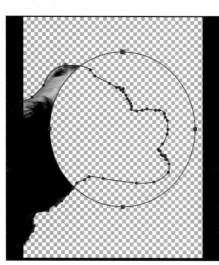

After Effects processes masks from the top down. So, make sure your top mask is the one that's adding pixels. A mask on the bottom can't reintroduce pixels that have already been removed from a mask above it.

> ☐ 1	📄 **This Majestic Creature**	⚓ /
∨ Masks		
> ☐ Mask 1		Add ∨
> ☐ Mask 2		Subtract ∨

Intersect shows only where multiple masks overlap. Difference hides where multiple masks overlap.

Intersect

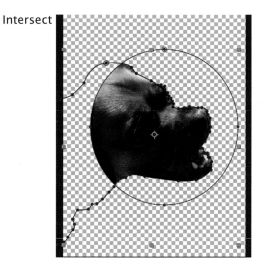

Difference

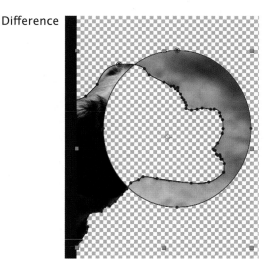

Less commonly used are Lighten and Darken. If you have several masks with different Mask Opacity settings, Lighten will show only the highest transparency value, and Darken, the lowest.

Finally, the mask mode drop-down contains an option for None, to disable the mask.

Mask Options

Mask Feather softens the edge of the mask, blending it with the background. It's usually a good idea to have some feathering. Mask Feather operates on the entire mask at once, but you can deselect Constrain Proportions 🔗 to feather X and Y separately. To customize feathering to a specific part of the mask, see the Mask Feather tool below.

Mask Opacity can be used to lower the transparency of the area inside a mask.

Mask Expansion expands or shrinks the boundaries of a mask.

The Mask Feather Tool

To increase the feathering on specific parts of your mask and not just apply the same value all around, we'll need to use the Mask Feather tool. Find it by clicking and holding on the Pen tool in the Toolbar, or pressing G a second time after the Pen tool is selected.

With the Mask Feather tool selected, make sure the mask you want to add feathering to is also selected in the timeline. Click anywhere on the mask path, then drag inward to create a new mask feathering path.

Shapes, Masks & Mattes

Effects

3D

Special Tools & Features

Expressions

The Interface
& Editing

Animation

Text

**Shapes, Masks
& Mattes**

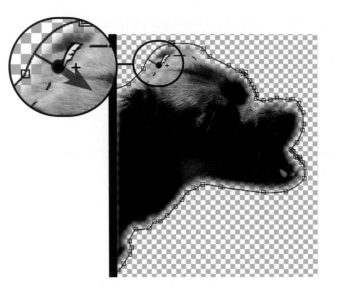

The mask is now feathered between the mask path and the mask feather path. The greater the distance between the two, the more feathering you'll get. Using the Mask Feather tool, you can add more points along the mask feather path and drag them inward or outward to create a custom shape for your feathering amount. You will need at least three points to create feathering within a specific area.

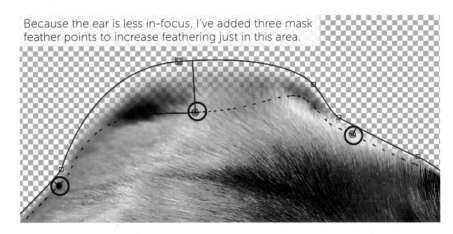

Because the ear is less in-focus, I've added three mask feather points to increase feathering just in this area.

Animating a Mask

If your mask is on a video, you'll likely need to keyframe the mask so it follows the subject. This process is known as rotoscoping, and it can be very time-consuming. Luckily, the folks at Adobe have blessed us with the Roto Brush tool, which does its best to automatically animate what's masked. The Roto Brush tool is covered in chapter 7 of the Compendium.

In some cases you might still need to manually keyframe mask points. To do so, first refill your coffee mug, then click the stopwatch next to Mask Path. You might be here for a while.

Mask Path keyframes are special in that a single keyframe can hold data for potentially hundreds of points. As such, these keyframes won't appear in the Graph Editor's Value Graph, only the Speed Graph. To manage interpolation and velocity for mask keyframes, use the Mask Interpolation panel, as outlined in chapter 1 of the Compendium.

Even without the Roto Brush tool, After Effects can still attempt to automatically track a mask to a subject (track meaning to follow). Once a mask is set around an object on a video layer, right-click the mask in the timeline and select Track Mask. Doing so brings up the Tracker panel.

Analyze Backward   Analyze Forward

Analyze One Frame Backward   **Analyze One** Frame Forward

Assuming you're at the beginning of where you'd like to track from, hit Analyze Forward and hope for the best. This works best on objects with high contrast.

After the tracker processes, you'll be left with Mask Path keyframes on every frame. If the mask gets off track, you can attempt to reposition it and hit Analyze again.

Mask Tracking Methods

The Method drop-down offers some customization on how the tracker works. The default is Position, Scale & Rotation, in which your mask points will mimic Transform controls. Find options for Position or Position & Rotation if you want to limit the mask transforms. Position, Scale, Rotation & Skew allows the shape of the mask to be distorted to follow a subject more accurately. Perspective is best for tracking a mask around a flat surface, such as a billboard.

Human faces only.

There are two options for Face Tracking, both of which are optimized to recognize faces. Face Tracking (Outline Only) will redraw your mask so it outlines a subject's face, and follows where it moves. This might be helpful if you're masking a color correction effect to just a subject's face.

Face Tracking (Detailed Analysis) tracks a subject's eyes, nose, mouth, cheeks, and chin. It then places keyframes for each in the timeline.

Shapes, Masks & Mattes

Effects

3D

Special Tools & Features

Expressions

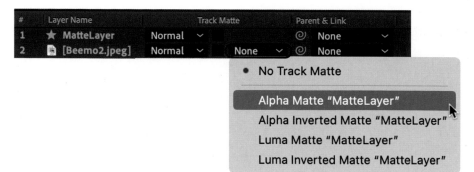

Observe: We can now see Beemo only within the confines of the layer above. Furthermore, the layer above also had varying transparency; with alpha at 100%, Beemo is fully opaque, and this value fades toward the edges of the star.

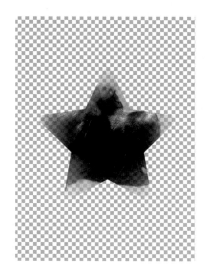

Also observe: The timeline now displays information telling you that Beemo has a matte ▣ and that MatteLayer is the matte ▣. The matte layer also has its visibility unchecked, assuming that you don't need to see the matte itself. You could even take this a step further and set your matte to be a shy layer, if you truly don't need to work with it much.

Indicates the layer is a matte.

⊙ ◀) ● 🔒	🏷	#	Layer Name		Mode		T	TrkMat
> ▣		1	★ ◉	MatteLayer	Normal	⌄		
⊙ > ▣		2	📄 ▣	[Beemo2.jpeg]	Normal	⌄		Alpha ⌄

Indicates the layer is matted.

Since these are two separate layers, we can transform one without transforming the other, either moving Beemo around within the confines of the star, or moving the star around to reveal other parts of her glorious mug.

Note that there are three other options for mattes under the TrkMat drop-down. Alpha Inverted Matte reverses the alpha of the matte, so full opacity hides the bottom layer, full transparency reveals it.

Less common are Luma Matte and Luma Inverted Matte, which translate a matte layer's brightness to opacity.

Squiggle, Ben Goldsmith, digital, 2021

Used as a **Luma Matte**, in which black = transparency and white = opacity.

Used as a **Luma Inverted Matte**, in which black = opacity and white = transparency.

The Set Matte Effect

Sometimes, the above process is cumbersome—especially when it comes to using one layer as a matte for several, or if the layer order limitation is restrictive. Keep in mind there's an effect called Set Matte that can do everything described above, but can choose from any layer. Find it in Effects > Channel > Set Matte.

Shapes, Masks & Mattes

Effects

3D

Special Tools & Features

Expressions

The Interface
& Editing

Animation

Text

**Shapes, Masks
& Mattes**

In the following groups of examples, I'll show a consistent pair of layers, one slightly offset from the other, so the Blend Modes can be compared. The top layer, a photo of a plush fruit named Peachy, is the one to which I've applied the Blend Modes. In some cases, I'll show additional, practical examples as well. In each grouping, I'll start with the most useful or definitive Blend Mode, then show the others that appear in the same section of the Blend Mode menu. As the table above shows, some modes can be put in multiple categories, but I'll show them with others nearby in the menu.

If you wish to have a deep understanding of what Blend Modes actually do, you'll have to know a little bit about how After Effects does math with color numbers when you apply a Blend Mode. For example, when we use the Multiply Blend Mode, just what numbers are being multiplied?

When blending colors, think of black as 0 and white as 1. When we use a Blend Mode called Subtract or Multiply, it'll be numbers between 0 and 1 that are subtracted or multiplied. As fascinating as that is, the arithmetic doesn't necessarily bring an image to mind. So I rely more on visual metaphors to explain the Blend Modes whenever possible. For a few modes, I'll also let you know what math is happening.

Normal Modes

Normal
Every layer's default Blend Mode: Normal means no blending at all.

Dissolve
Dissolve doesn't do much, unless the layer's opacity is lowered. Then, you'll see random noise on the layer's opacity.

Dancing Dissolve
Nearly identical to Dissolve, but the randomness changes frame-to-frame. (Ben adds: If random movements thirty times a second qualifies as dancing, sign me up for the next Adobe rager.)

Darkening Modes
All of these make white disappear; that is, white is the so-called "neutral color" for these modes. Multiply is the most definitive mode of this group.

Multiply

Multiply is the most useful of the modes in its section.

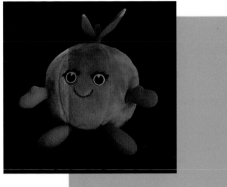

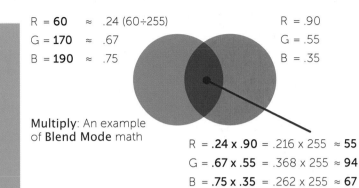

$R = 60 \approx .24 \ (60 \div 255)$
$G = 170 \approx .67$
$B = 190 \approx .75$

$R = .90$
$G = .55$
$B = .35$

Multiply: An example of **Blend Mode** math

$R = .24 \times .90 = .216 \times 255 \approx 55$
$G = .67 \times .55 = .368 \times 255 \approx 94$
$B = .75 \times .35 = .262 \times 255 \approx 67$

Recall that when blending, each pixel's colors use numbers in the range of 0–1. When we choose the Multiply mode, those are the numbers that literally get multiplied. Since each pixel value for white would be exactly 1, white has no impact on the colors below, and essentially disappears. A fine metaphor for this effect is slide (transparency) film. Hopefully some readers will remember this twentieth-century technology. Picture two slides on a light table that's shining light through them.

Now imagine overlapping the slides. Wherever the top image is white, the slide is clear, and we see the image under it. Where it's black, it's completely opaque, obscuring the image below.

Overlapping slides simulate the **Multiply Blend Mode** very well.

Color Dodge

Color Dodge is the opposite of Color Burn: It gives a light result and hides black, as the others in this section do, and it can intensify the color of the layer to which its applied more than the one below it (as Color Burn does).

Linear Dodge (Add)

Mathematically, this is one of the simplest Blend Modes. Linear Dodge literally adds the normalized RGB values of each pixel. If the result exceeds 1, it's simply set to 1 (white).

Lighter Color

Lighter Color not only makes black invisible and gives a light result like the others in this section, but it is more comparative than the others. Imagine that both the layer being blended and the one with which it is blended are completely desaturated (black and white). Each pixel's brightness is then compared and the lighter of the two is shown. Of course, neither layer is visibly desaturated, but After Effects uses that adjustment invisibly to determine the luminance values to compare.

Contrast Modes

Hard Light

Hard Light and Overlay tie for the title of "most definitive" in this section of Blend Modes.

In fact, Hard Light and Overlay are closely related: You can achieve the same visual result as Hard Light by inverting the layer order and using Overlay on the layer that's now on top. Think of Hard Light as a combination of Screen (when lighter than middle gray) and Multiply (when darker). Middle gray vanishes. In the window image above, a black-to-white gradient layer above the window is set to Hard Light. The center of the gradient disappears.

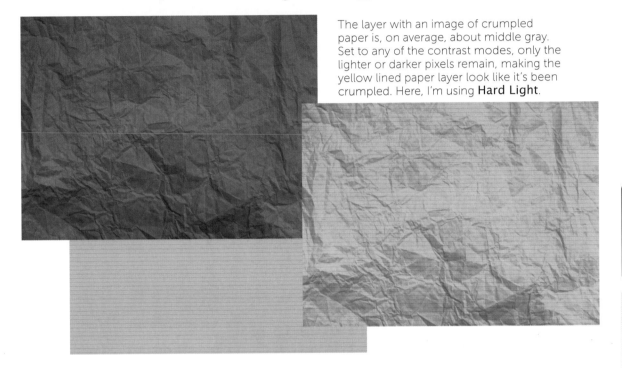

The layer with an image of crumpled paper is, on average, about middle gray. Set to any of the contrast modes, only the lighter or darker pixels remain, making the yellow lined paper layer look like it's been crumpled. Here, I'm using **Hard Light**.

Overlay

You can think of Overlay as a visually less intense version of Hard Light.

You can see above that neither black nor white are truly opaque; they merely darken or lighten the pixels under them. In the crumpled paper example, the paper looks less violently crumpled. The wall surrounding the window is less obscured than with Hard Light.

Shapes, Masks & Mattes

Effects

3D

Special Tools & Features

Expressions

Difference

The word "difference" means the result of a subtraction. And indeed, Difference mode is very similar to Subtract. The only difference (I couldn't help it!) between the two is that this mode always subtracts the darker pixel values from the lighter ones. So when the pixels to which Difference is applied are lighter than the ones underneath, the underlying pixels get inverted.

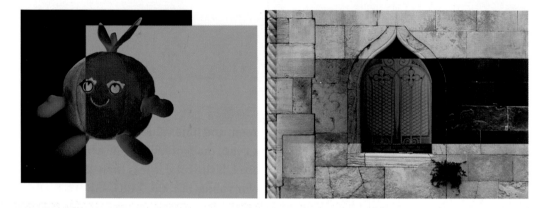

The most common use for the Difference mode is getting two similar layers aligned or registered to each other.

Consider two identical layers, one atop the other. That is, the difference between them is exactly 0. Thus, if the top one is set to Difference mode, everything turns black.

Here, a close-up of the window image we've been using. The window layer has been duplicated then offset 1 pixel up and 1 pixel to the left.

This image would be boringly black if the layers were lined up again.

Exclusion

Think of Exclusion as a weaker form of Difference. It uses the same rules, but produces a lower-contrast result. When two identical images are aligned to one another, the result will not be completely black.

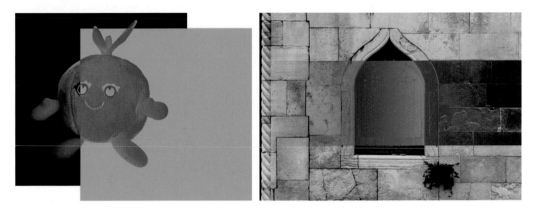

Divide

More math! Divide produces a lightening result by dividing the color numbers. The values of the pixels below are divided by the values of the pixels to which the mode is applied. If you divide by white (1), the underlying layer remains unchanged. Dividing by black, which is dividing by 0, creates a singularity that destroys civilization. Or it produces white. I'll let you find out!

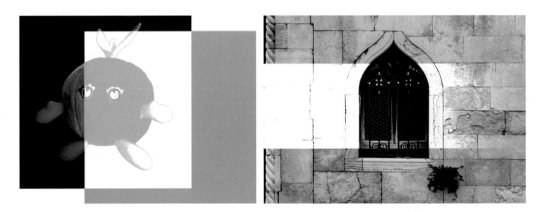

Component Modes

This group can be both very practical and wonderfully creative. To understand these modes, consider separating an image into two parts: its color and its luminosity, or brightness. A simple black-and-white image is one in which the color is removed, leaving only its luminosity behind. The color is, well, everything else. And that, too, can be thought of as having two components: hue (which part of the color wheel) and saturation (how intense the hue).

I find it easier to explain them in nearly the opposite order than they appear in the menu.

Shapes, Masks & Mattes

Effects

3D

Special Tools & Features

Expressions

We'll use the following images to explore these four modes:

A mostly colorful image atop our familiar
window image that features mostly browns.

Note that the image that will be our top layer, the one to which we'll apply these Blend Modes, is very colorful except for the grayscale across the top. Where there is color, it's quite saturated (except for the clouds and little else).

Luminosity

Luminosity mode essentially removes the color component, leaving only the luminosity (the tonal part) of the image. Any color we see comes from the layer(s) underneath—in this case, the blue-green below Peachy or the beige-and-brown window image below the tree layer. Where the underlying layer is either white or black or otherwise desaturated, the result is desaturated.

Color

This mode is the exact opposite of Luminosity. Color retains only the color from the layer to which it's applied, and any tonal detail you see comes from below. The grayscale at the top of the tree image has no color, and thus gives a grayscale look to the underlying image (the window). The rich, saturated colors elsewhere get applied to that underlying image.

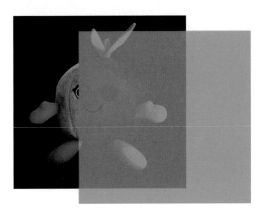

Hue

At first glance, Hue is very similar to Color. The grayscale makes the underlying image colorless, and tonal details come from the layer below. But note that the colors are not that saturated in the tree/window image, but are in the Peachy image. The level of saturation, like the tonal detail, comes from the layer below. Where the browns of the window image are saturated, so is the result. Since the layer below Peachy is very saturated, so is that result.

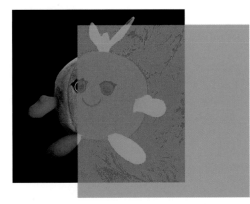

Shapes, Masks & Mattes

Effects

3D

Special Tools & Features

Expressions

Saturation

I think you're on to me at this point. When we set the top layer to Saturation, the hue and luminosity come from below. However intense (saturated) the bottom layer is, and however light and dark, so is the result.

Stencil Modes

Wait, Steve, don't go! We still have more Blend Modes that are unique to After Effects! Ah, he left, so you're stuck with Ben again.

Stencil modes are very similar to mattes, but they can affect multiple layers below them.

Stencil Alpha

When we apply Stencil Alpha to Peachy, we can see layers below only if there's opacity to Peachy. So it basically uses a layer as a cookie cutter for layers below. This is similar to Preserve Underlying Transparency, except the top layer provides the shape and the bottom layers provide the color.

The Interface & Editing

Animation

Text

Shapes, Masks & Mattes

Stencil Luma

Perhaps you're noticing the correlation to mattes by now. Stencil Luma is another cookie cutter to layers below, but the top image's brightness is what dictates opacity.

Stencil Alpha

Stencil Luma

Sillhoutte Alpha and Silhoutte Luma are simply inverse versions of their above counterparts.

Utility Modes

These are two features that exist to solve specific problems.

Alpha Add

Sometimes, effects like masks give you slightly transparent seams when edges ought to be totally opaque. In this instance, switching to Alpha Add should cover up those seams.

Luminescent Premultiply

This solves an error when the edge of an asset with partial transparency looks too bright.

Shapes, Masks & Mattes

Effects

3D

Special Tools & Features

Expressions

Additional Helpful Stuff

There are a few preferences and plug-ins that will make the above section easier for you.

Preferences

Preferences in the Mac edition are found in After Effects > Preferences. On a PC, that's Edit > Preferences. Some of these options might tailor After Effects to your needs.

Under the General category, find Preserve Constant Vertex and Feather Point Count when Editing Masks. This is on by default. Generally, if you have keyframes on a mask path, then add mask points to the path, those keyframes will appear throughout the animation. By deselecting this option, you can have the number of points on your mask path change during your animation. This may lead to some unexpected mask movement, so use it cautiously.

Pressing G multiple times switches between the Pen tool and the Mask Feather tool. By deselecting the preference for Pen Tool Shortcut Toggles Between Pen and Mask Feather Tools, pressing G will cycle through the Pen tool, the Add Vertex tool, the Delete Vertex tool, the Convert Vertex tool, and the Mask Feather tool. This is helpful if you don't want to memorize the various hotkey variations for the Pen tool.

Center Anchor Point in New Shape Layers—turn this on! By default, the Anchor Point of new shape layers is in the center of the comp, not the shape, which is annoying.

Plug-Ins

There are some fantastic companies out there who make additional tools for After Effects that can speed things along. Here are some that are relevant to this chapter:

Overlord by Battle Axe is a bridge between Illustrator and After Effects. With a layer selected in Illustrator, a single click sends that shape to After Effects and automatically converts it to a shape layer. This is an indispensable tool if Illustrator is a big part of your workflow. Find it here: https://www.battleaxe.co/overlord.

Explode Shape Layers by Zack Lovatt is a very handy tool to separate a single shape layer with multiple shapes out into individual layers, or merge multiple shape layers into one. It works fantastically with *Overlord*, since you might need different organization mechanisms in Illustrator than you do in After Effects. Find that here: https://aescripts.com/explode-shape-layers/.

5 Effects

It's in the name—effects in After Effects can do a lot. Whether it's something simple, like a glow, or advanced, like a particle simulation, the effects bundled with AE are a fun rabbit hole of tools to enhance your video.

Working with Effects

Applying an effect is simple. With a layer selected, choose an effect from the Effects menu or from the Effects & Presets panel.

The Effect Controls Panel

After an effect is applied, the parameters for the effect are listed in the Effect Controls panel, which is generally nested with the Project panel. This is the quickest way to modify an effect.

Some effects, such as CC Power Pin, can utilize controls within the Composition panel. To show those controls, the effect itself must be selected within the Effect Controls panel.

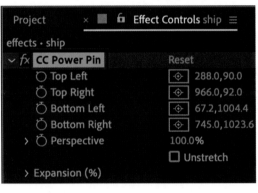

The helpful on-screen controls in the **Comp panel** are available only when the effect is selected in **Effect Controls panel**.

Effects are processed from the top down in the Effect Controls panel. This can be important—if a Ripple effect is placed *before* a Mosaic effect, the ripple will look pixelated. But a Ripple *after* a Mosaic effect will pixelate, then ripple the pixels. You can click and drag to reorder your effects.

Some effects won't accurately process the effects above them. For example, CC Force Motion Blur will ignore a Shatter effect that's directly above it. In some cases, you must precompose a layer with an effect on it (moving the effect into the precomp), then add the effect to the top layer.

On that note, precomping layers is a great way to add a single effect to multiple layers.

Clicking the fx badge *fx* in the Effect Controls panel turns an effect off without deleting it. The same button in the timeline switches off all effects for that layer. You can delete an effect by selecting it and pressing delete/backspace. You can delete all effects on a layer by selecting Remove All from the Effect menu.

Keyframing Effects

Nearly all effects have keyframable attributes. The Effect Controls panel has stopwatches to activate keyframes, which work identically to the stopwatches in the timeline. However, the

Effect Controls panel does not contain a timeline, so it's difficult to see where your keyframes live. It's always best to work with keyframes in the timeline.

    If you've activated keyframes on a layer, selecting the layer in the timeline and tapping U reveals all keyframed attributes. Selecting a layer in the timeline and pressing E reveals all effects applied to it. The effects portion of the timeline is identical to the Effect Controls panel, so you can work in either space— the panel is a little quicker to access, the timeline is better for keyframing.

Adjustment Layers

If you want to apply an effect to most of the layers in your scene (say, Lumetri to add some color grading to everything), you can apply the effect to an Adjustment Layer. Adjustment Layers are invisible, but their effects are applied to all layers below them.

    Create a new Adjustment Layer with Layer > New > Adjustment Layer. Then, apply the effects to the Adjustment Layer, and place it above the layers you'd like to affect.

    Lowering the opacity of an Adjustment Layer can be a great way to lower the visibility of the effect, especially if an effect doesn't have a global intensity slider (such as Lumetri). Also, Adjustment Layers can be masked and trimmed, which can allow you to apply an effect to only part of a composition.

    Convert any layer to an Adjustment Layer by toggling the Adjustment Layer icon ⬤ in the timeline switches. Note that this will make the layer invisible.

Masking Effects

Let's say you want to blur out someone's face. Normally, effects are applied to the entirety of a layer, but it's possible to add a mask to an effect so it applies only to a certain region.

    In this case, I would add my effect (Gaussian Blur) and a mask to the layer. Revealing Effects in the timeline shows a feature called Compositing Options. By clicking the + button, the effect is then assigned to the mask of my choosing, and my mask is no longer masking the whole image.

Indicates the mask is used for an effect

Indicates the effect is masked

Add or delete a mask

Choose a mask

Effects

3D

Special Tools & Features

Expressions

Reverb

Emulates the acoustic conditions of various rooms.

Stereo Mixer

Moves audio from one channel to the other.

Tone

Replaces your audio with a pitch. Here's your homework: Use the Track Faces feature to generate keyframes of someone's mouth moving, then parent the Tone frequencies to the Position keyframes.

Blur

Finally, the good stuff! You'll be amazed by how many different ways there are to blur. Often, a blur effect will blur the edges of your frame into nothingness, so look for a Repeat Edge Pixels setting if you want to fill your frame.

Bilateral Blur

Camera Lens Blur

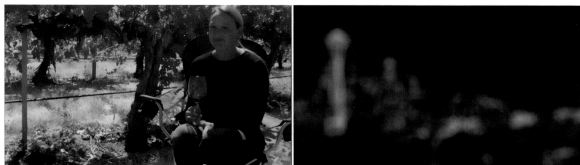

CC Cross Blur

CC Radial Blur & CC Radial Fast Blur

CC Vector Blur

CC Vector Blur below, utilizing another layer's brightness (below right) to define the direction of the blur

Channel Blur

Compound Blur below, utilizing another layer's brightness (below right) to define the amount of blur

Directional Blur   Fast Box Blur

Effects

3D

Special Tools & Features

Expressions

The Interface
& Editing

Animation

Text

Shapes, Masks
& Mattes

Effects

Gaussian Blur Radial Blur

Sharpen before and after

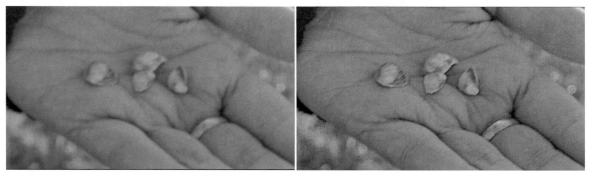

Smart Blur

Unsharp Mask before and after

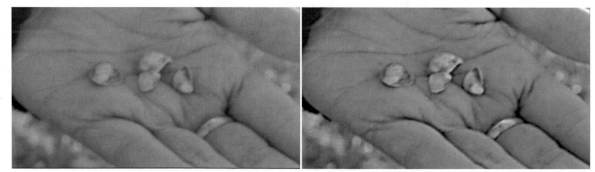

Bilateral Blur

Achieves a dreamy, Vaseline-on-the-lens effect by blurring areas of low contrast and preserving edges. Increase the blur amount with Radius and use Threshold for the cutoff that activates the blur.

Camera Lens Blur

A gorgeous blur that emulates an out-of-focus camera and introduces a bokeh effect, in which highlights can create hexagons (or other shapes).

Camera-Shake Deblur

Attempts to reduce blur caused by a moving camera, which happens with a slower shutter speed. This might be a good effect to combine with Warp Stabilizer, so your stabilized footage doesn't randomly go blurry.

CC Cross Blur

Blurs about the X or Y axes, and can transfer that blur effect onto your original with a built-in blend mode.

CC Radial Blur & CC Radial Fast Blur

Blur around or into a single point. Radial Fast Blur is similar, but has fewer options and processes faster.

CC Vector Blur

Not vector as in Bezier curves, but vector as in a direction. This effect blurs in a direction using another layer (and a designated channel) as an input, then distorts based off one of the Type settings. You can use a layer's own input to create some interesting, unpredictable blurs. Or, use another layer to specify the direction you want the blur to go.

Channel Blur

Blur just the red, green, blue, or alpha channels.

Compound Blur

Uses another layer's brightness to control the blur of a layer.

Directional Blur

Smears your image in any direction.

Fast Box Blur

Box Blur is considered by most to be a higher-quality blur than the default Gaussian Blur, and the new Fast edition computes quickly. Control the Radius of the pixels that get blurred together, and increase the quality of the blur with Iterations.

Gaussian Blur

The simplest blur that averages pixels. See if you can tell the difference between this example and the one for Fast Box Blur.

Radial Blur

Similar to CC Radial Blur, but this one also has a Spin setting.

Sharpen

Sharpen attempts to correct blurry footage by increasing contrast around edges. Unsharp Mask often performs better.

Smart Blur

This effect attempts to maintain hard edges and lines, but blurs the interiors of objects. Define the edge threshold with Threshold, and adjust the blur with Radius.

Unsharp Mask

More advanced than Sharpen, this effect allows you to control the Radius of sharpening, and has a Threshold to leave parts of the image unaffected.

Effects

3D

Special Tools & Features

Expressions

Boris FX Mocha

Detailed in chapter 7, the one effect in this category, Mocha AE, launches the Mocha AE plugin.

Channel

This set of effects operates on the raw data channels of a picture, and can also utilize data from other layers for complex interactions.

Blend

CC Composite

Invert

Minimax

Arithmetic

Performs one of several math operations on your video channels.

Blend

This works a bit like a Blend Mode, with the advantage of being a singular effect on a layer. Choose the layer you'd like to blend with, and choose from a slightly altered list of Blend Modes.

Calculations

Very similar to Blend, but this effect actually contains a list of all the Blend Modes.

CC Composite

This effect, when placed after a series of effects, can duplicate your original footage after all the effects have been processed. This creates a "clean" version of your original shot, which can be composited alongside your effects. In this example, I have some effects that would make the original text hard to read. By placing CC Composite after the effects and setting the Blend Mode to In front, I place my original text in front of the effects listed above this one.

Compound Arithmetic

This is similar to Arithmetic, but it uses the channels of another layer to perform math functions, instead of performing them on itself.

Invert

Not only will this invert RGB channels so darks are lights and lights are darks, but there are several functions of different channels you can swap.

Minimax

This effect scans pocket of your image based on a specified Radius, and derives either the lowest (Minimum) or highest (Maximum) value within that pocket.

Remove Color Matting

A simple cleanup tool to reduce fringe on an alpha layer.

Set Channels

Hardwires RGB values from one layer into another. For example, plug the red channel from layer X into the blue channel for layer Y.

Set Matte

For all intents and purposes, this is basically an alpha matte (as described in the previous chapter) in effect form. This is very useful when you want to use one layer as a matte for multiple layers. Plus, it skips the restrictive rule of setting the matte layer directly above the matted layer.

Shift Channels

Similar to Set Channels, but the channels are derived from this layer, instead of another.

Solid Composite

Composites your image with a solid color of your choosing. Choose from the Blend Modes.

Cinema 4D

The single effect in this category, CINEWARE, launches Cinema 4D Lite, which will be touched upon in the next chapter.

Color Correction

Fine-tunes colors in your image. Note than many of these effects can be found within the Lumetri Color effect.

CC Color Offset   CC Toner

Effects

3D

Special Tools & Features

Expressions

The Interface
& Editing

Animation

Text

Shapes, Masks
& Mattes

Effects

Change Color

Colorama

Equalize

Leave Color

Photo Filter

Tint

Tritone

Auto Color

A tool to detect your scene and automatically keep colors consistent. This is helpful if you're working with an image shot on a camera with auto white balance enabled.

Auto Contrast

Same as above, but for brightness controls. It might help with correcting video from cameras with auto exposure turned on.

Auto Levels

The same as above, but operates on each color channel individually, and can change both color and contrast.

Black & White

Surprisingly robust, this effect can adjust the brightness of colors before colors are desaturated, giving you good control over certain elements in your image.

Brightness and Contrast

While this effect gives you quick access to these parameters, adjusting curves in Lumetri Color is far more precise and powerful.

Broadcast Colors

If you're delivering to broadcast TV, this effect will limit the luminance or saturation to keep it within the legal range.

CC Color Neutralizer

This effect is meant to desaturate unwanted tints in the shadows, midtones, or highlights of your image. It works similarly to Lumetri Color's Color Wheels, but moves a color in the opposite direction of what's selected to attempt to bring the color closer to white.

CC Color Offset

Shift the hues of your red, green, and blue channels individually.

CC Kernel

The most cryptic effect, CC Kernel performs math on your pixels and is capable of adjusting brightness, blur, and glow using raw data. Don't stress yourself over this one—premade effects were built for a reason.

CC Toner

This effect can map your colors to two, three, or five arbitrary colors. The Duotone and Tritone settings are identical to the Tint and Tritone effects.

Change Color

Change a color by selecting it, adjust the Tolerance (which pixels are selected) and Softness (soften the selection mask), and shift that color using Hue, Lightness, and Saturation. Note that Lumetri Color's HSL Secondary is more powerful.

Change to Color

Same as above, but a new color is assigned instead of shifted. Again, Lumetri Color's HSL Secondary is more powerful.

Channel Mixer

Shift your red, green, and blue color channels. Lumetri Color offers tools that are more intuitive than this effect.

Color Balance

Not to harp on the whole Lumetri thing, but you should use Lumetri Color's Color Wheels instead of this effect.

The Interface & Editing

Animation

Text

Shapes, Masks & Mattes

Effects

Color Balance (HLS)

Quickly adjust the hue, saturation, and lightness of your image. Unlike the Hue/Saturation effect, this can be keyframed.

Color Link

Allows you to sample the average, median, brightest, or darkest pixel in an image. You can sample your current layer, or draw from another layer, either as a solid composite, or incorporate it with a built-in Blend Mode.

Color Stabilizer

If you're working with time-lapse or stop motion and the brightness is varying from frame to frame, this effect allows you to set certain brightness points, and have other frames in the timeline match to the set frame. Be sure to select Set Frame to designate the frame you'd like to match to, and place black, mid, and/or white points where you'd like them.

Colorama

Think CC Toner, but even more powerful. Colorama takes an input (say, your layer's lightness) and plots it onto a gradient (represented by a circle). This gradient is called the Output Cycle. You can assign any color you want to any point along the Output Cycle, allowing you to shift your image's colors to wildly arbitrary values. It even comes with some preset pallets. These can be helpful, since the Output Cycle often looks best when it's going from darkest to lightest.

Curves

Nearly identical to the ones found in Lumetri Color, Curves allows you to plot the brightness of any value, any way you want. The lower-left point on the graph indicates your blacks, and the upper-right point indicates whites. Moving a point up makes it lighter; down, darker. Add points to the curve by clicking anywhere along it. You can also adjust individual red, green, or blue channels. The advantages of this effect are the ability to save and open curve presets (which is cross-compatible with Photoshop), smooth uneven curves, or use the Auto feature, which compares your image with a database of images and chooses a nice curve for you.

Equalize

Automatically spread your red, green, and blue values so they fill the spectrum, and evenly distribute values throughout the spectrum.

Exposure

Adjust the brightness of your image, but with a method that's modeled after an f-stop level in a camera—in terms of both the interface and how each f-stop affects brightness.

Gamma/Pedestal/Gain

Each of these functions can be compared to an adjustment in the Curves effect. Gamma moves a curve's midpoint vertically, Pedestal moves a curve's bottom point vertically, and Gain moves a curve's top point vertically.

Hue/Saturation

Adjusts hue and saturation, either operating on the entire image (Channel Control: Master) or per individual color. When an individual color is selected, you can choose the high, low, and falloff of the selected color to be affected. You guessed it—Lumetri Color's HSL Secondary controls are more precise.

Leave Color
Desaturates an image except for the selected color.

Levels/Levels (Individual Controls)
Similar to Curves, but with less control. Plot the black, white, and gamma (midpoint) of all channels, or perform on each channel individually. This effect does come with a nice histogram, plotting the brightness values of each color onto a graph. Remember that a more powerful version of this graph can be pulled up with the Lumetri Scopes panel.

Lumetri Color
I know you're all waiting for me to shut up about Lumetri Color, but we're going to give this effect its own section, since it has so much built into it. Hang tight.

Photo Filter
A simple effect that allows you to utilize a warm, cool, or color preset as a color cast.

PS Arbitrary Map
This effect was meant to import Curves presets from Photoshop, but it's now obsolete. Use Curves instead.

Selective Color
Yet another way to tweak individual color channels, but this one uses CMYK colors instead of the usual RGB.

Shadow/Highlight
Independently boost shadows and lower highlights. This effect also has an Auto Amounts feature to keep your image in a comfortable range. Similar to Auto Levels, but with more control.

Tint
Map your black and white values to arbitrary colors.

Tritone
Similar to Tint, but maps highlights, midtones, and shadows to arbitrary colors.

Vibrance
This effect allows you to adjust both Vibrance and Saturation. The difference? Saturation saturates all pixels, while Vibrance introduces saturation into desaturated pixels.

Video Limiter
Similar to Broadcast Colors in that it limits the brightness of your image based on IRE broadcast standards.

Lumetri Color
It's finally here—a peaceful place where I get to discuss all the amazing benefits of the Lumetri Color effect in exquisite detail. Note that for many of these images, I'm looking at the Lumetri Scopes panel, which can be found in Window > Lumetri Scopes and is detailed in chapter 1 of the Compendium.

Basic Correction
These are quick tools to adjust your image, many of which will seem familiar to us. I don't often spend a lot of time in this section, as many of the following areas can do the same things with more control.

Input LUT

LUTs, or look-up tables, are presets that adjust your pixels in specific ways. The ones included with After Effects are quick ways to "undo" a low-contrast camera preset and reintroduce contrast. They're ordered here by camera manufacturer and setting, but even if you don't own an ARRI Alexa, you can try playing with LUTs until you find one that makes your image look the way you want it to.

You can also install LUTs from other sources. Choose Browse… from the LUT drop-down and select a file from your desktop. Your camera manufacturer may have some on their website. While these are okay to use, we're going to ignore LUTs for the rest of the chapter in order to gain a deeper understanding of the color tools available to us.

White Balance

If your footage looks like it's not correctly white balanced (often with an unwanted blue or yellow hue), you can use the Eyedropper tool to select an object in the scene that you think ought to be white (assuming there is a white object in your shot). This will automatically adjust your Temperature and Tint sliders until that color is white. You can also manually adjust the Temperature slider to shift your image between blue and orange, or the Tint slider to shift your image between green and magenta. If you're going for white, the Parade (RGB) scope in the Lumetri Scopes panel is helpful.

Saturation

Increase the intensity of the colors. Just don't go too nuts with this one—we'll have a more refined control momentarily. Check your Vectorscope scope in the Lumetri Scopes panel to view saturation levels.

Light

While good for quick adjustments, I tend to skip this entire section and go directly to Curves for my brightness and contrast controls. Nonetheless, let's look at what we can do. Exposure uniformly makes all your pixels brighter or darker. Contrast increases the distance between your darkest and lightest pixel. Adjust your semi-bright and semi-dark pixels with Highlights and Shadows, or your brightest and darkest pixels with Whites and Blacks. Or, click Auto to set your pixels in a decent, yet wholly unspecified range.

Auto

Harness Adobe Sensei AI to automatically grade your footage.

Creative

This is a section for creative LUTs, which are presets to give your footage a certain look.

Look

You can use the Look drop-down to browse many creative LUTs that come preinstalled. We can also adjust the Intensity of the LUT.

Just as with our Input LUTs, we can browse for more LUTs downloaded from the web. A quick web search will get you countless LUT packages, many of which claim to have the *Game of Thrones* or *Breaking Bad* look with a single click. While these are okay to use, we're going to ignore LUTs for the rest of the chapter in order to gain a deeper understanding of the color tools available to us.

I've applied **SL Blue Day4Nite**, a color-grading technique used to make shots appear as if it's nighttime.

Adjustment

A few quick effects. Faded Film decreases your shot's contrast. Sharpen is just an instance of the Sharpen effect built-in. We also have a second Saturation control, as well as a Vibrance control. The difference? Saturation saturates all pixels, while Vibrance introduces saturation into desaturated pixels.

This section also lets us adjust the hue of our Shadows and Highlights. This is a weaker version of the effect coming up in Color Wheels, so I tend to avoid this one.

Curves

We've arrived at my hands-down favorite color-correction tools! While some controls—like Exposure, Contrast, and Levels—allow you to move your pixels to the brighter or darker side, they do so in broad strokes. Curves allows you to control which bright, dark, or middle pixels are moved, and the amount by which they're moved. In fact, I generally start my color effects here.

RGB Curves

Curves allows you to plot the brightness of any value, any way you want. The lower-left point on the graph indicates your blacks, and the upper-right point indicates whites. Moving a point up makes it lighter; down, darker.

We can push this even further by adjusting the pixels directly between the lowest and highest points. Add a point to the curve by clicking on it. Often, an S-shaped curve allows you to darken your darks and lighten your lights, creating gorgeous contrast. If you wish to remove a point you've added to this graph, hold down ⌘/Ctrl and select a point. A double-click on a curve resets it.

The effect defaults to adjusting the Luma Curve. But we

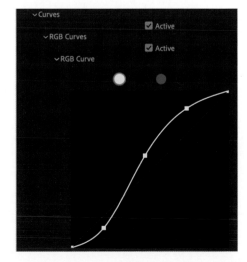

Effects

3D

Special Tools & Features

Expressions

The Interface
& Editing

Animation

Text

Shapes, Masks
& Mattes

Effects

can also adjust the curve of our red, green, and blue channels individually by clicking on the corresponding buttons. These adjustments go hand in hand with the Parade (RGB) scope.

Hue Saturation Curves

What if we wanted to use the power and specificity of Curves to not only adjust the brightness of our image or individual color channels, but also to manipulate things like hue and saturation? We can with the Hue Saturation Curves. They all operate under the same format: feature 1 versus feature 2 (e.g., Hue vs Sat). Select the aspect of feature 1 you'd like to manipulate by adding points along the X axis (click on the line to add, ⌘/Ctrl-click to remove, just like with our other Curves), or use the eyedropper to select a sample from the image. Adjust feature 2 by moving the selected point up and down about the Y axis. You'll likely need at least three points—one in the center to move, and two on either end to hold the rest of the values in place.

Hue vs Sat takes a range of hues and desaturates them. I often use this to desaturate my skin tones—overly saturated skin tones are yucky. A good way to do this is to use the eyedropper to select a skin tone, then adjust the selected point downward until you've reached the desired level of desaturation, adjusting the range of values selected as needed.

Hue vs Hue changes the color of a selected color. For example, I could change the blues in this image to orange. This one can be tricky to use for anything dramatic—HSL Secondary will do a better job of being specific.

Hue vs Luma changes the brightness of a selected color. Again, difficult to use.

Luma vs Sat can be used to saturate or desaturate based on brightness. Since saturation is more apparent in midtones anyway, sometimes simply desaturating your darks and highlights makes your colors pop.

Sat vs Sat allows you to desaturate your already desaturated colors even further, or introduce saturation where there wasn't any already (similar to Vibrance).

Color Wheels

Color Wheels adjust the hue, saturation, and brightness of your image, but broken down into Shadows, Midtones, and Highlights. They're a fantastic tool for color grading. A great place to start is to decide whether you want your image to be warm or cool. Start by pushing your Midtones toward the direction you'd like. Then, see if you can create color contrast by pushing your Shadows and Highlights in the *opposite* direction.

Use the sliders to adjust brightness.

Drag the crosshair away from the center to introduce saturation, and choose a hue by pushing the crosshair toward the desired color.

HSL Secondary

While we could use our Hue Saturation Curves to manipulate colors in broad strokes, it's not the most accurate tool. If we want to take a color and change it to another color, HSL Secondary is our friend. It has two components: selecting the color you want to manipulate by choosing from a range of hue, saturation, and brightness levels, then manipulating said color.

Key

Choose the color to change. Set color is a great place to start—select its eyedropper, then choose a color you'd like to change. Note Add color and Remove color, which are ways to add and subtract from the color range. I prefer to use the HSL sliders. Also note that you can choose specific colors from the color picker beneath the eyedropper—again, let's start with the eyedropper and refine with our HSL tools.

Off the bat, it's difficult to tell which colors are selected. Once we start playing with our HSL sliders, the effect will display only the affected colors. We can bring up this view manually by selecting Show Mask.

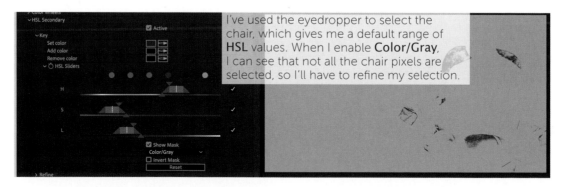

I've used the eyedropper to select the chair, which gives me a default range of HSL values. When I enable **Color/Gray**, I can see that not all the chair pixels are selected, so I'll have to refine my selection.

Next, we'll have to expand or shrink our HSL sliders until they contain only the pixels we want them to. This may take more than one pass through each control.

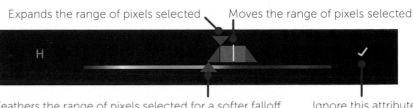

Expands the range of pixels selected   Moves the range of pixels selected

Feathers the range of pixels selected for a softer falloff   Ignore this attribute

If your mask has rough edges, use the Denoise and Blur effects under Refine to soften the selection.

Once you're all set, you should see just the pixels you want to change isolated. If you're unable to deselect rogue pixels you don't wish to change, remember that you can add masks to effects to crop out unwanted pixels.

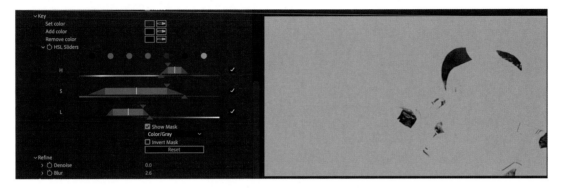

I'll now deselect Color/Gray and move on to Correction.

Correction

These controls should be fairly familiar by now—just know that they affect only the keyed pixels we've just selected. Also note that the default color wheel affects all pixels, but you can switch to the Shadow/Midtone/Highlight wheels by clicking .

Vignette

A Vignette darkens pixels around the edges of your frame. It's a great way to darken background elements and draw the viewer's eye to the center of the frame. I apply a Vignette to almost all my shots, as do many colorists—look out for it the next time you're watching a movie or TV show. It's one of those "can't unsee" things that you never noticed before.

Effects

3D

Special Tools & Features

Expressions

The Interface
& Editing

Animation

Text

Shapes, Masks
& Mattes

Effects

This effect has four simple controls. Amount controls how much darkening is applied. Make sure you drag this into the negative—positive values add a white halo, which should be reserved for the most egregious wedding videos. Midpoint is how far into the image the Vignette creeps. Roundness controls the shape—a negative extreme gives you a rectangle, and a positive extreme gives you a linear gradient with a highlight in the middle and dark sides. Use Feather to adjust the softness of your Vignette, with a low value being a hard circle.

Distort

These effects move parts of your image around. Want a pixel to be somewhere else? Distort it! Many of these effects utilize on-screen controls. Select the effect in the Effects Controls panel to see them.

Bezier Warp   Bulge

CC Bend It   CC Blobbylize

CC Flo Motion   CC Griddler

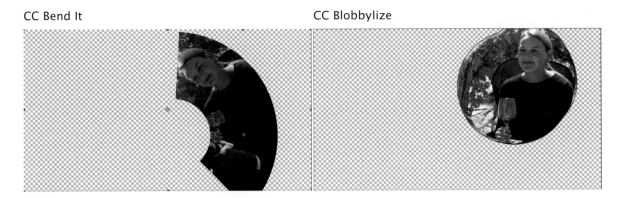

CC Lens   CC Page Turn

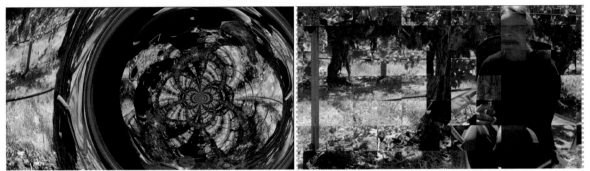

CC Power Pin   CC Slant

Effects

3D

Special Tools & Features

Expressions

CC Smear

CC Split

CC Tiler

Displacement Map

Liquify

Magnify

Mesh Warp

Mirror

Offset

Polar Coordinates

Reshape

Ripple

Rolling Shutter Repair before (left) and after (right)

Smear

Turbulent Displace

Effects

3D

Special Tools
& Features

Expressions

The Interface & Editing

Animation

Text

Shapes, Masks & Mattes

Effects

Twirl   Warp

Wave Warp

Bezier Warp

Similar to CC Corner Pin in that you can place the corners of your image wherever you like, but this one includes Bezier handles to bend your image's edges however you'd like. Perfect for bulgy old CRT TV screen simulations.

Bulge

Enlarge an elliptical-shaped area.

CC Bend It

Mask your image by defining start and end points, then bend it.

CC Blobbylize

Uses a layer's input to define the shape of a blob, which is a gooey distortion with depth.

CC Flo Motion

Choose a point to "pull" your footage into or out of, creating some psychedelic effects.

CC Griddler

Chops your image into tiles, which can be scaled and rotated.

CC Lens

A crystal ball–like effect.

CC Page Turn

Animate an image as if it's a page in a book turning.

CC Power Pin

Place the corners of your image anywhere you'd like. Great for compositing images onto TVs or phones. This effect has a slightly better interface than Corner Pin, so I prefer it.

CC Ripple Pulse

Similar to Ripple, except you manually trigger ripples leaving the specified point by keyframing Pulse Level.

CC Slant
Slide the edges of your frame.

CC Smear
Smear pixels from a point of your choosing to another point.

CC Split
Tear a portal-like hole in between two points of your choosing.

CC Split 2
Nearly identical to the above effect, but you can create asymmetrical tears.

CC Tiler
Shrinks your image down and replicates it.

Corner Pin
Similar to CC Power Pin, but with fewer controls.

Detail-Preserving Upscale
AE's most powerful technique for increasing the scale of raster images while preserving quality. It also comes with a built-in denoiser. This is great for upscaling standard definition footage.

Displacement Map
Uses channels from a layer to offset pixels. For example, if you point this effect to displace based off a paper texture, your pixels will be moved based off the brights and darks of the paper, giving your image a wrinkled look.

Liquify
Apologies to our subject for this one! Liquify is for when you want to grab pixels and move them around. Select from one of the ten available tools: Warp (best for pushing and pulling pixels), Turbulence (good for randomness), Twirl Clockwise and Counterclockwise, Pucker, Bloat, Shift Pixels, Reflection, Clone, and Reconstruction (reverts distortion back to normal). Adjust the size of the application brush by holding ⌘ / Ctrl and dragging the mouse. While this effect can't be keyframed in the traditional sense, you can keyframe the Distortion Percentage, which can transition from undistorted to your fully distorted version.

Magnify
Enlarge a portion of your image in a circle or square shape.

Mesh Warp
Another powerful "put this pixel here" effect, Mesh Warp overlays a grid on your image. You can move the corner points around wherever you want (and even adjust their Bezier handles), pushing the pixels within each box. It's a good idea to set a grid size that's small enough where you can adjust detail where it's needed, but not so dense that you have to move many points around.

Mirror
Choose a spot to reflect your image, then choose the angle of reflection.

Offset
Slides the image within the frame, with repeating edges.

Optics Compensation
This effect is intended to undo lens distortion, such as excessive fish-eye.

Effects

3D

Special Tools & Features

Expressions

Polar Coordinates
Bends your image into a sine wave.

Reshape
This effect is useful when you want the shape of an image to fit into another shape—plus, you can keyframe between the two for smooth changes. The shape you want your image to become should be defined by mask points. Select that mask from the drop-down for Destination Mask. In my example, the Destination Mask is green. For smooth motion, it's a good idea to duplicate that mask, then reshape it around your original shape. This mask gets selected in the Source Mask drop-down. In my example, the Destination Mask is red. To move from one to the next, keyframe Percent, and choose how stiff or fluid you want your distortion to be from the Elasticity drop-down.

Ripple
Distorts from a point outward and automatically animates, like ripples in a pond.

Rolling Shutter Repair
Many DSLR and smartphone cameras record an image from the top to the bottom of the sensor, and not simultaneously. With fast-moving images, this can sometimes create distortion, as the object may be in a different place by the time the sensor has captured the frame. This can easily be repaired with Rolling Shutter Repair.

Smear
This is similar to Reshape in that two masks are used to define a start and end point for your distortion. However, instead of entirely reshaping your image, this effect allows you move, rotate, and scale the Source Mask, which will distort pixels close to the Source Mask and leave pixels close to the Boundary Mask untouched. In my example, the Source Mask is red, the Boundary Mask is green, and destination is represented by the yellow lines.

Spherize
Nearly the same as Bulge, but with fewer controls.

Transform
These are the same as each layer's Transform controls, but in effect form, allowing you to adjust Position, Anchor Point, Scale, Rotation, and even Skew. This may be helpful if a layer's transforms are inaccessible due to an effect or expression, or if you want to more easily duplicate transforms to other layers.

Turbulent Displace
Adds random distortion in a variety of patterns. Animate the Evolution to see it move.

Twirl
Treat your footage like digital spaghetti.

Warp
Choose from some preset patterns that distort your whole image.

Warp Stabilizer

If you have shaky camera footage, Warp Stabi-lizer does a fantastic job of minimizing camera movement by punching in on your image and offsetting the camera's translation. And After Effects does most of the work for you. Your main considerations with this effect are choos-ing what type of Method to use—the default, Subspace Warp is the most powerful, but may cause unwanted distortion. Note that this effect may need a few minutes to analyze your footage before operating.

Wave Warp

I'd say that ninety-nine percent of the time I use Wave Warp it's because I'm trying to select Warp Stabilizer. The other one percent is for a wavy effect, with a few different shape options.

Expression Controls

None of these effects do anything—that is, until you parent features to them. Consider them place-holders if you want effect controls to manipulate your expressions, such as adding and keyframing a slider to control Wiggle amount. Expressions are detailed in chapter 8 of the Compendium.

3D Point Control

For controlling points in 3D space.

Angle Control

For controlling expressions that utilize degrees.

Checkbox Control

For true/false statements in expressions.

Color Control

A color picker for expressions.

Dropdown Menu Control

For choosing between various options in expressions.

Layer Control

A variable to select layers.

Point Control

For controlling points in 2D space.

Slider Control

The simplest control, allowing you to easily keyframe a number value into your expression.

Effects

3D

Special Tools & Features

Expressions

The Interface & Editing

Animation

Text

Shapes, Masks & Mattes

Effects

Generate

This section is all about creating stuff from scratch. Most of these effects are generally placed on Solid layers, since they can remove all content currently in a layer.

4-Color Gradient

Advanced Lightning

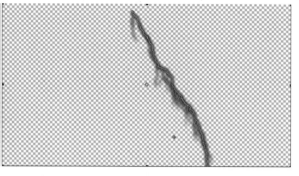

Audio Spectrum/Audio Waveform

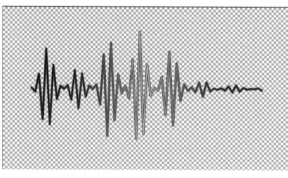

Beam

CC Glue Gun

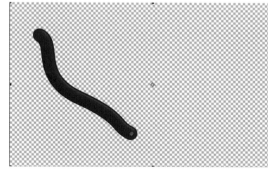

CC Light Burst 2.5

CC Light Rays   CC Light Sweep

CC Threads   Cell Pattern

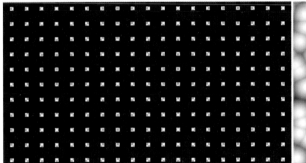
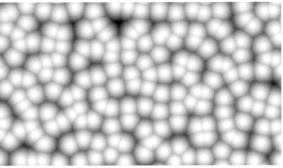

Checkerboard   Circle

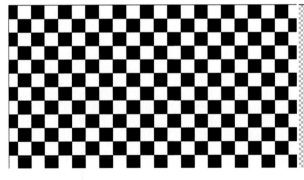

Ellipse   Fractal

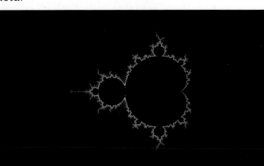

Effects

3D

Special Tools & Features

Expressions

The Interface & Editing

Animation

Text

Shapes, Masks & Mattes

Effects

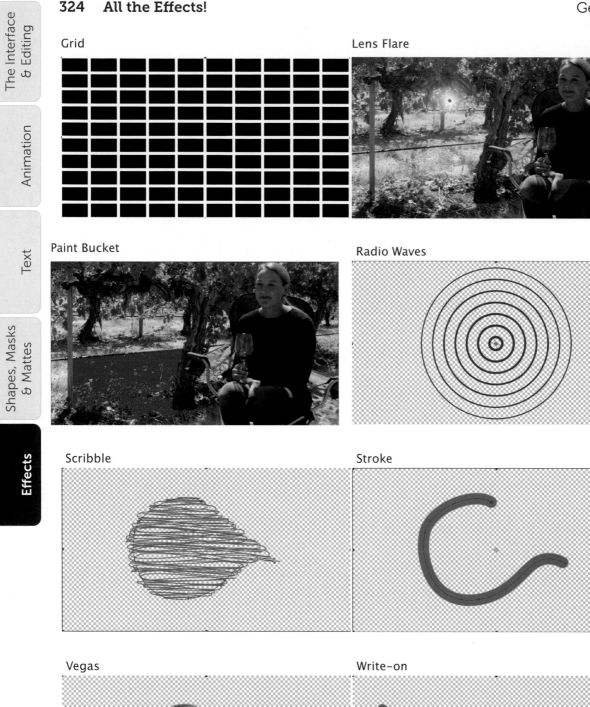

Grid

Lens Flare

Paint Bucket

Radio Waves

Scribble

Stroke

Vegas

Write-on

4-Color Gradient

This is slightly more advanced than a radial gradient, as this effect allows you to plot your four colors anywhere you'd like.

Advanced Lightning

The renderer strikes back.

Audio Spectrum

I love this effect. Set your Audio Layer to any layer that has an audio track, and this effect generates a spectrum of your audio, plotting the amplitude of your bass to treble ranges. There's tons of customization on this one, so have fun.

Audio Waveform

Very similar to the above effect, but this one continually draws an audio peak and moves it down the path.

Want to do more with audio data? You can right-click any layer than has an audio track and select Keyframe Assistant > Convert Audio to Keyframes. You can parent anything to those keyframes to have a layer's volume drive any parameter you want.

Beam

Ostensibly a glowing shape path, this effect can be used for photons, lasers, and lightsabers.

CC Glue Gun

After keyframing this effect's Brush Position, the effect renders a blobby line that leaves its mark wherever the brush has landed.

CC Light Burst 2.5

A radial glow from the point of your choosing.

CC Light Rays

Select a point in your scene to make it appear as if it's emitting light.

CC Light Sweep

Emulates a "God ray" from a cloud.

CC Threads

A complex interwoven pattern with built-in shading and texture.

Cell Pattern

Create many tiny things bunched together with some randomness. There are many different types of patterns to choose from.

Checkerboard

When ska comes back, you'll be ready.

Circle

Look, there was a time before shape layers when this effect might have been kinda useful.

Ellipse

Awesome.

Eyedropper Fill

This effect samples the color selected by Sample Point and sets the layer to that color. Increasing the Sample Radius averages the pixels within that area.

Fill

Sets the layer to a color. This can be an easier way to set many things (text and shape layers) to a certain color—it's easy to copy and paste an effect to multiple layers.

Fractal

Generates one of several fractal patterns, which is a shape with a theoretically infinite circumference, as the entirety of the shape is repeated on its edges. Fractals were discovered by Benoit B. Mandlebrot. His middle name? Benoit B. Mandelbrot.

Effects

3D

Special Tools & Features

Expressions

The Interface & Editing

Animation

Text

Shapes, Masks & Mattes

Effects

Gradient Ramp

Another way to create a linear or radial gradient that predates shape layers.

Grid

It's a grid!

Lens Flare

J. J. Abrams's favorite effect.

Paint Bucket

This effect attempts to fill in an area of your frame by coloring in objects that are similarly contrasted, chosen by Threshold. In a few rare instances, I've been able to enhance a poorly lit green screen by starting with this effect to paint the unevenly lit green screen the same color before I keyed it.

Radio Waves

Automatically create and animate circles that emanate from a point of your choosing.

Scribble

This powerful effect generates scribbles, utilizing a path on the same layer. The scribble can be a fill or a stroke of the path. It's also automatically animated with a wiggle control.

Stroke

This effect renders a layer's path as a visible line. This is very similar to a shape path, complete with Start and End controls that work identically to Trim Paths.

This effect can be used to make text (or anything, for that matter) appear as if it's being drawn on.

- Add a mask path to the layer in the same shape as your text.
- Apply the Stroke effect.
- Set the Brush Size so that the effect covers the entire layer.
- Animate the End from 0 to 100%.
- Switch the Paint Style to Reveal Original Image. This uses the effect as a matte.

Vegas

This effect can generate lines or points, along either a mask or an image's edge. These can then be animated to rotate around the object, like lights on a Las Vegas marquee.

Write-on

A simpler version of CC Glue Gun in which a line is rendered based on Brush Position.

Immersive Video

These effects were designed for virtual reality shots; however, they can also be used on regular footage.

VR Blur

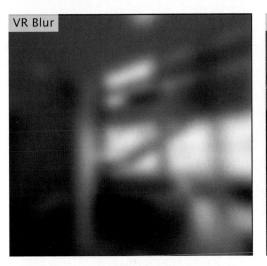

VR Chromatic Aberrations

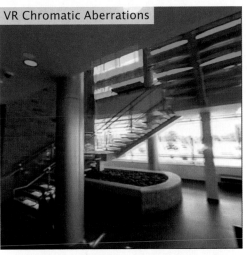

VR Color Gradients

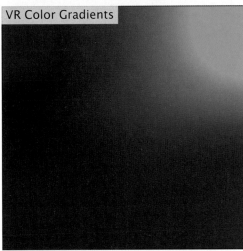

VR De-Noise

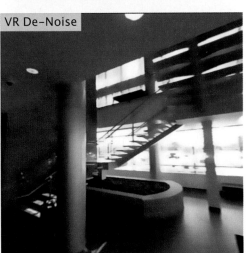

VR Digital Glitch

VR Fractal Noise Basic

VR Fractal Noise
Turbulent Sharp

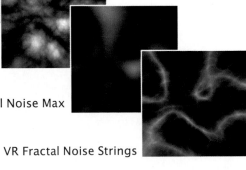

VR Fractal Noise Max

VR Fractal Noise Strings

Effects

3D

Special Tools
& Features

Expressions

The Interface & Editing

Animation

Text

Shapes, Masks & Mattes

Effects

VR Blur

Gaussian blur, that is.

VR Chromatic Aberrations

Emulate a prismatic-lens effect that separates your red, green, and blue channels based on the distance from the camera.

VR Color Gradients

Similar to 4-Color Gradient, except the color points occupy space within the VR sphere.

VR Converter

A utility to convert between various VR layouts.

VR De-Noise

This effect attempts to reduce noise in your footage by adding blur in low-contrast areas.

VR Digital Glitch

Emulate the effect of your cat chewing on your headset cord, without the mess! Color Distortion is very similar to VR Chromatic Aberrations. Use Noise to add randomness to your pixels.

VR Fractal Noise

Choose one of four fractal patterns to generate: Basic, Turbulent Sharp, Max, or Strings. These are similar to the Cell Pattern effect.

VR Glow

Glow is a blur that occurs above a brightness threshold. Control which bright pixels have glow with Luma Threshold, then control the Glow Radius, Brightness, and Saturation. If you'd like your glow to be a specific color, enable Use Tint Color, then pick that color.

VR Plane to Sphere

Turns your VR footage into an image placed on a sphere. Adjust the size of the sphere with Scale, edge softness with Feather, and rotate either the footage or the sphere with the Rotate controls.

VR Rotate Sphere

Rotate your environment. May induce nausea.

VR Sharpen

Increases the contrast around the edges of pixels.

VR Sphere to Plane

The opposite of VR Plane to Sphere, this effect projects 2D footage onto a sphere. Move your image about a sphere with the Pan, Tilt, and Roll controls.

Keying

Keying, also known as green screening or chroma keying, is the art of removing a color (usually green or blue) from an image. If you have something shot in front of a green screen, this suite of effects can help you remove the background.

Effects

3D

Special Tools & Features

Expressions

Advanced Spill Suppressor before (left) and after (right)

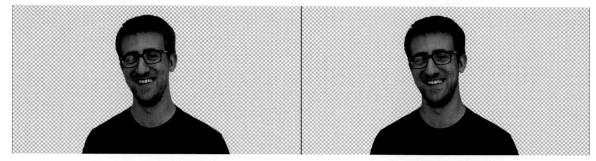

Difference Matte foreground   **Difference Matte** background

Difference Matte final output

Extract before (left) and after (right)

Advanced Spill Suppressor

Spill is when light from a green screen is reflected onto the subject. You don't want your perfectly keyed footage to have a weird green tint, so if the built-in spill suppression in Keylight doesn't work, you can try this effect to quickly desaturate your greens.

CC Simple Wire Removal

This effect is made to remove wires, such as those hanging actors from the ceiling.

Color Difference Key

I recommend Keylight as the go-to effect for keying, but this effect might work better when keying partially transparent objects, such as smoke or glass. This effect utilizes two keys— Matte Partial B contains the color data for your green screen, and Matte Partial A contains colors that *aren't* green. The two are then combined for your final output matte.

Color Range

A simple keyer in which the Eyedropper and Eyedropper+ buttons are used to include colors you wish to key out.

Difference Matte

If you have footage of a subject and footage of the background without the subject, this effect can attempt to subtract the similar pixels, leaving you with just the subject. It's similar to how the background gets removed in a video conference call. It's rarely perfect, but it's not a bad idea to shoot a clean shot of your green screen with nothing in it, so you can use a Difference Matte in addition to keying. This is called a clean plate.

Keylight (1.2)

Let's learn Keylight, After Effects' most powerful keyer! I'll walk you through the most commonly used features.

Extract

A wonderfully simple keyer that lets you key based on the histogram. I use this effect as a luma key, which is a key based on brightness instead of color. With the Channel set to Luminance, simply dial down the White Point until the whites in your image are keyed out.

Inner/Outer Key

This effect allows you to say, "key in THIS spot!" Step one is to draw a mask around the edges of your object—including the green. Then, use the drop-down for Foreground (Inside) to select that mask. Keying will happen within the boundaries of your mask. Or, you can use two masks—one just outside your subject, which you'll set to Background (Outside), and a second one just inside the borders of your subject, which you'll set to Foreground (Inside). Keying will only happen between these two masks.

This effect is probably only useful for static objects.

Key Cleaner

After you've keyed, you can use this effect to grow or shrink the boundaries of your key, and reduce chatter, which is noise on your matte edge.

Effects

3D

Special Tools & Features

Expressions

The Interface
& Editing

Animation

Text

Shapes, Masks
& Mattes

Effects

View

This effect allows you to see not just the end result, but the steps it takes to get there. The most helpful of these is Source, which tells Keylight to display the pixels it's deemed green as black, and the pixels it's deemed not green as white.

Screen Colour

Start here. Use the eyedropper to select the color (or colour, if you're fancy) you wish to remove. It's best to choose a median color—not the brightest nor the darkest green. And hopefully your green screen is evenly lit, so there isn't too much variation.

If your screen has a texture on it, you can dial up Screen Pre-blur, which blurs your image before the keying happens. This might make your green more smooth, but it will be more difficult to get a crisp edge.

Screen Matte

A single click of Screen Color might look good at first, but you'll likely need to refine the effect and set thresholds for what is and isn't green. Setting View to Status may reveal something like this:

Our task is to make the green stuff black and the not green stuff white. This happens by dialing open the Screen Matte portion of the effect. Increase Clip Black and decrease Clip White until the background is black and the foreground is white.

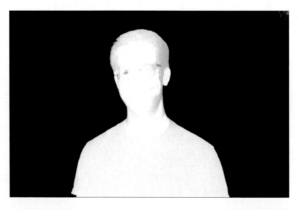

Got green? That's okay. Green means an area is included in the foreground, but has a partial green tint to it. We'll decide what to do about that in a bit. Also notice that I still have some fuzziness in the top-right corner of my frame. Sometimes, it's best to clean things up with a rough mask instead of trying to include everything in the key effect.

I like my edges to have partial transparency, so I'll increase Screen Softness a little. This will create a more realistic blend with the background. Doing so may reveal the green screen behind the subject. To counter this, I'll decrease Screen Shrink/Grow to have my matte chew into my footage ever so slightly.

Replace Method is a built-in suppression effect that operates on the green stuff in Status view. Since Keylight automatically desaturates the greens in your shot, it might color-correct your footage in an undesirable way. Set Replace Method to Source to leave your footage uncorrected. Otherwise, choose between Hard or Soft Colour for the best look.

None   Source   Hard Colour   Soft Colour

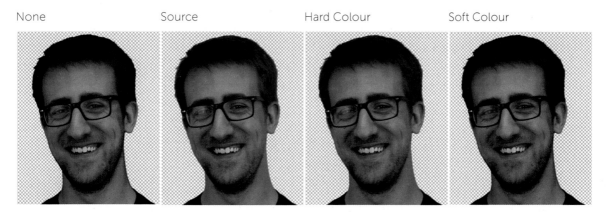

Inside Mask
By adding a mask to a section on your foreground, this section can give you some further refinement. First, it can include an area that may have been keyed out. Second, you can choose a custom Replace Method for just this section.

Outside Mask
Similarly, a mask set to Outside Mask will exclude the area from your key.

Foreground and Edge Color Correction
Like a mini Lumetri built into the effect. This also contains further spill-suppression controls and the ability to correct only the color or your edges.

Source Crops
As an alternate approach to masking out the edges of your frame, this portion can repeat, reflect, or wrap your green screen on the edge, which might eliminate ugly corners.

Linear Color Key
A simple keyer without many bells and whistles. Use Keylight instead.

Effects

3D

Special Tools & Features

Expressions

Matte

These effects help clean up the edges of your image.

Matte Choker

If your image has rough edges, this effect can soften and choke (that is, shrink) the edges.

Mocha Shape

If you've applied the Mocha AE effect to cut out a shape, this effect can borrow that shape's alpha channel and use it on another layer.

Refine Hard/Soft Matte

Choose the effect best suited for your matte. These effects can add feathering to edges and reduce chatter, which is random noise on your matte edge.

Simple Choker

Brings the edges of your matte inward.

Noise and Grain

Add (or remove) noise, which is randomness over your image. Noise on a still image makes it look more convincingly video-y, and for making two shots look similar, matching noise to a noisy shot is easier than removing noise.

Add Grain

Noise/Noise Alpha/Noise HLS/Noise HLS Auto

Turbulent Noise

Add Grain

A fantastic effect for adding film or video grain to your image, with lots of customization options. By default, this effect operates only within the Preview Region. Set Viewing Mode to Final Output before rendering.

Dust & Scratches

Despite how the name sounds, this effect is meant to remove dust and scratches from old film. It does so by searching for erroneous pixels (with the search area defined by Radius) and blurring them (based on Threshold).

Fractal Noise

This effect has largely been replaced by Turbulent Noise.

Match Grain

Want to make the noise of one shot match that of another? This powerful effect is similar to Add Grain, but it analyzes the grain of another shot and attempts to automatically match it. Hang tight, as this is a very processing-intensive effect with long render times.

Median

Similar to a blur, this effect averages pixels around a certain radius, which can be a quick way to reduce noise.

Median (Legacy)

Included for compatibility with older versions of After Effects. Do not use.

Noise/Noise Alpha/Noise HLS/ Noise HLS Auto

Simpler than Add Grain, these effects add randomness to your pixels. Choose the effect that adds noise to the channel you want.

Remove Grain

Another powerful effect that analyzes footage and removes unwanted noise. This effect is a beast and can take a long time to render—as such, I recommend going down the list of features and only increasing the power of each one if needed. This effect utilizes the Preview Region to operate on a sample of your image at first—set Viewing Mode to Final Output before rendering.

Temporal Filtering is the big gun here—enabling this analyzes frames before and after the current one to detect irregularities between the two. Enabling this effect turns your computer into a small furnace, which is great for long winter nights.

Turbulent Noise

More of a generative effect, Turbulent Noise is fantastic for creating random patterns, which can be used to make clouds, lava, grunge, oil, terrain—if it needs randomness, Turbulent Noise can make it. Animate Evolution to watch the effect churn.

Obsolete

These effects have all been replaced by better features, and are only here to preserve backward compatibility with old versions of After Effects. Please disregard.

Effects

3D

Special Tools & Features

Expressions

Perspective

When your film teacher tells you to give your characters more depth, look no further than the Perspective effects.

3D Glasses Stereo Pair

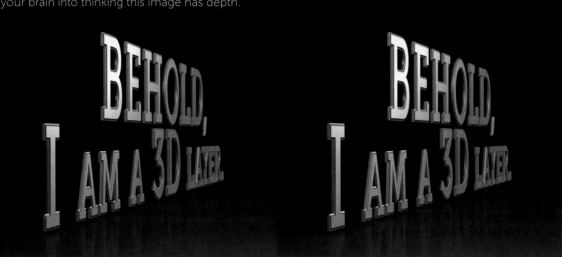

By crossing your eyes until the images align, you can trick your brain into thinking this image has depth.

3D Glasses Red Blue LR

Viewing this with red-blue 3D glasses also tricks your brain into seeing depth.

Other ways of tricking your audience into thinking your video has depth: shooting in black and white, having a non-linear storyline, speaking French. *Ce n'est pas la profondeur!*

Bevel Alpha

Bevel Edges

CC Cylinder

CC Environment

This is a high-resolution image taken from all angles mapped onto a 2D plane.

Author: ESO/S. Brunier,
http://www.eso.org/public/images/potw1105a/

CC Sphere

CC Spotlight

Drop Shadow

Radial Shadow

Effects

3D

Special Tools & Features

Expressions

The Interface & Editing

Animation

Text

Shapes, Masks & Mattes

Effects

3D Camera Tracker

This effect analyzes a camera's movement and recreates your camera with a 3D After Effects camera, so you can composite in 3D objects. We'll cover this in chapter 6 of the Compendium.

3D Glasses

Your brain perceives 3D when your left and right eyes show slightly different images. Using this effect, you can produce images that trick your brain into thinking it's seeing in three dimensions, by either placing images side by side, or generating an image that can be viewed with red-and-blue 3D glasses.

In this example, I've duplicated my 3D scene. In the second version, I've shifted my camera over slightly, emulating the distance between two eyeballs. By plugging the original image into this effect's Left View and my shifted duplicate into Right View, the effect can render a "3D" image, with a few different options.

Bevel Alpha

If your image has an interesting alpha channel, you can make the edges pop out, as if the image has depth. Control the thickness of the pop-out with Edge Thickness. This effect simulates a light hitting your object and casting a shadow, so control the Light Angle, Color, and Intensity.

Bevel Edges

This is the same as Bevel Alpha, but it operates on the edges of the image irrespective of alpha.

CC Cylinder

Wraps your image into a 3D pipe, which you can rotate. When animators talk about working within a 3D pipeline, this is not what they mean.

CC Environment

This effect allows you to use an environmental map (spherical, probe, or vertical cross styles) in conjunction with an After Effects 3D camera. To use this effect with After Effects' 3D camera, do the following:

- Add the environment map to your comp.
- Turn off that layer's visibility.
- Add a Solid layer to the comp, matching your comp's dimensions.
- Apply the CC Environment effect.
- Set the effect's Environment to the environment map layer, and choose the correct Mapping algorithm.
- Add a camera to the scene.

The environment will now respond to your camera's movements.

CC Sphere

Plots your image onto a 3D sphere. This is great for globes—ideally using this effect on a pre-comp containing a map that has a 2:1 aspect ratio.

CC Spotlight

An effect that mimics an After Effects 3D spotlight, but this one functions all within 2D. You can control where the light sits, where it points, and how high off your image it is.

Drop Shadow

Replicates the alpha of your image as an offset monochromatic layer. Yeah, Drop Shadow is a better way of phrasing that. While this effect works just fine, I prefer the simplicity of the Drop Shadow Layer Style. Right-click a layer and select Layer Styles > Drop Shadow.

Radial Shadow

This is similar to Drop Shadow, except it can emulate a light source directly in front of your subject, which essentially adds a scale factor to the shadow. If your clip has semi-transparency, Glass Edge (under the Render drop-down) can emulate the effect of light shining through it and create a colored shadow.

Simulation

A complex suite of effects that simulate particles, which are tiny elements controlled by parameters such as emitters and physics. Great for water, fire, smoke, and killing hours at a time.

Most of these effects are best applied on a dedicated layer, such as a Solid.

Card Dance   Caustics

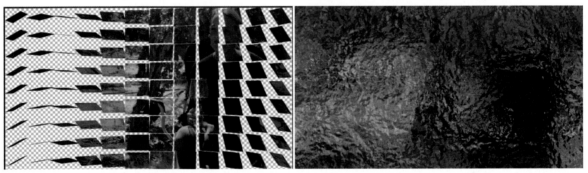

CC Ball Action   CC Bubbles

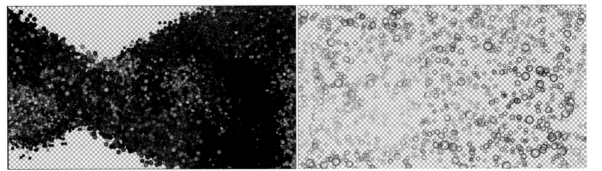

Effects

3D

Special Tools & Features

Expressions

The Interface & Editing

Animation

Text

Shapes, Masks & Mattes

Effects

CC Drizzle

CC Hair

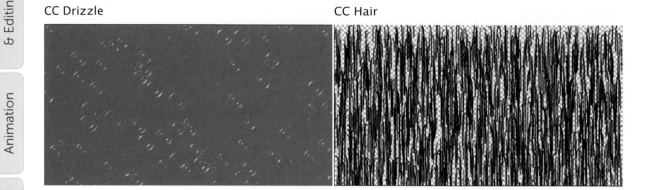

CC Mr. Mercury

CC Particle Systems II

CC Particle World

CC Pixel Polly

CC Rainfall

CC Scatterize

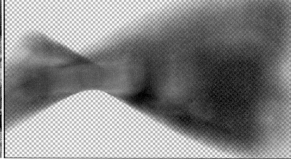

CC Snowfall

CC Star Burst

Foam

Particle Playground

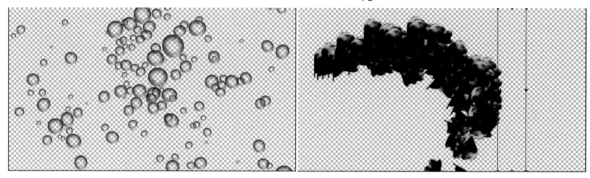

Shatter

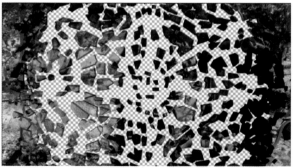

Wave World

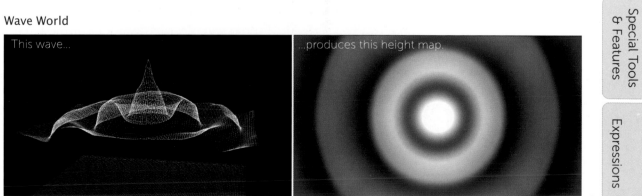

This wave...

...produces this height map.

Effects

3D

Special Tools & Features

Expressions

The Interface & Editing

Animation

Text

Shapes, Masks & Mattes

Effects

Card Dance

This effect divides your image into cards. The number of divisions is determined by Rows and Columns. Cards can be uniformly positioned, scaled, or rotated. Or, you can select a layer with Gradient Layer, and use a channel to determine the order of events. For example, in this sample image, I have Gradient Layer 1 set to a gradient going from light to dark. This means the card rotation can be affected more by the light part of my image than the dark.

Caustics

Mimics the effects of light hitting water. In this image, I have Water Surface set to a layer with the Turbulent Noise effect.

CC Ball Action

Balls are the new pixels. This effect renders your image into a 3D plane made out of... well, balls. There are some options to rotate and twist the plane.

CC Bubbles

Bubbles! These are automatically animated floating upward.

CC Drizzle

Mimics raindrops falling onto a surface. When combined with CC Rainfall, you can utilize this effect to make water droplets appear on the ground. It works well on a 3D layer, rotated to match your scene, and utilizing a Blend Mode.

CC Hair

This doesn't come with many animation options, so use this if you want to create the worst background imaginable.

CC Mr. Mercury

Not only does this effect render your image with metallic globules, but it also has a built-in particle system, so it can churn and spit out globs continuously. It uses many of the same parameters as CC Particle Systems II.

CC Particle Systems II

Particle systems generate many small things, so you don't have to worry about hand-animating each flame, puff of smoke, or magic sparkle. Instead, you give the system a set of guidelines on which to operate. Those principles are:

- Birth Rate: How many particles are being generated per second? Keyframing this to 0 stops emission.
- Longevity: Do your particles die on-screen, or last forever? Having some limits on Longevity will reduce render times.
- Producer: Where and how big is the thing that is emitting particles?
- Physics: There are several different types of ways the particles can leave the emitter, and you have control over velocity, gravity, and more.
- Particle: What does the thing look like? This effect gives you a few options. You can also tell it what to do with the particle as it's spat out: it can change color, size, opacity, etc.

Want to do more with particles? CC Particle World and Particle Playground are both more powerful than this one. To go even further, check out Red Giant's Particular plug-in, which can do way more.

CC Particle World

Similar to the effect above, but slightly more complex and with a few more features. For one, you can assign another layer to be the particle, so you're not beholden to the presets. For two, this effect can utilize a floor, which particles can bounce off of.

To use another layer as the particle, set the Texture Layer to Textured Disc, then select another layer (best used on a precomp, and make sure that precomp's dimensions are quite small; otherwise, you'll hit huge render times).

CC Pixel Polly

A simpler version of Shatter, this effect automatically explodes your image into tiny triangles or squares.

CC Rainfall

Simulates rain. This effect can be fairly convincing on wide shots, but for scenes with characters, you'll want to spray your actors with a hose for splashes and drips.

CC Scatterize

Randomly scatters pixels, which could be used for a character disintegrating. Like CC Ball Action, this effect lets you twist your image.

CC Snowfall

An unexpected snowfall in wine country means that vintage is likely going to be bad.

CC Star Burst

Turns your images into balls and flies through them. This is the Millennium Falcon at light-speed effect.

Foam

A powerful bubble generator. This functions similarly to the other particle generators, but has options for displaying your environment as reflections in the bubbles, and using a layer as a flow map, which uses whites for a faster flow and blacks for a stickier flow.

Particle Playground

Another fantastically fun particle effect, but the most complex one. This one lets you generate particles from either a canon (a single point) or a grid (a wide surface area). Adding a mask on the same layer as the effect lets you use it as a wall, which your particles can bounce off of. Finally, you can set any layer to be a map for just about any property, giving you complete control over how your particles are affected. Use the Persistent Property Mapper to set permanent values for particles, and the Ephemeral Property Mapper to have particles change based on their current position relative to the map.

Shatter

This effect subdivides your image into many small shapes based off of preset patterns, and automatically explodes them outward based on the settings under Force. This effect defaults to a preview of the effect under View, but make sure to change this to Rendered before export. Also note that this effect will always start on frame 1 of your layer, so you'll likely need to precomp your layer so it begins at the desired time.

Wave World

Many effects use another layer to define an attribute, such as a Displacement Map using a layer's brightness to control the amount of displacement. Wave World is meant to generate one of those maps, but does so by emulating the physics of waves to produce a black-and-white output. Use the Wireframe Preview to check out what the waves look like, and turn it into a usable map by switching the View to Height Map.

Effects

3D

Special Tools & Features

Expressions

The Interface & Editing

Animation

Text

Shapes, Masks & Mattes

Effects

Stylize

"Artistic" effects meant to emulate different mediums.

Brush Strokes

Cartoon

CC Block Load

CC Burn Film

CC Glass

CC HexTile

CC Kaleida

CC Mr. Smoothie

CC Plastic

CC RepeTile

CC Threshold

CC Threshold RGB

CC Vignette

Color Emboss

Effects

3D

Special Tools
& Features

Expressions

The Interface & Editing

Animation

Text

Shapes, Masks & Mattes

Effects

Emboss

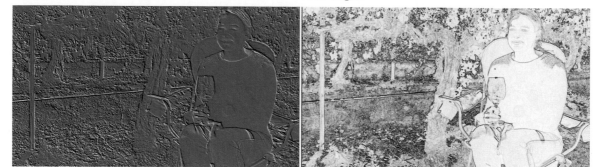

Find Edges

Glow

Mosaic

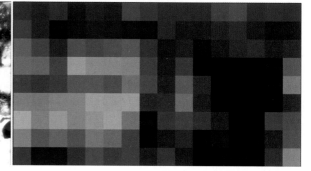

Motion Tile

Posterize

Roughen Edges

Scatter

Texturize

Brush Strokes
Averages pixels into streaks.

Cartoon
This effect has two components. Fill groups similar areas and colorizes them with a limited palate, replacing detail with blobs of color. Stroke looks for edges, then renders them as a black line. You can choose to use either or both components.

CC Block Load
This effect emulates how jpegs load on your grandma's computer that's still running Netscape on Windows 95.

CC Burn Film
Like holding a lighter under a photograph, except this effect doesn't produce harmful vapors.

CC Glass
Emulates stained glass, displacing based off this or another layer's brightness.

CC HexTile
Turns your footage into the strangest Settlers of Catan map. This effect offers some fun kaleidiscopic options.

CC Kaleida
After Effects' most psychedelic effect, this one emulates looking through a kaleidescope and has many different options to play with.

CC Mr. Smoothie
I like to imagine Mr. Smoothie is the nemesis to the Kool-Aid Guy. His effect blobs your image and phases the colors through it.

CC Plastic
Shrink-wraps your footage for plastic shine.

CC RepeTile
Repeats your footage outward, with a few options for flipping the duplicates.

CC Threshold
Converts your image to high-contrast black and white, with a slider to control where the black or white point lands. This effect is more powerful than the other Threshold effect, as it can also operate on your RGB channels.

CC Threshold RGB
Same as above, but you can control the thresholds for each color channel individually.

Effects

3D

Special Tools & Features

Expressions

The Interface & Editing

Animation

Text

Shapes, Masks & Mattes

Effects

CC Vignette
Darkens the edges of your image, which is a nice way to draw the eye to your image's center. This effect will likely work best on an Adjustment Layer.

Color Emboss
Emulates shadows catching a 3D relief.

Emboss
Similar to the one above, but the main elements are gray.

Find Edges
Renders the high-contrast areas of your image.

Glow
"Making it glow" is one of the client requests that we motion designers hear all too often. Glow is basically an additive Blend Mode and blurs over a brightness threshold.

Mosaic
Great for pixelization.

Motion Tile
Shrinks your image down to a repeating tile, which can be offset with Phase.

Posterize
Posterize reduces the amount of color stops in an image.

Roughen Edges
Makes your image a little rough around the edges.

Scatter
Moves your pixels to a random nearby location.

Strobe Light
Periodically replaces your image with a solid color.

Texturize
Uses another layer as a texture.

Threshold
A more limited version of CC Threshold.

Text
Simple yet limited ways of generating counting numbers on-screen.

Numbers
Upon applying this effect, you'll be prompted to pick Font, Style, Direction, and Alignment—none of which can be changed later. However, you are then able to create an animated counter by keyframing number values.

The limitations of Font and Style are frustrating. It's far preferable to parent the Slider Control effect to a text layer's Source Text. This process is outlined in chapter 8 of the Compendium.

490

Timecode
Generates on-screen timecode.

Time

Effects capable of looking forward and backward on the timeline and affecting images with time-based effects.

CC Force Motion Blur

CC Wide Time

Echo

Time Difference

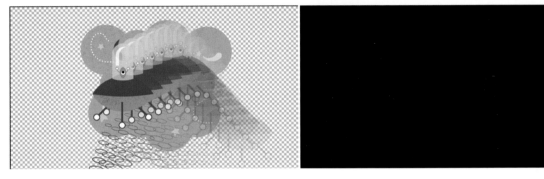

Time Displacement

In this example, I used a vertical gradient over the subject's face as the **Time Displacement Layer**, so the center of her face borrows pixels from the future, and the effect dissipates outward.

Effects

3D

Special Tools
& Features

Expressions

The Interface
& Editing

Animation

Text

Shapes, Masks
& Mattes

Effects

CC Force Motion Blur

After Effects' built-in motion blur is only capable of analyzing keyframes. CC Force Motion Blur looks at visual changes between frames and draws its own motion blur. This is helpful for effects like Shatter, which won't otherwise display motion blur.

CC Force Motion Blur will generally ignore effects placed above it, so you'll likely need to precomp any effects before applying this one.

Pixel Motion Blur is a nearly identical effect, but it runs faster than this one.

CC Wide Time

This effect blends frames before and after the current one into your image.

Echo

This effect can bring frames before or after the previous one into your composition. I find it works best if the layer has an interesting alpha channel, so you can see the previous iterations of the image trailing behind it.

Pixel Motion Blur

This effect is very similar to CC Force Motion Blur, but will likely render faster.

Posterize Time

Lowers the frame rate of your footage.

Time Difference

Compares two frames—either on a different layer or at a different time on the current layer—and only displays pixels that have changed between the two.

Time Displacement

Think back to the Displacement Map effect, which shifts pixels based off another layer's brightness. Time Displacement borrows the pixels from another time, based on another layer's brightness. Whites in the Time Displacement Layer borrow pixels from the time as defined by Max Displacement Time. This can be used to produce a slit-scan effect.

Timewarp

This is a complex effect that gives you total control over a clip's speed. With it, you can easily keyframe a clip to speed up or slow down. When slowing a clip down, you can introduce a Method to generate new frames to keep your footage playing smoothly. Pixel Motion analyzes your image and creates new frames, and Frame Mix fades between the outermost whole frames.

Transitions

These control how images enter or leave the frame. While these all need to be manually keyframed to be used as classic transitions, the Presets menu has some automatically key-framed for you.

Block Dissolve

Card Wipe

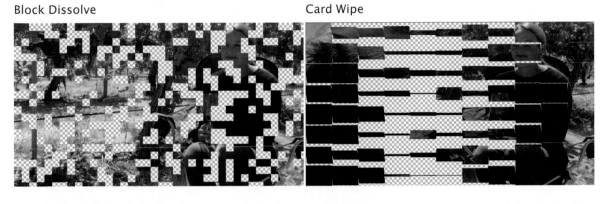

CC Glass Wipe

CC Grid Wipe

CC Image Wipe

CC Jaws

Effects

3D

Special Tools & Features

Expressions

The Interface & Editing

Animation

Text

Shapes, Masks & Mattes

Effects

CC Light Wipe

CC Line Sweep

CC Radial Scale Wipe

CC Scale Wipe

CC Twister

CC WarpoMatic

Iris Wipe

Linear Wipe

Radial Wipe   Venetian Blinds

Block Dissolve

Transitions with random blocks. You can control the size and softness of the blocks.

Card Wipe

Very similar to Card Dance, but designed around the cards flipping from one layer to the effect's Back Layer.

CC Glass Wipe

Similar to CC Glass, but the threshold of the effect is animated to reveal the Layer to Reveal.

CC Grid Wipe

Transitions by manipulating your image in a grid pattern.

CC Image Wipe

Allows you to create your own transition pattern by designating a channel from another layer.

CC Jaws

Is it shark week already?

CC Light Wipe

There are a few shapes to choose from, but the takeaway is the bright glow around the transition.

Venetian Blinds

Equal-sized slits that all open simultaneously.

CC Line Sweep

Staggered lines.

CC Radial Scale Wipe

A circle with distortion around the edges.

CC Scale Wipe

Stretches your image in a direction. This one is controlled by animating the Center point.

CC Twister

Twists an image around a center point to reveal the Backside layer.

CC WarpoMatic

Blends and distorts between two layers.

Gradient Wipe

Similar to CC Image Wipe.

Iris Wipe

The classic sitcom ending.

Linear Wipe

A simple crop.

Radial Wipe

I like to use this transition for animating pie graphs.

Effects

3D

Special Tools & Features

Expressions

Utility

Less-than-creative effects meant to solve practical problems.

Apply Color LUT

Identical to applying a LUT with Lumetri.

CC Overbrights

If you have RAW footage that exceeds maximum brightness levels, this effect can colorize your whites.

Cineon Converter

Cineon is a file format commonly used when digitizing film negatives.

Color Profile Converter

Converts your footage into a different color profile, such as Rec.709, sRGB, or ACES.

Grow Bounds

If a precomp contains an image that is cropped by the boundaries of the precomp dimensions, this utility can expand the edges of that precomp.

HDR Compander

You may have noticed the little icons next to effects that look like this: 8 16 32 . These numbers represent the bit depth on which the effect can operate. Since most footage is 8-bit, you can likely ignore this. However, if you're working with 32-bit HDR footage, some effects won't operate on the higher values. This utility compresses HDR footage into 8- or 16-bit for the purpose of applying effects to it.

HDR Highlight Compression

Lowers the values of highlights in HDR footage so they're within the visible range.

Layer Styles

Somehow, there's still more. Layer Styles are similar to regular effects, but they work somewhat differently. First off, these are identical to Photoshop's Layer Styles. In fact, if you import a Photoshop document with Layer Styles and select Editable Layer Styles, you can further manipulate the styles created in Photoshop, in After Effects.

Secondly, Layer Styles are applied after all other effects and masks. So if you want to continuously render a stroke around a masked image with the Roughen Edges effect applied, the Stroke Layer Style will draw the stroke *after* the layer has processed the other effects. However, this also means that Layer Styles are applied after motion blur, which can sometimes create some undesirable blobs. You don't want to draw a stroke around your motion blur!

Applying a Layer Style

To apply a Layer Style, right-click a layer and choose one from Layer Styles. You can then edit the Layer Style by unfurling the layer's triangle.

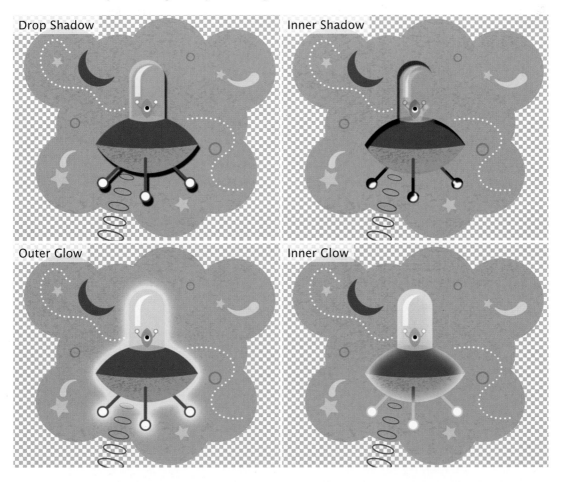

Effects

3D

Special Tools & Features

Expressions

The Interface
& Editing

Animation

Text

Shapes, Masks
& Mattes

Effects

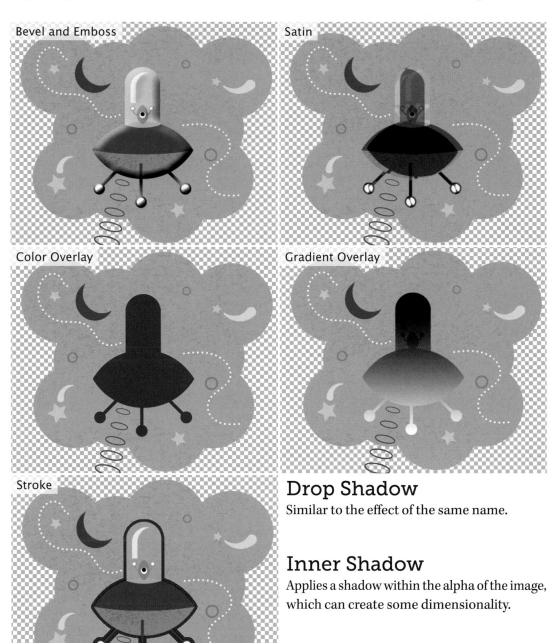

Drop Shadow
Similar to the effect of the same name.

Inner Shadow
Applies a shadow within the alpha of the image, which can create some dimensionality.

Outer Glow
Similar to the Glow effect, but this one uses a glow color (or gradient) of your choosing.

Inner Glow
Applies a glow within the alpha of the image.

Bevel and Emboss

There are five different options to create a 3D relief effect.

Satin

This style creates two duplicates of your original image and overlays both with a Blend Mode. All of this is contained within the original alpha boundary of your image.

Color Overlay

Similar to the Fill effect. You can utilize a Blend Mode with the color and lower its opacity.

Gradient Overlay

Similar to the Color Overlay, but using a linear or radial gradient. Combining this with a Multiply Blend Mode creates some shading on your graphic.

Stroke

Outlines the alpha boundary of your image with a color.

Effects

3D

Special Tools & Features

Expressions

6 3D

Let's set some expectations. "True" 3D software (such as Cinema 4D, Maya, or Blender) can create just about anything imaginable in a fully fleshed-out, three-dimensional interface. After Effects' 3D capability is affectionately referred to as "2.5D," since it's not nearly as robust as the software mentioned above.

That said, After Effects is great at 3D-ifying 2D assets, in which 2D objects can be positioned like postcards in 3D space, creating the illusion of depth. Activating 3D also enables lights, cameras, and a plethora of other advanced features.

Image by Emanuele Mara
https://www.behance.net/MaraniEmanue
Used with permissi

3D Basics

To utilize 3D features, we must first convert a layer to a 3D layer. Doing so is simple. Select the Enable 3D Layer Switch from the switches portion of the timeline.

3D Position

The main difference between a 2D and 3D object is the ability to move in three dimensions. 2D layers can be moved about the X (horizontal) and Y (vertical) axes; 3D layers can be moved about the X, Y, and Z (depth) axes.

As per usual, X and Y movement for a 3D object can be achieved by clicking and dragging the image within the Composition panel. However, 3D objects also have the 3D gizmo, an object that enables movement in all three axes. Select a 3D object to see the gizmo.

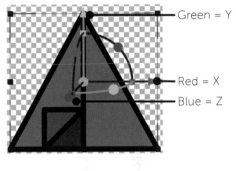

Green = Y

Red = X
Blue = Z

Clicking and dragging the red arrow moves about the X-axis, green moves about the Y, and the new blue arrow moves about the Z-axis.

The stacking order of layers in the timeline isn't as important with 3D layers (unless 2D layers are also present—see "Interactions with 2D Layers," page 363). With 3D, the layer with the lowest Z position will be viewed on top of layers with higher Z positions. **Remember**: Low Z values bring the object toward you; high Z values, away.

Also keep in mind that position values are now represented by three values—again, X, Y, and now Z, in that order.

#	Layer Name	⊕ ✳ ↘ ⨍ 🖪 ◎ ◐ ⊗
1	⭐ tent	⊕ ✳ / ▢ ⊗
	○ Position	242.6,855.8,0.0

3D Orientation and Rotation

3D rotation is where things start to get fun. Default 2D rotation actually rotates about the Z-axis. Picture a pen tip touching your computer screen. Objects rotate about the tip of the pen, and the pen is pointing toward you, in Z space. With 3D enabled, we can now rotate about the X and Y axes as well. Rotating about the X-axis is like sticking a pen in the side of an object, where it can now bow to and away from you. Rotating about the Y-axis—probably the most useful of the bunch—is like sticking a pen in the top of an object, and having it rotate around it, like a spinning ballerina. To rotate about any of these axes, click the ball in the midpoint of the rotation handles of the gizmo.

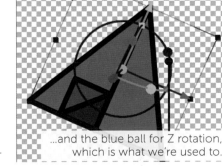

Click and drag the red ball for X rotation...

the green ball for Y rotation...

...and the blue ball for Z rotation, which is what we're used to.

3D

Special Tools & Features

Expressions

Orientation vs. Rotation

There are actually two ways to rotate a 3D object. With a layer selected in the timeline, tapping R reveals both Orientation and Rotation properties.

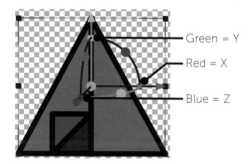

Both controls can orient a 3D object. However, the Orientation control is a single keyframe for all three dimensions. This is useful when you want an object to look around and move about all three axes at once. X, Y, and Z Rotation are all controlled by individual keyframes. These are useful if you want an object to move about only a single axis at a time, such as a gas station's spinning sign. I recommend choosing one or the other—it can get confusing if two keyframes contradict one another.

Note that manipulating the gizmo changes Orientation by default. If you select the Wotate tool (W), you'll see an option in the Toolbar to decide whether the tool sets Orientation or Rotation.

Scaling

While we now have three dimensions about which we can scale an object, scaling about the Z-axis doesn't really do anything, as objects will remain as flat postcards (for now, anyway). Take note that we can scale a 3D object by clicking and dragging the colored boxes near the arrows of the gizmo.

Green = Y
Red = X
Blue = Z

Gizmo Options

With both a 3D layer and the Selection tool selected, we can view some options in the Toolbar for how the gizmo works.

Local, World, and View Axis
Universal, Position, Scale, and Rotation gizmo styles

Local, World, and View Axes

By default, Local Axis is selected ⊼. This means that your gizmo is aligned to your object. If you rotate the object, the gizmo rotates as well, with the Z-axis pointing wherever the object is facing.

World Axis ⊼ keeps the gizmo oriented so that Z is pointing toward you, even if the object is rotated. This is helpful when you want a rotated object to move about your scene's X, Y, and Z coordinates.

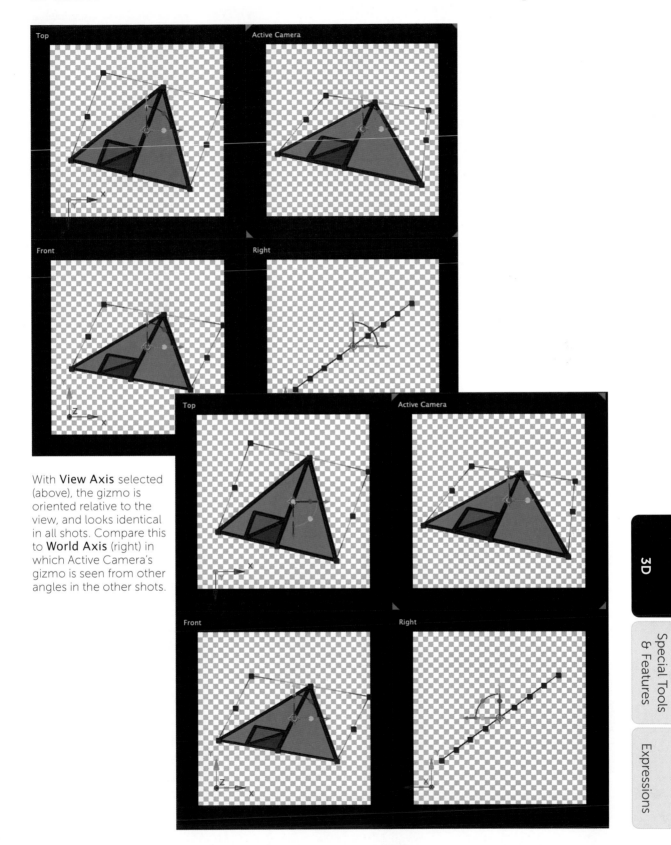

With **View Axis** selected (above), the gizmo is oriented relative to the view, and looks identical in all shots. Compare this to **World Axis** (right) in which Active Camera's gizmo is seen from other angles in the other shots.

Special Tools & Features

Expressions

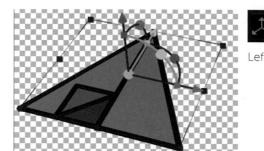

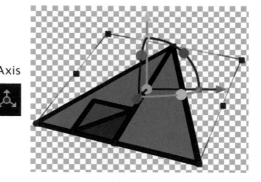

Left: **Local Axis**
Right: **World Axis**

If you're looking at multiple views (described in the next section), the orientation of the gizmo in Active Camera will look different in each shot. However, with View Axis selected , each view will display the gizmo in its own world axis. X is horizontal, Y is vertical, and Z is depth, relative to each view. See previous page.

Gizmo Styles

The default Universal Gizmo Style can manipulate position, rotation, and scale of your 3D object, depending on which part of the gizmo is selected. This tool is also the default when the Selection tool is selected (with V). If you want control over just one of these parameters, you can choose from another gizmo style.

The Position gizmo style displays handles that can easily move your object diagonally, about the XY, YZ, and XZ axes. This can quickly be called up with the hotkey 4.

The Scale gizmo style displays handles so you can scale simultaneously about the XY, YZ, and XZ axes. This can quickly be called up with the hotkey 5.

The Rotation gizmo style displays handles for easy access to rotation. This can quickly be called up with the hotkey 6.

Position gizmo style   **Scale** gizmo style   **Rotation** gizmo style

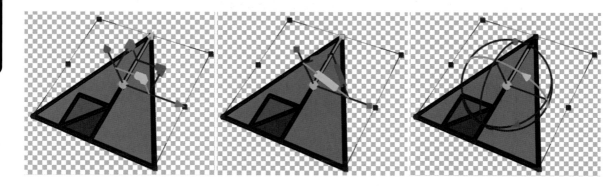

Interactions with 2D Layers

Got both 2D and 3D layers? That's fine. Just note that After Effects will process 3D layers from the top down as a whole unit. As soon at it spots a 2D layer in the stack, it stops processing the 3D, processes the 2D, then goes back to processing the other layers. You can think of a group of stacked 3D layers as a bin. In fact, bins are now visualized in the timeline.

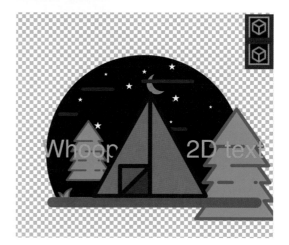

In this example, the 2D layer sits between two sections of 3D layers. Notice the boxes drawn around groups of 3D cubes. So, After Effects will process the tent and the ground as one block of data, then render the text, then the trees, bush, and sky. The scene looks like this:

Notice how the ground sits *above* the foreground tree, even though it's further away from the camera! That's because the introduction of the 2D layer segregates the other 3D layers, and establishes an order of how After Effects processes. Pay attention to how the boxes around your 3D layers are grouped to avoid confusion.

3D

Special Tools
& Features

Expressions

The Interface & Editing

Animation

Text

Shapes, Masks & Mattes

Effects

3D

The 3D Interface

When it comes to working with 3D, After Effects has some options to make your life easier. By having at least one 3D layer in your composition, you'll see the following options in the lower-right of the Composition panel:

Toggle **Draft 3D**   Change renderer   View options

Draft 3D   Classic 3D   ∨   Active Camera   ∨   1 View   ∨

Draft 3D

If your big 3D composition is previewing slowly, toggling Draft 3D can help. Not only does it use a faster, lower-quality render algorithm, but this feature temporarily disables lights, shadows, and camera depth of field.

With Draft 3D enabled, you can also toggle the Ground Plane by selecting the corresponding button ⊞. This is a helpful user interface feature that allows you to align objects to the ground and keep your bearings while moving around in three dimensions.

Also within Draft 3D is the Extended Viewer, toggled by pressing the corresponding button ▣. This lets you view elements outside of the composition's frame boundaries. Click and hold on the icon to bring up an interface to change the opacity of the outside elements.

Without **Extended Viewer**   With **Extended Viewer**

Change Renderer

By default, 3D in After Effects uses the Classic 3D renderer, which is a relatively fast and straight-forward algorithm, but it does have some limitations. Switching the renderer to the Cinema 4D renderer unlocks more features, but disables others. See "The Cinema 4D Renderer" (page 380).

View Options

By default, the Composition panel displays the Active Camera, which is what you'll see upon export. If your scene has a Camera layer, the Active Camera is what your camera sees—otherwise, it's just your regular-old view of the scene.

Clicking on the 3D View Popup (that is, the text that currently says Active Camera) allows you to change what you see in the Composition panel. You can choose from Front, Left, Top, Back, Right, and Bottom views to view your scene from alternate angles. So, if you're displacing layers about the Z-axis, switching to the Top or Right views might give you a better sense of how far back your layers are being pushed.

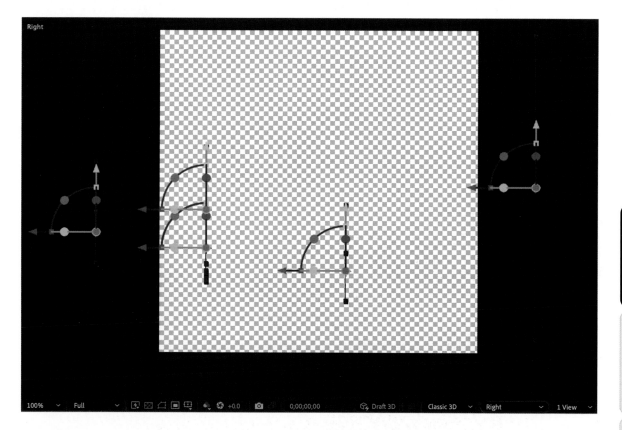

Note that you can use the camera controls to reposition these views as if they were cameras, but these cameras cannot be orbited. See "Cameras" (page 367).

This menu also contains Custom Views. By default, these are presets that view your scene from alternate angles. Using the camera controls, you can change the angles of view as if the Custom Views were cameras. See "Cameras" (page 367).

3D

Special Tools & Features

Expressions

If you're viewing an angle that you like and want to convert it into a camera so you can render from that angle, select Create Camera from 3D View from this same drop-down.

Multiple Views

Computer monitors are 2D, so it can be difficult to accurately tell where an object is moving in 3D. However, by viewing from multiple angles at once, we're able to catch any perspective errors before they happen. As such, it's a great idea to bring up more than one view at a time. Do so with the Select View Layout drop-down that reads 1 View by default, and choose from 2 or 4 Views.

Each view has its own view controls. By selecting a view in the Composition panel (a selected view has blue corners ◥) you can change the view angle, move the camera, toggle Draft 3D, or toggle the Ground Plane per view.

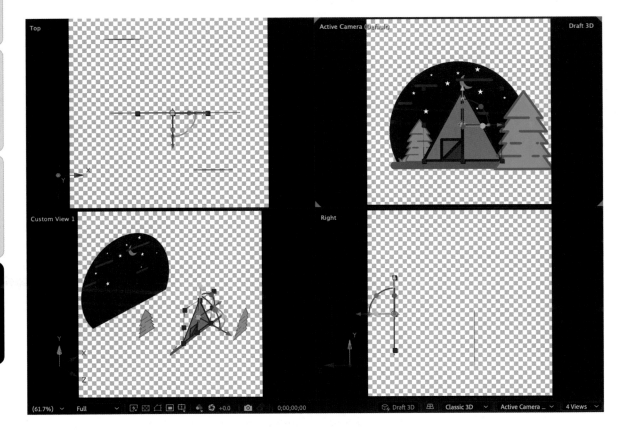

The Interface
& Editing

Animation

Text

Shapes, Masks
& Mattes

Effects

3D

Cameras

When using 3D layers, you have the option to add a camera. This is a quick and powerful way to move through your 3D scene and show off that excellent parallax you've created, or simply to "pan" over your layers. Note that only 3D objects are affected by cameras; 2D layers will appear normally.

Create a Camera

Add a camera to your composition with Layer > New > Camera. You'll be presented with a Camera Settings dialog box.

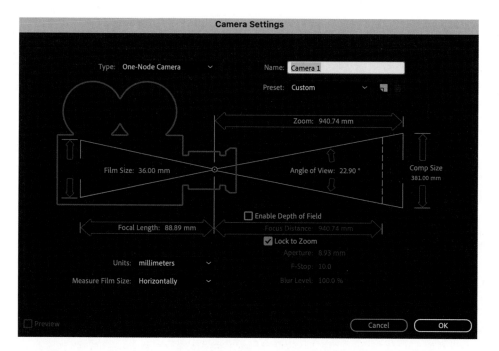

I tend not to worry about this screen, since all of these options can be changed later, and the default settings generally place and frame a camera identical to your composition's default view. Access this dialog box a second time by selecting the camera, then going to Layer > Camera Settings. We'll get to these in a minute in "Camera Options" (page 370).

With a camera created, note that it appears as a layer in the timeline, but obviously functions quite differently from other layers, as it's not a visible object. Toggling the layer's visibility temporarily removes the camera from your scene.

One-Node vs. Two-Node Cameras

One important decision to think about when creating a camera is deciding whether to create a One- or Two-Node Camera. A One-Node Camera is simpler and has more freedom. Picture a camera operator who can freely move around the scene and point the camera any which way.

3D

Special Tools & Features

Expressions

A Two-Node Camera consists of two parts, a camera and a Point of Interest. The camera is always oriented toward (that is, looking at) the Point of Interest. Picture a string coming from the camera operator's belly button that is always fixated on an object. While more restrictive, this restriction can be a benefit if you always want your camera to be viewing an object.

Moving the Camera

Now that there's a camera in the scene, you can move it around and view your 3D objects from different angles. First, make sure your composition view is set to Active Camera to look through the camera's lens. Or, view the scene from multiple angles by using one of the multiple view options, above.

1	Camera 1	
⌄ Transform		Reset
⏱ Point of Interest		540.0,540.0,0.0
⏱ Position		540.0,540.0,-2666.7
⏱ Orientation		0.0°,0.0°,0.0°
⏱ X Rotation		0x+0.0°
⏱ Y Rotation		0x+0.0°
⏱ Z Rotation		0x+0.0°

First off, note that cameras have Position and Orientation/Rotation controls in the timeline, just like any other 3D layer. This is one way we can move the camera, and is a great place for keyframing to add camera movement.

When using a Two-Node Camera, you'll notice 3D position controls for the camera's Point of Interest here as well.

You can also directly move a camera when viewing the scene from any angle other than Active Camera. The camera appears as a pink cube with a cone emanating from it, representing its field of view (that is, the things it can see). Cameras have their own gizmo, so you can move it around like any other 3D object. You can also move the Point of Interest with the Selection tool.

However, the simplest and quickest way to move a camera is with the Camera tools, found in the Toolbar. Cycle through the Camera tools by pressing C multiple times, or with 1, 2, and 3.

The Orbit Tool—One-Node Camera

With the Orbit tool selected, clicking and dragging within the Composition panel changes what the camera is looking at. It's as if the camera person's feet are planted, and they're moving the camera around, like that video you took of Niagara Falls that you'll never watch.

While the Orbit tool is selected, the Toolbar shows a few more options.

Freeform allows you to look in any direction, Constrain Horizontally allows you to orbit only about the Y-axis (which makes you look left and right) and Constrain Vertically allows you to orbit only about the X-axis (which makes you look up and down).

Note that the Orbit tool affects a camera's Orientation, not Rotation. Furthermore, the Orbit tool doesn't do a lot with rotating a camera about the Z-axis, which is akin to cocking your head sideways to create what's called a Dutch angle. Since this is less common, you can achieve this by manually adjusting a camera's Z Orientation in the timeline.

The Orbit Tool—Two-Node Camera

The Orbit tool is extremely useful with a Two-Node Camera, as it can orbit about the Point of Interest to have the camera fixate on a certain object. This happens by default when using the Orbit tool and a Two-Node Camera.

Clicking on the Orbit tool icon in the Toolbar reveals a few more options, some of which may be useful with a Two-Node Camera. You can also cycle through these options with shift-1.

With a Two-Node Camera, Orbit Around Cursor and Orbit Around Camera POI pretty much do the same thing—Two-Node Cameras default to orbiting around a camera's Point of Interest in either case. Orbit Around Scene does just that, utilizing the center of the 3D Ground Plane as the scene's center.

The Pan Tool—One-Node Camera

There's an ongoing joke in the film-making community that clients call all camera movements "pans," even when they're not (a pan is a horizontal orbit). Embarrassingly, the Pan tool doesn't really pan either—it moves the camera's position about the X- and Y-axes, as if the camera operator is moving left, right, up, or down. Click and drag within the Composition panel with the Pan tool selected to change the camera's X and Y position.

The Pan Tool—Two-Node Camera

With a Two-Node Camera, the Pan tool will move the Point of Interest *and* the camera. There are two options for this tool, which you can access by clicking on the icon in the Toolbar, or cycling through them with shift-2.

The distinction here is subtle, and won't likely matter too much. The default Pan Under Cursor tool reads, "Pan speed changes relative to the cursor hit point." The Pan Under Cursor POI tool reads, "Pan speed remains constant relative to the Point of Interest."

The Dolly Tool—One-Node Camera

Since the Pan tool moves the camera about the X- and Y-axes, a click and drag with the Dolly tool must then move the camera about the Z-axis, moving it closer to and farther from the action.

The Dolly Tool—Two-Node Camera

With a Two-Node Camera, the Dolly tool moves the camera toward and away from the Point of Interest. Again, we have three tool options that can be cycled through with shift-3.

Dolly Towards Cursor Tool	3, Shift+3
Dolly to Cursor Tool	3, Shift+3
Dolly to Camera POI Tool	3, Shift+3

These distinctions are quite subtle. The Dolly Towards Cursor tool reads "Dolly towards the cursor hit point and away from the center of the composition." The Dolly to Cursor tool reads "Dolly towards and away from the cursor hit point." The Dolly to Camera POI tool reads "Dolly towards and away from the camera's point of interest."

Classic Camera Mode

In ye olde days of After Effects, the camera worked differently. It was one tool to rule them all—a single camera control that changed based on which mouse button you pressed. You can still access this mode by simply holding option/alt (provided you have at least one 3D layer in your composition). Holding option/alt and dragging the left mouse button orbits the camera; option/alt and dragging the right mouse button dollys the camera; option/alt and dragging the middle mouse button (pressing the scroll wheel, provided your mouse has one) pans the camera.

Camera Options

Camera options can be controlled either in the Camera Settings dialog or in the timeline by unfurling the Camera Layer's triangle and selecting Camera Options.

Zoom

Zoom is linked to a camera's Focal Length and Angle of View. You can adjust any of these settings in the Camera Settings dialog, but just the Zoom is available for adjustment in the timeline's Camera Options. However, controlling any controls all three.

The lower the Zoom, the lower the Focal Length, and the wider the Angle of View. That is to say that by lowering the Zoom, you can see more stuff in the camera, and expand the pink cone of view. A lower Zoom value also exaggerates distance, so if the depth of your scene isn't quite popping, you can try lowering the Zoom and bringing the camera closer to the action to compensate. Conversely, a higher Zoom will flatten the look of your scene. This is how Alfred Hitchcock's famous *Vertigo* shot was created—by lowering the amount of zoom and dollying the camera in at the same time, the background seems to recede from the character, while the character stays fixed in place.

At right, a low **Zoom** and a camera close to the action exaggerates the scene's depth.

At left, a high **Zoom** and the camera far away lessens the scene's depth.

Depth of Field

This effect emulates a camera's ability to keep some objects in focus and others out of focus. It's a great way to give your scene film-like depth. It's off by default, so be sure to switch it on here.

Once Depth of Field is enabled, there are several other settings to keep in mind. You can change the Focus Distance to tell the camera which object ought to be in focus. The focus plane is visible when the camera is selected in an alternate view, which makes aligning to an object much easier.

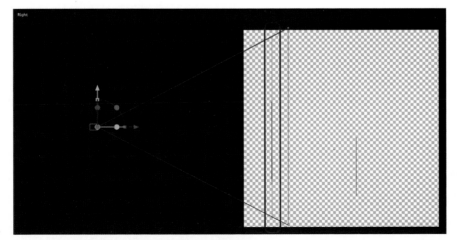

There are a few other tools to help get things in focus. Right-clicking a camera layer and selecting Camera reveals some options. Link Focus Distance to Point of Interest does just that— your camera will always be focused on the Point of Interest. With a camera and another layer selected, you can either do a one-time Set Focus Distance to Layer, or Link Focus Distance to

Layer. By linking focus distance to a null object, you can easily animate the focus in your scene, allowing for realistic camera rack focuses.

Increase the Aperture to decrease the Depth of Field—that is, the area in which things are in focus. High Aperture = low Depth of Field = a thin plane where things are in focus = your in-focus objects are in focus and your out-of-focus objects are very out of focus. You can then further the amount of blur applied with Blur Level.

While the default camera blur settings work great for most purposes, you can tweak what your camera blur looks like further. Doing so can introduce bokeh, which are blurry shapes caused by bright objects in your scene.

If you want to get bokeh going on, you should first change the Iris Shape. The default, Fast Rectangle, is great because it uses less computation time, but it doesn't produce great bokeh. Choose from one of the shapes in the drop-down. Most camera bokeh is octagonal, but you can go more round. However, the more sides, the slower the render time.

It's unlikely that you can see bokeh at this point. You'll likely need to dial down Highlight Threshold until some highlights in your screen are included—only objects within this threshold will produce bokeh. You can bump up the brights with Highlight Gain, and introduce Saturation if you wish.

Now that we're cooking with bokeh, you can further adjust the look of it with Iris Shape, Rotation, Roundness, Aspect Ratio, and Diffraction Fringe (edge hardness). These are somewhat more prominent on the triangle- and square-shaped bokeh.

Not seeing it? Make sure Draft 3D is off, as it will disable this entire section. This can be a boon, as depth of field and bokeh effects will tank your render times.

Lights

Lights are another optional component of the 3D work-space, but they can dramatically change the look of your scene. Note that only 3D objects are affected by lights; 2D layers will appear normally. If you wish to use lights on 2D objects, check out the CC Spotlight effect.

Creating a Light

Add a light to your scene with Layer > New > Light. You'll see the dialog at right.

These options can all be changed later, either in Layer > Light Settings or by unfurling the layer's triangle and selecting Light Options. For now, let's look at the four types of light that can be created, and the properties unique to those lights.

Spot Light

A Spot light is perhaps the most intuitive light. Like a camera, it points in a direction and casts light in a cone. The position and angle are both important to getting the light to hit just where you want. You can control where the light points either by selecting a Point of Interest, just like a Two-Node Camera, or with its Orientation.

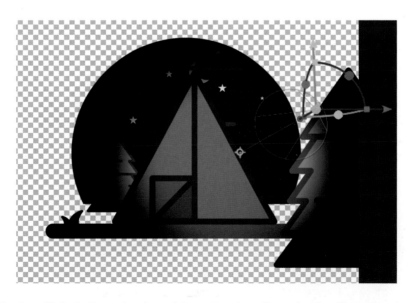

Unique to the Spot light is Cone Angle and Cone Feather. Cone Angle affects the size of the light hitting the scene. Control the softness of the Spot light's edge with Cone Feather.

3D

Special Tools & Features

Expressions

Parallel Light

A Parallel light will illuminate everything in your scene from a certain angle. You can think of it as a massive Spot light, with an infinitely wide cone. This is most commonly used for sunlight, when your whole scene needs to be lit from a single source. You can control the light's position and Point of Interest.

Point Light

Like a single light bulb floating in your scene, a Point light emanates light outward in all directions. You can control only its position, since this light doesn't need to be pointed in any particular direction.

Ambient Light

An Ambient light illuminates everything in your scene evenly. It doesn't use position at all, since everything is affected. If I've added a single Spot light that's creating dark areas that aren't illuminated at all, an Ambient light can bring up those darks. Or, bring an Ambient light's Intensity to the negative to darken a scene with too many hot lights.

Using an **Ambient** light at 50% **Intensity** plus a **Spot** light, I'm able to lighten areas unlit by the **Spot** light.

Common Light Attributes

All lights have an Intensity (that is, brightness) value and Color, which can be used to cast warmth, coolness, or a vivid style to your scene. Having multiple Spot lights with varying colors within a palette can look super nifty. Also note that Intensity can be cranked into negative values—meaning you can use lights to darken parts of your scene.

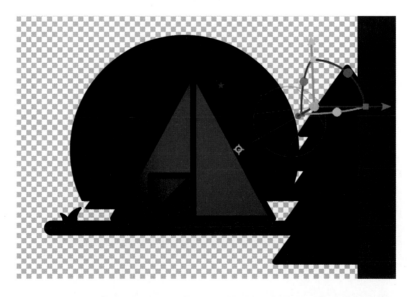

By default, the light from a Spot, Parallel, or Point light will travel infinitely into your scene. By giving it a Falloff, you can have the light travel only to a certain distance. Choose one of

3D

Special Tools & Features

Expressions

the two Falloff algorithms, either Smooth or Inverse Square Clamped. Smooth evenly feathers your light's intensity from the start to the Falloff Distance. Inverse Square Clamped keeps your light's value consistent within the Radius, but feathers it from the edge of the Radius to the Falloff Distance.

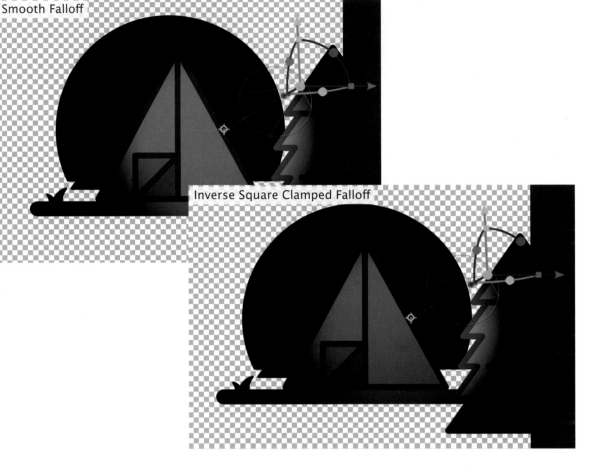

If you want only certain objects to be affected by lights, you can unfurl the affected layer's triangle and select Materials Options> Accepts Lights, then choose Off or On.

Shadows

Lights can also cast shadows—but they might not by default. In order for shadows to appear, three things must be in place:

- Under Light Options, Cast Shadows must be set to On.
- For the layer you want to cast shadows, unfurl its triangle and select Material Options > Cast Shadows > On.
- For the layer you want to receive shadows, unfurl its triangle and select Material Options > Accepts Shadows > On.

Obviously, the layer that is casting shadows must be within the line of sight between the light and the object receiving shadows.

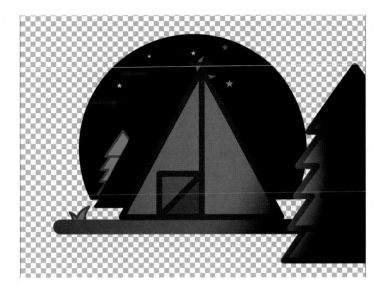

If your shadow is looking a little in-tents (ha, ha), under the Light Options, you can control the Shadow Darkness (that is, its opacity) and Diffusion (edge feathering).

The third option under Cast Shadows is Only, by which an object is invisible, but casts a shadow. Spooky!

Conversely, Accepts Shadows > Only is another option, by which a layer is invisible except for the shadow it receives. This is helpful when compositing 3D objects into footage, and you need a "shadow catcher" to exist just to place shadows in your scene.

If an object is casting a shadow, increasing Light Transmission allows light to "pass through" the object, tinting its shadows with the object's original color.

With my **Shadow Darkness** lowered and **Light Transmission** on the tent cranked up, notice the orange cast to the stars within the tent's shadow.

3D

Special Tools & Features

Expressions

Materials

Let's explore the settings under a 3D layer's Material Options further. These define the ways that light can hit an object.

Ambient controls how much a layer is affected by an Ambient light. With an Ambient light in the scene, you can dial down Ambient to quickly darken individual objects.

If Ambient controls affectivity by Ambient light, think of Diffuse as affectivity by the other three types of light. This one starts at 50%—dialing it down dulls the effect of light hitting the object, but increasing it has the light hitting the object hotter.

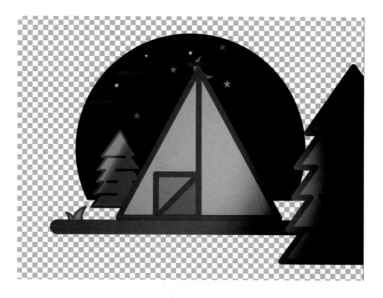

Think of Specular as the shiny part of an object—the small part that bounces off light directly. Increasing Specular Intensity increases the brightness of that light's hot spot. Increasing Specular Shininess makes that hot spot smaller, which gives more of an intense hot spot.

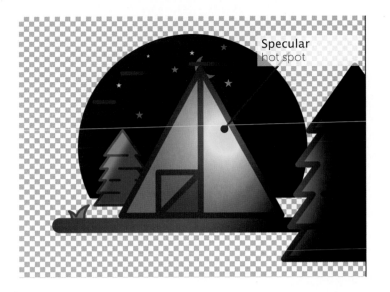

When Metal is set to 100%, the color of the Specular is derived from the color of the layer. When Metal is set to 0%, the color of the Specular is derived from the color of the light.

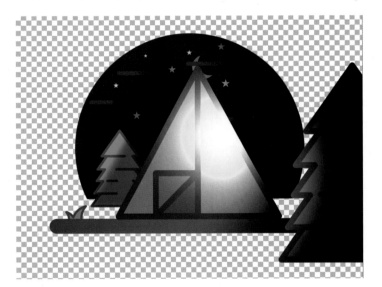

3D

Special Tools & Features

Expressions

The Cinema 4D Renderer

So far, everything we've been working with has utilized After Effect's default Classic 3D renderer, and we've reached the end of its list of features.

However, there is another renderer—that is, a different algorithm for producing 3D—than the Classic 3D. It's called the Cinema 4D renderer, because it uses the same rendering algorithm as the 3D software with the same name. There's a lot that it can do, but there's also quite a bit it can't do. Understanding the differences between the renderers is key to producing the 3D look you want.

Switch renderers with the drop-down in the lower-right of the Composition panel, or in Composition > Composition Settings > 3D Renderer. For the remainder of this chapter, we'll look at features that are only available with the Cinema 4D renderer.

Cinema 4D's Limitations

It's important to note that by enabling the Cinema 4D renderer, the following attributes in your composition will not display:

- Blend Modes
- Track Mattes
- Layer Styles
- Masks and Effects on Continuously Rasterized Layers, Text and Shape Layers, and Collapsed 3D Precompositions
- Preserve Underlying Transparency
- Light Transmission
- Transparency and Index of Refraction
- Accept Shadows Only
- Motion Blur

Yeah, that's a lot. Consider putting attributes that utilize the Cinema 4D renderer in a pre-comp, and any of the above attributes in a top-layer comp that doesn't have the Cinema 4D renderer enabled.

Now that we've gone over what we can't do, let's see what we can do with this renderer.

Reflections

Enabling the Cinema 4D renderer unlocks the ability to add reflections to your scene. These options live within the Material Options within the layer's triangle. Similar to with shadows, each layer has an Appear in Reflections option, allowing you to toggle what appears in reflections and what doesn't. If there are any vampires in your scene, Appear in Reflections ought to be set to Off.

Assuming you have objects set to Appear in Reflections, the second step is to increase an object's Reflection Intensity. This is the amount that objects appear in reflections.

Here, I've added a **Ground Plane** and set its **Reflection Intensity** to 50%, so I can see both the original plane color and the objects reflected in it.

You can adjust the look of your reflected objects with Reflection Sharpness. A value of 100% is a perfect reflection. Lowering this blurs your reflected objects. It's the difference between a reflection in a perfectly polished mirror versus an icy pond.

Reflection Rolloff dictates how deep the reflection goes. A value of 0% shows everything in the reflection; increasing this displays only reflections close to the surface.

Geometry Options

The Cinema 4D renderer also allows shape and text layers to have geometry—that is, actual 3D depth. You can extrude objects in Z space, thereby increasing their bulk and physicality.

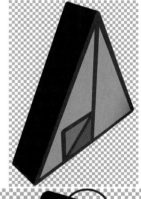

To start, unfurl a layer's triangle, choose Geometry Options, and increase the object's Extrusion Depth.

Bevel refers to the shape of the extrusion's edge. Choose one of the three Bevel Styles: Angular, Concave, and Convex (or None, if you prefer the hard edge). Increase the size of the bevel with Bevel Depth.

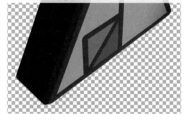
Angular creates a 45° bevel on the edge of the extrusion.

Concave carves into the bevel, as if it's been whittled with a lathe.

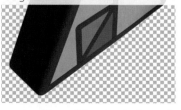
Convex creates a smooth curve on the edge of the extrusion.

If your shape or text has a hole in it, such as the letter A, you can control bevel for the hole with

Hole Bevel Depth. A value of 100% uses the same bevel for the hole as for the rest of the object, and 0% turns off bevel for the object's hole.

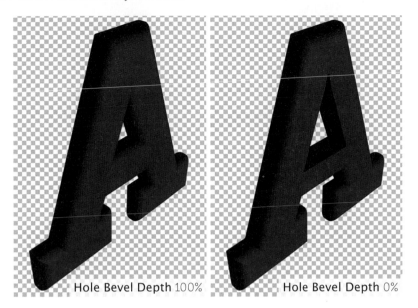

Hole Bevel Depth 100%   Hole Bevel Depth 0%

Render Quality

Geometry, reflections, shadows, lights—After Effects might choke on render times for these, which can be frustrating while you're working. Selecting Renderer Options from the renderer drop-down allows you to change the quality of the Cinema 4D renderer. These changes are the most obvious in shadows and reflections.

It's a good idea to work within the Draft values while working. Before exporting your scene, you should dial up the Quality. A value of 100% might be overkill, but pick a value that produces high-quality shadows and reflections and doesn't cause your graphics card to catch fire.

Going Further with 3D

While After Effects' 3D capabilities offer some great looks, there are certainly limitations to it. Want more 3D? Read on.

Cinema 4D Lite

After Effects comes with a free version of Cinema 4D Lite, a pared-down version of Cinema 4D, which is a fully fledged 3D software in which you can create anything. You can fire it up with File > New > MAXON CINEMA 4D File.

Cinema 4D is a robust piece of software, to say the least. Head to cineversity.com to find the official tutorials to get started.

Export to Cinema 4D

After Effects and Cinema 4D can talk to each other. You can export 3D layers, cameras, and lights from After Effects into Cinema 4D. To do so, select File > Export > Maxon Cinema 4D Exporter. This saves your composition as a Cinema 4D file. Open that sucker up and experience your whole scene in true 3D!

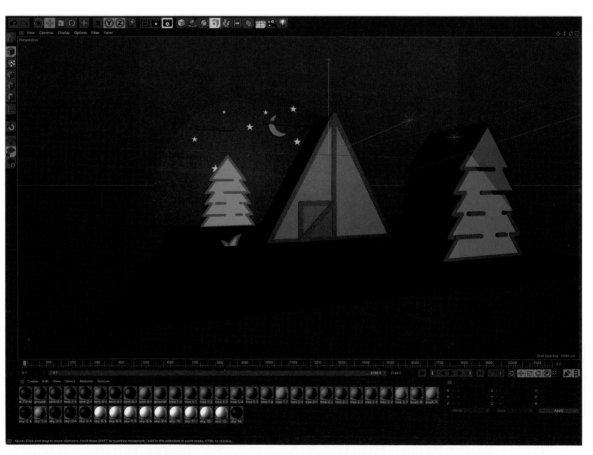

The Interface & Editing

Animation

Text

Shapes, Masks & Mattes

Effects

3D

James Curran of slimjimstudios.com is perhaps the master of the After Effects–to–Cinema 4D workflow. Check out his website to get inspired by 3D-ifying shape layers.

Import from Cinema 4D

You can have a layer in your composition that dynamically links from a Cinema 4D file. Whatever you see in Cinema 4D will be visible in After Effects. You can create a new Cinema 4D project with Layer > New > Maxon Cinema 4D File. Or, import a Cinema 4D scene into the Project panel as you would any other type of file.

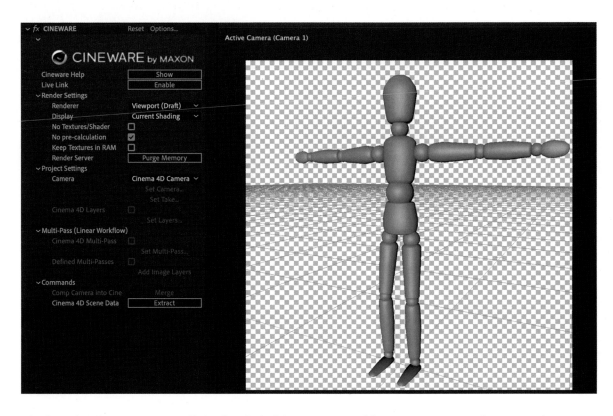

The layer's Effect Controls offer a few helpful options. Enabling Live Link synchronizes the playhead position between the two softwares. You must enable Live Link in both softwares (in Cinema 4D, that's Edit > Preferences > Communication > Live Link > Live Link Enabled at Startup). Under Camera, you can choose whether the scene uses the camera in Cinema 4D, or the one in After Effects.

Element 3D

Element 3D is an awesome plug-in by the great folks at videocopilot.net. This plug-in allows you to import fully 3D models, complete with textures, directly into After Effects. Check out their website for more details.

7 Special Tools & Features

Because "special" sounds so much better than "miscellaneous," we're going to take this chapter to dive into some extra features in After Effects that live on their own. Not quite effects, these are powerful tools that work a little differently than the rest of the software.

The Roto Brush Tool

In video, separating an object from the background is a common yet excruciatingly challenging task. Traditionally, this is done with rotoscoping, a brutally time-consuming process of making masks (yes, like those described in chapter 4) and animating them to match the subject's movement.

The folks at Adobe don't want to watch us suffer, so they've bestowed upon us the Roto Brush tool, a technique for leveraging Adobe's Sensei AI to automatically detect what "stuff" is foreground and what is background. This makes rotoscoping much easier.

Selecting the Subject

Hey, remember the Layer panel? To use this tool, you have to be in the Layer panel, so double-click your footage layer from the timeline to view just that layer in its own panel. This isolates the shot so you're not bothered by effects and other things in your comp.

Select the Roto Brush tool ![icon] from the Toolbar, or hit option–W/Alt–W.

The first step is to tell After Effects what the foreground object is (that is, the thing that you're trying to isolate). This is done by painting a green selection more or less over your object. This does not require precision—the tool looks at similar pixels and automatically includes them in your selection.

To tell the Roto Brush tool what to include, simply click and drag in the Layer panel to include stuff. Try not to select your object's edges.

The Interface & Editing

Animation

Text

Shapes, Masks & Mattes

Effects

3D

Special Tools & Features

I find Alpha Overlay to be very useful, as it really shows the subject separated from the background. With this selected, you're able to change the color and opacity of the overlay.

Propagating
Ready to roto? Let's take a look at the Roto Brush timeline at the bottom of the Layer panel.

| 0f | 02f | 04f | 06f | 08f | 10f | 12f | 14f | 16f | 18f | 20f |

The frame on which you've defined the Roto Brush will look like this: ▮◆▮ . Kind of like a keyframe, right? This means that you've recorded Roto Brush data, and your input is stored in this frame.

The next step is to have After Effects take your input and apply it to subsequent frames. All you have to do is press the spacebar and the Roto Brush tool will work its magic. The tool detects changes and similarities between frames, and does its best to preserve its boundary. Frames that have been processed turn green in the Roto Brush timeline.

If the Roto Brush becomes misaligned or loses track of what it needs to follow, simply navigate to the first frame where the error occurs and correct it with the Roto Brush tool. You'll then need to repropagate the subsequent frames—again, simply by playing the footage. For this reason, it's best to catch mistakes early on.

Freeze and Unfreeze

When you're satisfied with the roto job, the next step is to freeze the calculations. This tells After Effects you're done with propagation, and it will reduce the resources required to process the effect. Do so with the Freeze button ![Freeze]. After it processes, playback on your roto-brushed footage will now be much faster. If you decide you need to go back and refine things, hit the Freeze button again to unfreeze.

Switching back to the Composition panel—we can see that our roto is nearly complete!

Roto Brush Refinement

We're done with the Layer panel for now. Footage that has been roto-brushed contains an effect visible in the Effect Controls panel. This Roto Brush & Refine Edge effect gives you some global controls over the look of your alpha layer.

Special Tools & Features

Expressions

The Interface
& Editing

Animation

Text

Shapes, Masks
& Mattes

Effects

3D

**Special Tools
& Features**

The Brushes Panel

This panel allows you to affect not the paint that's about to appear on-screen, but the brush that applies it.

We start off with some quick presets to choose from, but let's focus on customizing our own. Diameter is the size of the brush. You can change it in this menu, or by holding down ⌘ / Ctrl and clicking and dragging. Most brushes start off circular, but you can make it an ellipse by decreasing Roundness, then adjusting the Angle. Hardness refers to the edge of the brush—decreasing it feathers the brush stroke. While painting, a low Spacing value groups blots close together for a continuous line, while higher numbers space out blots.

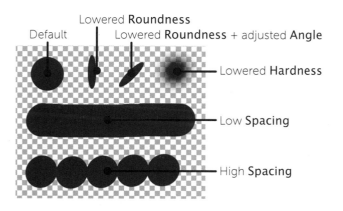

If you're using a stylus to paint, you can set the parameters affected by Pen Pressure, Pen Tilt, and the Stylus Wheel all within the Brush Dynamics category. These can be assigned to your brush's Size, Angle, Roundness, Opacity, and Flow. For example, assigning Opacity to Pen Pressure means a harder pen press makes a more opaque stroke. Now, paint away!

Editing and Animating Brush Strokes

Since After Effects' workflow is entirely nondestructive, you can go back and edit all paint attributes after they've been applied. Select a layer that's been painted on in the timeline, and unfurl its triangle, then unfurl Effects > Paint > Brush to see the parameters for each brush stroke you've added.

Click to edit the brush path
Keyframe brush **Path**
Stroke duration

You can retroactively change all the above attributes, and more. Note that each stroke has its own duration in the timeline, allowing you to lengthen or shorten the timing of each stroke. With Brush selected in the timeline, you can redraw the path of the brush to have it appear in a new place. Hey, is that a keyframe I see? Enabling keyframes for Path lets you redraw the brush's path on new frames and watch it automatically change shape. Finally, keyframing Start or End allows your stroke to be drawn on.

Since all your paint is technically an effect applied to your shot, disabling the Paint effect turns off all your paint.

The Clone Stamp Tool

The Clone Stamp tool works very similarly to the Brush tool. However, instead of painting with a color, it samples another part of your footage and paints with that. This is a quick and easy way to paint out a microphone that dips into the top of your frame, especially if it's over a wall. Select this tool from the Toolbar, or cycle to it with ⌘-B/Ctrl-B.

The first step is to choose which part of your image you'd like to sample from. With the Clone Stamp tool selected, hold down option/Alt and click on part of your image (again, all in

Special Tools
& Features

Expressions

The Interface
& Editing

Animation

Text

Shapes, Masks
& Mattes

Effects

3D

**Special Tools
& Features**

the Layer panel).

Then, by painting with the Clone Stamp tool, you'll resample your originally selected pixels and clone them elsewhere in your shot.

A soft brush (created by lowering the Hardness in the Brushes panel) is key to selling the effect.

I want to get rid of this rope dangling in my shot...

...and replace it with these grapes. So I first **option/
Alt** click the grapes to sample from that spot.

By painting here, I clone my
pixels from where I selected.

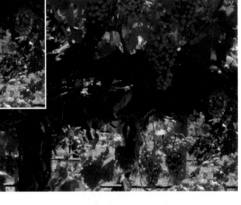

Clone Stamp Options

Some options in the Paint panel become available when the Clone Stamp tool is selected.

By selecting one of the Preset icons, you can save your current settings to that icon so it's faster to call up.

Often, the Clone Stamp tool is used to clone something from your current layer. However, you can choose another layer to sample from with the Source drop-down.

Clone Options

Preset:

Source: P1070773.MOV

☑ Aligned   ☐ Lock Source Time

Offset: 972 ,   -124

Source Time Shift: 0 f

☐ Clone Source Overlay: 50 %

With Aligned selected, each click with the Clone Stamp tool resamples from the exact spot you sampled. This is helpful for cloning one thing several times. By deselecting Aligned, each subsequent stroke samples relative to how far your cursor has moved from your first click. This might be helpful for cloning larger items a single time, as you can release your mouse button and resume from where you left off.

By using an **Aligned Clone stamp**, I can repaint these grapes several times.

With Lock Source Time deselected, your clone paint is basically a tiny video that plays concurrently with the source you selected. This is great, since grain in your footage will be accurate. By selecting Lock Source Time, the Clone Stamp tool paints a still frame.

Source Position is simply a readout of the coordinates from where you last sampled. If you wish to change your Source Position of a clone you've already created, that must be performed in the timeline (as you can't use this panel to edit strokes that have already been drawn). The same goes for Source Time Shift.

Enable Clone Source Overlay to have an overlay of where you selected follow your cursor around, which might help with placement. If you're having trouble seeing both layers at once, you can adjust the Opacity or press this button ⬤ to apply a Difference Blend Mode to the overlay.

Editing Clone Stamp Strokes

You can retroactively edit most strokes created by the Clone Stamp tool in the timeline, just as we did above with the Paint tool. Also note that you can edit and keyframe the Clone Position and Time, so your sample can change if need be.

The Eraser Tool

Very straightforward and very handy: Use the Eraser tool to erase parts of your footage. Sometimes this is quicker than reediting a rogue splotch from a Roto Brush or chroma key. Or switch the Erase drop-down to Paint Only to undo paint strokes. Nab this tool by selecting it from the Toolbar or with ⌘–B/Ctrl–B.

Special Tools & Features

Expressions

The Interface
& Editing

Animation

Text

Shapes, Masks
& Mattes

Effects

3D

**Special Tools
& Features**

Content-Aware Fill

While the Clone Stamp tool is a simple tool for quick fixes, you might need something more elaborate to get rid of bigger unwanted objects in your shot. Something more advanced, something powered by Adobe Sensei, something built off of Photoshop's image-processing algorithms that have been around for years. That's where After Effects' Content-Aware Fill comes in—your trick for using AI to automatically fill unwanted stuff in your shot.

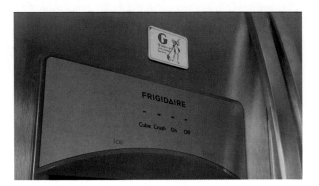

Choose What to Replace

This technique works best when there's an object or surface over a background that needs to go away. In this example, I'm going to delete an old, sexist fridge magnet from my shot and replace it with automatically generated textures of the fridge to fill it in.

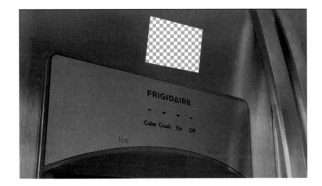

- I'll start by using the Pen tool to draw a mask around the object I want to get rid of. It doesn't need to be terribly precise.
- In the timeline, switch the Mask mode to Subtract.
- If the camera or object is moving, track the mask to the subject. Either manually keyframe it, or right-click the Mask in the timeline and choose Track Mask, then click the Play button in the Tracker panel to have AE track it automatically.

Your end result should have a hole chopped out of your footage.

The Content-Aware Fill Panel

The next step is to whip open the Content-Aware Fill panel, which is going to do most of the heavy lifting for us. If it's not already open, find it in the Window menu.

The Fill Target ought to display a boundary of where this effect intends to operate. You can expand this mask with Alpha Expansion.

Choose from one of the three Fill Methods. Object is best for removing an entire object altogether. Surface is best for removing a pattern or stain on a surface. Edge Blend is the simplest, as it simply uses the pixels near the edge of the object to estimate the fill. Choosing the correct method might involve trial and error—I would have suspected Surface to work the best in my case, but spoiler alert: It ended up being Edge Blend.

If the lighting changes in your scene (such as sunlight filtering in, or your phone's auto-exposure), select Lighting Correction, and choose Subtle, Moderate, or Strong. Again, trial and error is likely necessary. Finally, decide the Range of frames you'd like to process.

When you're good to go, hit Generate Fill Layer. After Effects will do its magic, and hopefully spit out a new layer that contains the corrected surface.

¿No bueno? Sometimes this effect works miracles, sometimes it falls flat on its face. The first step to correct a failed fill is to try the other Fill Method or Lighting Correction settings. If those still don't work, you may need to create the fill yourself. Do so by clicking Create Reference Frame. This will open up your masked image in Photoshop (provided it's installed). Here, you can use a nearly identical Clone Stamp tool and other techniques to draw your own fill layer.

- In Photoshop, paint in your own fill for the layer.
- Hit Save (not Save As, as After Effects is referencing that specific file).
- Switch back to After Effects.
- Note that the reference frame you've just created is sitting underneath your footage. This is dynamically linked, so you can keep working on it in Photoshop, saving it, and it will update in After Effects.
- The next time you click Generate Fill Layer, Content-Aware Fill will base the new fills off your reference frame.

How does this all work? Note that by clicking Generate Fill Layer, After Effects is generating brand-new frames and saving them to your computer. Those frames can be found next to the project file in a folder called Fills. The frames are automatically imported into After Effects and dropped into your composition as an image sequence, which is a type of video file composed of individual still images. You can individually edit these stills if need be.

You can change the location of these generated fills. By clicking the three lines in the top-right corner of the Content-Aware Fill panel ≡ followed by Content-Aware Fill Settings, you can change the Output Location. The other options in this window specify the bit depth and file type of the generated frames.

Special Tools & Features

Expressions

Motion Tracking

When it comes to realistically compositing assets into footage, you may want to match the movement of the asset to the movement of something within your footage. Basically, we're talking about converting the motion of something in-camera into keyframes that we can then parent to anything. This process is called Motion Tracking.

Types of Tracking

Let's start with the Tracker panel, which offers four means of tracking:

- Track Camera, which converts the motion of your camera into a 3D camera for placing 3D assets within your scene. See "Camera Tracking" (page 406).
- Track Motion, in which After Effects can follow the movement of an object and convert it into keyframes. This is what we'll cover in this section.
- Warp Stabilizer, which applies the Warp Stabilizer effect. See chapter 6.
- Stabilize Motion, which is set up similarly to Track Motion, but the end result is a stabilized shot.

For the rest of this section, I'll proceed by selecting Track Motion. Next, let's explore each option now available in this panel.

Motion Source

This is where we select the footage to track. Tracking motion works best when you have an element with high contrast to track.

Current Track

Each time you press Track Motion, you create a new track. This way, it's possible to either make multiple attempts to track using various methods, or track more than one element in your scene. Use this drop-down to revert to a previous track, if you've run more than one.

Track Type

This is important. Here, we choose from one of many methods to track footage.

Stabilize

This method uses one or two trackers to completely stabilize an object. This is different from using Warp Stabilizer to stabilize footage. Using a Stabilize motion track, you can choose what object you want to remain perfectly still, even if the camera is moving around it. In VFX shots, it can be helpful to Stabilize your shaky camera shot before compositing in effects. You can apply stabilization using any combination of Position, Rotation, and Scale, which will apply those keyframes to your footage.

By tracking this piece of lavender and applying **Stabilize**, the lavender stays perfectly still throughout the footage, even with a shaky camera. The footage now has **Position** and **Rotation keyframes** on it to compensate for the stabilization.

Transform

This is the dependable option when it comes to following something in your footage. With this option selected, choose if you want to track any combination of Position, Rotation, and Scale, and the following keyframes will be written accordingly. If Rotation or Scale is selected, you must utilize two trackers to extract your data.

By tracking the position of this bee, I can convert this bee's location on-screen into **Position keyframes** that are placed onto a **Null Object**. By parenting text to the **Null**, the text now accurately follows the bee's movement.

The Interface & Editing

Animation

Text

Shapes, Masks & Mattes

Effects

3D

Special Tools & Features

Parallel/Perspecitve Corner Pin

This option is the go-to for using four tracking points to track a rectangular object, such as a screen. Instead of placing keyframes on an object's Transform controls, this track applies the Corner Pin effect and keyframes each corner to match the corners of your object.

Parallel Corner Pin doesn't change the distance between each corner, which might be the case of moving a camera around a billboard. Perspective Corner Pin assumes the distance between corners changes, such as when a phone rotates away from the camera and the corners seem to "shrink" together in perspective.

By tracking the four corners of the phone and applying it to another **precomp**, the **Corner Pin** effect is applied to the **precomp** with the position of each corner applied to the corners of the effect. This makes the **precomp** follow the movement of the phone.

Raw

This option simply places a single tracker in your shot.

Target

This tells the tracker where to place the data. For Stabilize, the target is usually the same as the source—you want to place keyframes on the footage itself. For Transform, it's best practice to place a Null Object in your scene and have the target be the Null. This way, the Null contains the keyframe data, and you can have it be the parent of another object, giving you more freedom and flexibility to move the child around. For Corner Pin tracks, the target is whatever you'd like to apply the Corner Pin effect to—often a precomp.

The Edit Target button allows you to choose the target.

Analyze

Once you've chosen the type of track you'd like to perform, the next step is to have After Effects actually do the track. Depending on the type of track selected, you should see one, two, or four trackers on your footage.

Note: Analysis happens exclusively in the Layer panel. By selecting a tracker, the Layer panel should open automatically. If you can't see trackers, make sure you're in the Layer panel!

Placing Trackers

First, you must place the trackers over the object you want to track. Trackers are two concentric boxes with a target in the middle. Click and drag within the concentric squares (but not on the target) to place the tracker over the object you want After Effects to follow.

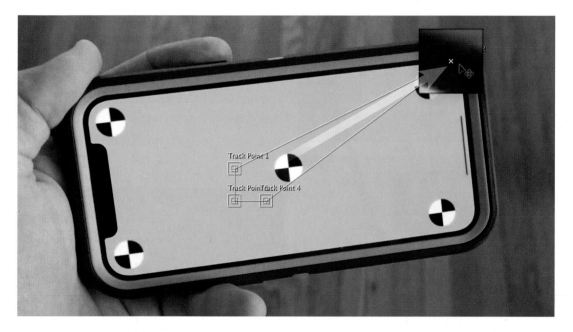

The inner box is an area of pixels that After Effects will attempt to follow. Frame by frame, After Effects will search for similar pixels, then place keyframes where it believes a close match is found. Click and drag the corner of the innermost box to resize it depending on which pixels you want After Effects to follow.

Pro tip: After Effects is searching for contrast. For best results, choose pixels that have decent variance from light to dark. If you're attempting to track a faint smudge on a dark wall, After Effects might have trouble distinguishing those pixels from the rest of the wall. This is why you often see high-contrast trackers placed on shots that are intended to be tracked, such as in my example. In some cases, I've even had to precomp my footage, increase the contrast with the Brightness and Contrast effect, then track the high-contrast precomp.

The outer box is After Effects' search area. After Effects will search for similar pixels only within the defined area. This is to both decrease the amount of time analysis takes (a small search radius means a faster calculation) and to prevent the match from jumping all over the screen. Resize this box according to the amount your object moves.

Special Tools & Features

Expressions

The Interface & Editing

Animation

Text

Shapes, Masks & Mattes

Effects

3D

Special Tools & Features

Camera Tracking

Another nifty feature to come from the Tracker panel is Camera Tracking, in which your footage's camera motion is analyzed and converted to a 3D camera. 3D objects placed in your composition will move as if they're being shot by the same camera. This is a really cool way to realistically composite elements in a scene with a moving camera.

Track Camera

To get started, select your footage layer in a composition, open the Tracker panel and select Track Camera. This applies the 3D Camera Tracker effect to your shot and analyzes your footage in the background.

Once analysis is complete, you'll see many colorful tracking points automatically placed throughout your shot. When scrubbing through your footage, these should remain attached to their respective objects.

3D Camera Tracker Options

Before moving forward, note some options in the Effect Controls panel.

By default, the effect assumes the Shot Type is

a Fixed Angle of View, which means the camera doesn't zoom in or out. If that's not the case, you can switch this option to Variable Zoom. This drop-down also lets you manually input the camera's angle of view, if you know what it was shot on. This will create a 3D camera with the same angle of view.

Most of the options in this panel are straightforward interface options. Selecting Create Camera is one simple way to just drop a corresponding 3D camera into your scene, but we'll get to a more robust way to do so shortly. If the camera solve didn't calculate correctly, you may wish to select Detailed Analysis under Advanced.

Incorporating 3D Objects

One may simply select Create Camera from the Effect Controls panel to drop a 3D camera into your composition that will mimic the motion of your footage's camera. Any 3D object in your composition will react as if it's being shot with the same camera. The problem is knowing where to place the object in Z-space. In the image above, what if I wanted to place text as if it's directly above the firepit? It's difficult to determine how far back in Z-space the object needs to be in that scenario. Instead, we can create objects at the same position as objects in the footage.

With the 3D Camera Tracker effect selected in the Effect Controls panel, hovering over the image in the Composition panel reveals targets. These targets are tracked and aligned to points in your scene.

Once you find a target that looks similarly positioned to where you want your 3D layer to go, right-click the target to reveal creation options: Create Text and Camera, Create Solid and Camera, Create Null and Camera, and Create Shadow Catcher, Camera, and Light. For the following examples, I'll create text. This ought to create an object aligned to the target.

The Interface & Editing

Animation

Text

Shapes, Masks & Mattes

Effects

3D

Special Tools & Features

The Mocha Workspaces

Like After Effects, Mocha has different workspaces that show or hide features depending on what you're likely to need. It defaults to the Essentials Workspace (⌘–1/Ctrl–1), which reveals most basic features. Change workspaces with the Workspaces menu.

The **Classic Workspace** (⌘–2/Ctrl–2) reveals just about every interface feature.

The **Big Picture Workspace** (⌘–3/Ctrl–3) dedicates most of the interface to your video, for detailed review.

The **Roto Workspace** (⌘–4/Ctrl–4) highlights rotoscope tools.

Special Tools & Features

Expressions

Mocha Tools

Select a tool either from the Toolbar at the top of the interface, or from the Tools menu. If you don't see one of these tools, the button might not appear in your current workspace.

Save Project

Save the project. Select this before exiting Mocha to return to After Effects.

Select (⌘-F/Ctrl-F)

The main tool used to manipulate splines. Clicking and dragging creates a square marquee selection. If you click and hold on this icon, you can switch it to a lasso selection, allowing you to draw a shape to select.

Select Both (⌘-Shift-B/Ctrl-shift-B)

This tool allows for the selection of both inner spline points and edge points. Hold this button down to select further options, listed below:

Select Inner

Only selects the inner spline points.

Select Edge

Selects only the outer edge points.

Select Auto

Automatically selects between inner and edge points.

Add Point (I)

With a spline already created, this tool can add points to it. It's basically the equivalent of the Add Vertex tool in After Effects.

Pan (hold X)

Move footage in the viewer. Similar to After Effects' Hand tool.

Zoom (hold Z)

With this tool selected, click and drag in the viewer to zoom in and out. Note that a quick tap of * (asterisk) on the numpad automatically frames your shot.

The Interface & Editing

Animation

Text

Shapes, Masks & Mattes

Effects

3D

Special Tools & Features

Create X-Spline Layer (⌘-L/Ctrl-L)

Similar to the Pen tool. Use this to draw an X-spline, which is Mocha's version of a path. Splines define the thing to track—for tracking footage, place splines around the thing you want to follow. For rotoscoping, place splines around the thing you want to roto.

With the tool selected, click on your video to place spline points. To finish and close the spline, right-click anywhere.

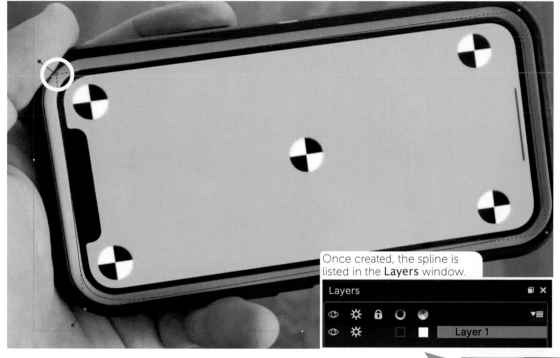

Once created, the spline is listed in the **Layers** window.

X-splines are similar to a traditional Bezier curve, but instead offer a single curve handle that sticks out of the spline vertex. Clicking and dragging the handle away from the point sharpens the curve, and dragging it inward creates a bigger curve.

Clicking and holding on this icon reveals some other tools, listed below.

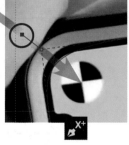

Add X-Spline to Layer

With a layer already created and selected, this tool adds a second spline to the same layer. This can be helpful for creating complex shapes for a roto.

Create Bezier-Spline Layer

B-splines are similar to X-splines, but might be a little more familiar to us. These have Bezier handles, just like a good ol' fashioned After Effects mask. While they offer more control, it can take more effort to get them to be even. Give X-splines a try first, then switch to B-splines if you can't get the precision you need.

Special Tools & Features

Expressions

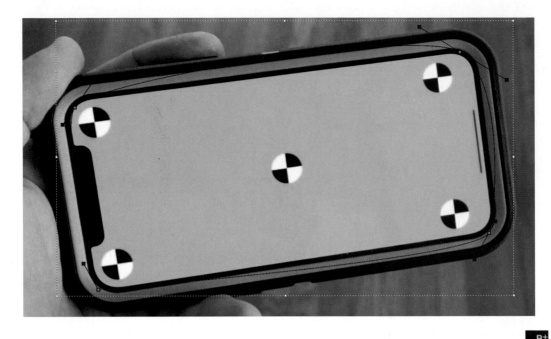

Add Bezier-Spline to Layer
Adds a B-spline to a preexisting (selected) layer.

Create Rectangle X-Spline Layer
Similar to the Shape tool, this quickly draws a rectangle using X-splines. Click and hold the icon to reveal a few other tools.

Add Rectangle X-Spline to Layer
Adds an X-spline rectangle to a preexisting (selected) layer.

Create Rectangle Bezier-Spline Layer
Same as above, but uses B-splines instead of X-splines.

Add Rectangle Bezier-Spline to Layer
Adds a B-spline rectangle to a preexisting (selected) layer.

Create Circle X-Spline Layer
This tool uses the same options as above, but draws a circle instead of a rectangle.

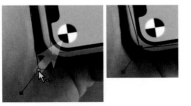

Attach Layer (⌘-M/Ctrl-M)
Use this tool to merge two spline points on two separate layers. With the tool selected and more than one layer visible, click and drag one vertex onto another. They'll now move as one.

Rotate, Scale, and Move

With multiple vertices selected with the Select tool, these tools let you move multiple points at once (similar to selecting mask points and double-clicking in After Effects). However, selection of these tools is not required. With vertices selected, Mocha automatically activates the Transform tool. Speaking of…

Transform Tool

This tool is on by default when vertices are selected. It's nearly identical to how we free-transform double-clicked mask points in After Effects—you can move, scale, and rotate points depending on where the cursor sits. Selecting this button toggles these controls.

Show Planar Surface

The planar surface is an important part of the tracking process. After points have been tracked, the planar surface must then be manually aligned to where you want your tracked plane to go. Here's comparable analogy from the After Effects tracker: Think of the spline as the search target and the planar surface as the crosshairs, where the corner pins are going to go.

After you've tracked, press this button to show the planar surface. Then, align its corners to the corners of your plane.

My splines set the area to track, but the planar surface is where my corner pins will end up. Here, I've aligned the corners of the planar surface to the corners of the phone.

Spline

Planar surface corner

Show Planar Grid

Toggles a grid relative to the planar surface view. You can adjust the number of grid lines under Viewer Preferences. See "Viewer Preferences" (page 417).

See "Viewer Preferences" (page 417).

Special Tools & Features

Expressions

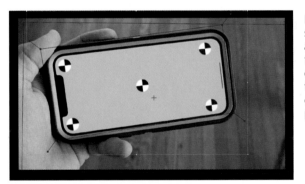

Is my planar surface aligned? The planar grid is a great way to check.

Align Surface

This expands the layer surface to fit the dimensions of the footage at the current frame. All tracked data is made relative to this new alignment. Why is this helpful? Let's think a few steps ahead. When we eventually convert this track to a Corner Pin effect to be applied to a new layer, that layer will be squished down and distorted. By selecting Align Surface, these corners will follow the track, but will be better suited for a 1920 x 1080 precomp. In short, the Corner Pin effect will likely distort your aspect ratio. Select this option to keep your aspect ratio between your track and precomp the same.

By selecting **Align Surface**, my planar surface still follows the track, but starts at the same dimensions as my original footage (note the blue box at the edge of the frame). When I eventually export this planar surface to a **Corner Pin** effect on a 1920 x 1080 **precomp**, that **precomp** won't change aspect ratios.

Viewer Controls

Some preferences for what the viewer displays. These are available only in the Classic and Roto Workspaces or the View menu.

Change Display | Selected layer ▾ |

Toggles between displaying different clips.

Show RGB

Shows your video's RGB channels.

Show Alpha

Shows your video's alpha channel.

Show Layer Mattes

Displays a solid fill within your splines.

The Interface & Editing

Animation

Text

Shapes, Masks & Mattes

Effects

3D

Special Tools & Features

Color Layer Mattes

Edit the color of your matte fill. The slider to the right of this icon controls the opacity.

Overlays

Toggles this to display the Mocha interface stuff, such as splines.

Show Layer Outlines

Toggles the visibility of your splines.

Show Spline Tangents

Toggles the visibility of your spline tangents.

Show Zoom Window

With the Zoom tool and this icon selected, a mini window of your entire comp displays.

Stabilize

This moves your tracked footage so the content stays in the center of the interface.

Trace

Displays the path of a the planar surface.

Adjust Brightness

Similar to the one in the Composition panel, this is for display only.

Viewer Preferences

Options for grid and trace displays.

Timeline Controls

Each workspace has some instance of the timeline, but not all features may be available unless you're in the Classic Workspace. You can also find these in the Movie menu.

Set In and Out Points

Think of In and Out Points in Mocha as the After Effects workspace, in which you'll only operate on these frames.

Reset In and Out Point

Sets your In or Out to the first or last frames of the shot.

Zoom Timeline to In/Out Points

Zooms in on the timeline.

Zoom Timeline to Full Frame Range

Resets the above option.

Play Controls

First frame, play backward, go back one frame, stop, go forward one frame, play forward, last frame.

Change Playback Mode

Toggle between Bounce (play forward, then reverse), Play Once, and Loop.

Tracking Controls

With a spline selected, use these controls to track it to your footage. In the Essentials Workspace, you'll find these **VERY IMPORTANT** controls under the Essentials panel. Find buttons for track backward, track backward one frame, stop, track forward one frame, and track forward.

Special Tools & Features

Expressions

Go to Previous and Next Keyframe

Unlike tracking in After Effects, keyframes in Mocha are frames with user input and are highlighted in green on the timeline.

Add/Delete Keyframe

With Autokey on, adjusting a spline automatically creates a new keyframe, so Add Keyframe isn't all that important. However, if the timeline is on a keyframe, this button allows you to delete it.

Delete All Keyframes

This doesn't delete your track, it just deletes adjusted keyframes you've added.

Autokey

Turning this off means you must select Add Keyframe to create new keyframes.

Überkey

Let's say you've created keyframes, but then decide you want to change the shape of your splines. By enabling Überkey, you can move your splines while preserving the relative motion of your other keyframes. Basically, you can reshape a keyframed spline without worrying about having to reshape it for all keyframes. Make sure this is turned off if you actually want to change the shape of your splines over time.

The Layer Panel

All your splines (and the tracking data within) are stored as layers. Manage them here. You can also rename layers in this panel, which is very helpful.

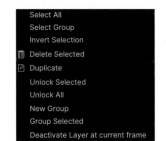

Toggle Layer Visibility

You should be pretty comfortable poking eyeballs at this point.

Toggle Tracking

Grays out the Tracking controls for the layer so it's can't be tracked. I think this icon should be a tinfoil hat.

Toggle Locking

Prevents any changes to the layer.

Change Spline Color

Mocha's color picker is quite robust.

Change Matte Color

Does what it says!

Layer Actions

Displays some self-explanatory features.

Group Layer

Creates a folder to help with organization.

Duplicate Layer

I often like to create duplicates of layers when mucking with tracks and trying things out.

Delete Layer

See ya!

The Interface & Editing

Animation

Text

Shapes, Masks & Mattes

Effects

3D

Special Tools & Features

Layer Properties

Affects the selected layer. We've seen some of this stuff before, but let's check out some new things.

Insert Clip

Displays a preset clip within your splines. Options include the Mocha logo or various grids. This might be easier to view than the splines.

Link to Track

Mocha's version of parenting, in which one layer may follow another. Selecting Adjusted means the track follows adjustments made in the AdjustTrack section (see below).

Essentials Panel

Only available in the Essentials Workspace, this is a handy panel that should contain all you need to track.

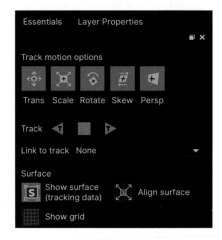

Track motion options determines which types of movement will be tracked. Select all you need for your track. Skew distorts your points but preserves your shape's volume, and Perspective allows total distortion of your shape (which, if it's rotating in three dimensions, you'll likely need).

When you've added some spline curves around the object you want to track and are ready to do it, hit Track forward or backward. Then, select Show surface (the same as Show Planar Surface) and align where you want your corner pin points to land.

Parameters Panel

Only available in the Classic Workspace, this panel provides many fine-tuning options. You may never need to touch this panel, but here we go all the same.

Clip

Details of the footage that's being tracked. You probably don't need to mess with this.

Track

Fine-tune the way Mocha handles your track. Only muck with these settings if things are truly going awry with your track.

AdjustTrack

When you need to manually adjust the way that Mocha tracks an object, this is the panel for you (you poor soul). Selecting this reveals four red corners where the planar surface is mapped.

Special Tools & Features

Expressions

Navigate to your first frame and select a corner to see what's being tracked.

Navigate to another frame. The new window that says Current Frame indicates the original position of your key-frame—as if it had not moved.

You can then click and drag the red box to reposition where you want it to go. Or, use the Nudge section to move it with great detail. The Auto button here lets Mocha guess. The goal is to match the position of the Current Frame with the original Master reference.

Speaking of the Master reference, the Reference Point section defines snapshots that Mocha uses to calculate the movement. Select Set Master to change the reference frame.

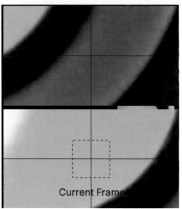

Dope Sheet

This is where the tracking keyframe data is stored, if you need to delete tracking keyframes.

Getting Back to After Effects

If you're happy with the way Mocha has tracked your footage, it's time to turn it into data After Effects can use. Save and close the Mocha window and return to After Effects' Effect Controls panel.

The Interface & Editing

Animation

Text

Shapes, Masks & Mattes

Effects

3D

Special Tools & Features

Matte

If you've used Mocha to track an object for rotoscoping, start here. If you have more than one layer in Mocha, click on Visible Layers to toggle off any layers you don't want to bring into After Effects, then make sure Shape is set to All Visible. You can have this effect directly matte your footage by selecting Apply Matte and adjusting the Feather, if need be. Or you can convert it to an AE mask by selecting Create AE Mask.

Tracking Data

If you've used Mocha to track an object for corner pinning, start here. Select Create Track Data to then select a layer from within Mocha. This will import that layer's data. Under Export Option, choose Transform (no distortion), Corner Pin, or Corner Pin with Motion Blur. Under Layer Export To, choose the layer you'd like to apply the pinning to. Then, hit Apply Export.

Mocha Pro

The free version of Mocha Lite that comes with After Effects is remarkably powerful, as you can see. Want to do more? The full version of Mocha, Mocha Pro, has many cool features, such as object removal, camera solving, and the ability to track just about any surface and match distortion—which means you can track footage onto faces, fabric, and liquids. Find out more at https://borisfx.com/products/mocha-pro.

Special Tools & Features

Expressions

The Interface & Editing

Animation

Text

Shapes, Masks & Mattes

Effects

3D

Special Tools & Features

The Puppet Tool

Imagine a spider made out of shape layers in which each leg is a stroke. Animating the legs moving would be pretty simple, right? Simply keyframe the stroke path. Now, imagine a spider that's an image layer, such as a JPEG or PSD. How would you animate that? The answer: The Puppet tool. It's a great way to bend limbs and add character to raster (that is, pixel-based) images.

Building a Puppet Rig

The technique of preparing an asset for animation is called "rigging." Imagine you're Jim Henson and you've just built a Kermit the Frog puppet. Rigging is the art of attaching a wire to Kermit's hand to enable him to gesticulate.

With the Puppet tool, we start rigging by adding pins to our asset. Some pins we will move, which will also move the surrounding pixels. Other pins are there to hold stuff in place, so it doesn't move.

Start pinning by selecting the Puppet Pin tool from the Toolbar. There are five types of pins in this drop-down; we'll start with the first, the Puppet Position Pin tool.

Puppet Position Pin Tool	Cmd+P
Puppet Starch Pin Tool	Cmd+P
Puppet Bend Pin Tool	Cmd+P
Puppet Advanced Pin Tool	Cmd+P
Puppet Overlap Pin Tool	Cmd+P

Add pins to your raster image by clicking on it. If you're using pins to move a character's wrist around, you'll obviously want a pin in the wrist. However, you'll also want to add pins to the edges of your image so they hold in place. This part can be a little unpredictable, but it's easy to go back and revise later. If you notice moving the wrist also moves the feet, simply place pins in the feet to lock them down.

It took some experimentation to get this right, but in order to move just the wrist around, I need a pin in the wrist, elbow, shoulder, and also the head, opposite elbow, torso, and feet to prevent extraneous movement. The pin in the wrist is the one I'll be animating.

Animating a Puppet Rig

Got pins? Move them! Each pin is automatically keyframed, so all you need to do is hop to a new time, move them around, and you're animating with puppetry!

Check out the timeline to view the keyframes on your pins. Find them under your layer's triangle, under Effects > Puppet > Mesh 1 > Deform > Puppet Pin. Since these are Puppet Position Pins, you can only change the pin's Position. More on that shortly.

Don't forget you can click on just about any attribute in the **timeline** and hit **return/Enter** to rename it. Renaming pins is very helpful!

The Interface
& Editing

Animation

Text

Shapes, Masks
& Mattes

Effects

3D

**Special Tools
& Features**

The Mesh

Before we start getting all fancy with our pins, let's rewind and take a look at what the Puppet tool is actually doing. As soon as you add your first pin to an image, After Effects divides the image into a bunch of small triangles. This is called a Mesh. We can look at the Mesh by selecting Show from the Toolbar, provided we've added a pin and we have any Puppet tool selected.

Mesh Expansion grows the boundaries of your Mesh just beyond your original artwork. This is helpful to prevent the Puppet tool from excluding little corners of your image—if this still occurs, increase Expansion. Mesh Density is the number of triangles drawn. A higher density produces smoother deformation, but will take more processing time (and increase the chances of After Effects crashing). Both options can also be accessed from the timeline.

Other Types of Pins

While the Puppet Position Pin tool is simple and good for changing an object's position, let's check out the other tools. You can either create a different type of pin by selecting it from the Toolbar, or swap Pin Type in the timeline.

The Puppet Starch Pin Tool

Adding a Starch Pin prevents an area from deforming. In my example, the subject's wrist bends a little too much when the arm moves. By adding a Puppet Starch Pin on the wrist, I prevent deformation from happening. This is different than adding a new Position Pin; a Starch Pin's position is influenced by the position of other Position Pins. Is that the most one can use the word "position" in

A **Starch Pin** prevents the nearby pixels from deforming, and its movement is influenced by the nearby **Position Pins**.

a sentence? I'm in no position to argue.

The Puppet Bend Pin Tool

This tool works very similarly to the Puppet Position Pin tool, but instead of manipulating a point's position, it can modify rotation and scale. When it comes to animating limbs, rotation can look more elegant than position.

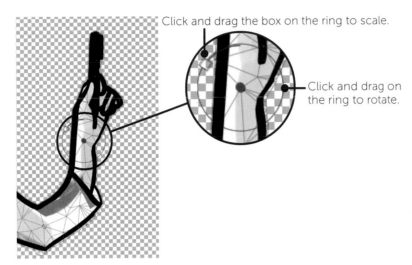

Click and drag the box on the ring to scale.

Click and drag on the ring to rotate.

The Puppet Advanced Pin Tool

The mother of all Puppet tools, this one has controls for Position, Rotation, and Scale. But it doesn't end there. The interaction between the Puppet Advanced Pin tool and the Puppet Bend Pin tool is where these two really shine.

While most pins interact independently of one another, the Puppet Advanced Pin tool and the Puppet Bend Pin tool work together. The Puppet Advanced Pin tool is capable of influencing the Puppet Bend Pin tool. I'll show you a common case study.

In the previous image, I have an Advanced Pin in the elbow and a Bend Pin in the wrist. If I move, rotate, or scale the Advanced Pin, the Bend Pin follows—and the classic Puppet Position Pin in the shoulder remains in place.

This is a great way to build an elegant rig—Advanced Pin at the base, subsequent Bend Pins down the rest. You get more control and are less likely to get weird deformation from two Position Pins not quite aligning.

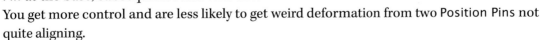

Special Tools & Features

Expressions

The Puppet Overlap Pin Tool

This tool gives layers to your rig. Consider this: Here, I have the pen going in front of the character's face.

What if I wanted it to go behind? The answer: Use the Puppet Overlap Pin tool. It basically assigns Z-depth to various parts of your rig, so you can determine what goes on top and what goes on bottom. If you don't use

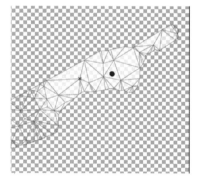

the tool, After Effects just guesses what you'd like to be on top. Sometimes it's right, sometimes it's not. If it's not, here's what to do:

First, select the Puppet Overlap Pin tool. Then, designate a thing to which you'd like to assign Z-depth. In this case, it's the wrist and pen. However, this tool operates *before* deformations. As you highlight over your illustration, you'll see an outline of where the wrist started before you started bending it every which way. *That's* what you want to click on.

From either the Toolbar or the new Overlap category listed in the timeline, dial up the Extent until you see the Mesh colored in up to where you'd like this designation to occur. In my case, I want the influence of this Overlap Pin to be the entire wrist.

In Front determines Z-depth. Objects default to 0%, so if I want an object to go behind the default, I dial In Front into a negative percent. In this case, anything lower than -1% is fine, but if one were to create interlocking fingers, one would have to assign each finger a higher percentage than the one below.

Here, I've added a **Puppet Overlap Pin** to the hand, increased the **Extent**, and lowered the **In Front** amount. The hand now moves behind the head.

Going Further with Character Animation

The Puppet tool is great for simple twists of the wrist and head nods. If you really want to fully animate a character in After Effects, you should look into plug-ins that are built specifically for this purpose.

The biggest character animation deficit in After Effects is the lack of what's called an IK Handle. IK, or Inverse Kinematics, is a special type of rig that allows you to move a wrist or ankle around, and have the elbow or knee automatically go where it needs to. Animating a wrist and elbow without an IK handle requires two keyframes and has tons of room for human error—an IK handle lets you do it with just one keyframe, which may not sound like much, but it's a colossal time-saver, and it leads to smoother animation.

So, what plug-ins create IK handles? DUIK is a popular one, particularly since it's free. It has a bit of a learning curve, but it can be used to create a very powerful rig for characters, in which you parent your shape layers to a prebuilt skeleton that's already accurately rigged. You can even animate a walk cycle with a single button-click. Find it at https://rainboxlab.org/tools/duik/.

Another one I like is Rubber Hose, which gives you prebuilt shape layers that you can use for arms and legs. It's by far the fastest way to slap an IK-ready limb into your shot. Find that at https://www.battleaxe.co/rubberhose.

When it comes to rigging faces, nothings beats Joysticks 'n Sliders. You can assign various face positions (say, a smile or frown) to a slider, which is an on-screen element that's very easy to keyframe. Or, animate a head turning with a joystick. Find it at https://aescripts.com/joysticks-n-sliders/.

Finally, with a Creative Cloud account, you have access to Adobe Character Animator, which lets you animate characters in real-time using your webcam.

Special Tools & Features

Expressions

8 Expressions

If you can dream it, After Effects can build it. Out of the box, After Effects' presets and effects can do a lot. With expressions, they can do so much more.

Expressions are lines of code added to any keyframable parameter. They're a means of customizing the way After Effects works. Want to link a single Adjustment Layer to Fill effects on multiple layers? Or loop animation? Or animate a number counter? Expressions!

Expressions could be their own book—in fact, those exist. This chapter does not intend to be a comprehensive list of everything possible with expressions. Rather, it's intended to be a place to get started and focus on a few practical case studies in which expressions may make your life easier. After finishing this chapter, you should be able to do a web search for comparable expressions that fit your needs, and understand them enough to be able to modify them to your liking.

Advanced Parenting

Chapter 2 of the Compendium explored basic parenting, in which a pickwhipped layer follows another layer's position, rotation, scale, and anchor point. Advanced parenting is a quick and simple means of generating an expression in which you can link just about anything to anything. And no code is required. It's a great way to get your feet wet with expressions.

Let's set up this scene. Say I have six shape layers all being colored in by the Fill effect. I know I want them to all be the same color. However, modifying an effect on six layers means doing something six times. If I know it's something that I'll frequently need to mess with, parenting the Fill of each layer to a single control layer means I can change all colors at once. This might save me time down the road.

This scene contains a Null Object that has the Fill effect applied. This isn't currently doing anything, but it will become our controller for all other Fill effects.

Expressions

Rocky Nook

http://www.rockynook.com

http://www.rockynook.com/information/newsletter

https://www.instagram.com/rocky_nook/

https://www.facebook.com/rockynookinc

https://twitter.com/rocky_nook